William Alexander, Lord Stirling

WILLIAM ALEXANDER, LORD STIRLING
(Portrait by Bass Otis, Courtesy of
Independence National Historical Park Collection)

William Alexander, Lord Stirling

PAUL DAVID NELSON

•

THE UNIVERSITY OF ALABAMA PRESS

Copyright © 1987 by
The University of Alabama Press
University, Alabama 35486
All rights reserved
Manufactured in the United States of America

Library of Congress Cataloging-in-Publication Data
Nelson, Paul David, 1941–
　William Alexander, Lord Stirling.
　Bibliography: p.
　Includes index.
　1. Alexander, William, 1726–1783. 2. Generals—
United States—Biography. 3 United States. Army—
Biography. I. Title.
E207.A3N45 1987　　　973.3′092′4 [B]　　　85-16473
ISBN 0-8173-0283-2

For Wade, Tom, and Peggy

Contents

	Preface	ix
One	The Making of an American Aristocrat, 1726–1754	1
Two	Service for Crown and Colony, 1754–1756	14
Three	The Provincial Becomes a Nobleman, 1757–1761	31
Four	The Whig as Royalist, 1761–1775	43
Five	The Republican Earl, 1775–1776	61
Six	Lord Stirling at Bay: Long Island to Trenton, 1776	79
Seven	Washington's Loyal Captain: The Campaign of 1777	103
Eight	Monmouth and Its Aftermath, 1778–1779	124
Nine	Military and Financial Stalemate, 1779–1780	144
Ten	The Rewards of Duty, 1781–1783	161
	Notes	177
	A Selected Bibliography	216
	Index	234

Illustrations

William Alexander, Lord Stirling	*frontispiece*
Residence of Lord Stirling	45

Maps

Stirling's New York Campaigns, 1755–1783	22
Stirling's Battles, 1776, 1777, and 1780	86
Stirling's New Jersey Campaigns	96
Battle of Trenton, December 26, 1776	101
Battles in Pennsylvania, 1777	111
Battle of Monmouth, June 28, 1778	129

Preface

William Alexander, Lord Stirling, is remembered in history as that curious character who merits two references in indexes of books on the American Revolution. Most writers see him as a flamboyant, pompous figure who need not be taken very seriously. Such characterizations, however, are incorrect because they are incomplete. Lord Stirling also served society loyally as a prominent New York provincial before 1775 and as a swashbuckling, brave major general in the Continental army under George Washington thereafter. Although he does not rank among the first figures of his age, his life is well worth studying. It is my hope that, as far as the historical record allows, the complete Lord Stirling is captured in this biography.

My work is not the first full-scale biography of Lord Stirling. In 1847 the earl's grandson, William Alexander Duer, published *The Life of William Alexander, Earl of Stirling: Major General in the Army of the United States, during the Revolution*. Although Duer's work was not complete or detailed, containing as it did mostly haphazardly edited letters by Stirling from the collections of the New-York Historical Society, it is considered the best biography to this time. Fifty years later, Ludwig Schumacher wrote *Major-General the Earl of Stirling: An Essay in Biography*, a book that contributed little to an understanding of its subject. Another work, published in 1920, Charles A. Ditmas's *Life and Service of Major-General William Alexander*, is not taken seriously by scholars. A doctoral dissertation on Stirling's career, entitled "The Rebel Earl," appeared in 1955, written by George H. Danforth at Columbia University. This thesis, which concentrated heavily on the earl's career to 1775, did little to clarify his record as a soldier. The only other biography, *Lord Stirling*, written by Alan Valentine and published in 1969, left the critics cold. All the critics expressed the opinion that a complete, modern biography of the general was still needed. I hope this work fills that prescription.

The records left by General Lord Stirling reveal no psychological quirks and no exciting pecadilloes to account for his behavior. I have, therefore, confined myself to evidence and leave to writers of fiction all further speculations about Lord Stirling's life and character. The source materials for this work are in numerous archives throughout the United States, a complete listing of which may be found in the bibliography. The major collections of papers are in the New-York Historical Society, New York Public Library, National Archives and Records Service, and Morristown (New Jersey) National Historical Park. I owe a debt of gratitude that I can never adequately express to the curators and librarians of all institutions possessing materials on Stirling's life. One of the rewards I gain from scholarly work is the unfailing assistance I receive from the keepers of historical records.

For financial support, I wish to thank Berea College, which has been generous in its aid for sabbatical leaves and for summer trips to archives. Without Berea's economic support, I could not have completed this book.

I owe special thanks to my wife, Rebecca, for giving unfailing countenance to my interest in historical study.

PAUL DAVID NELSON

One

•

The Making of an American Aristocrat, 1726–1754

William Alexander, claimant to the title of Lord Stirling, loved life and lived it fully. Always zealous in his enthusiasms, he never did anything by halves, and his eagerness to grasp the moment often led him into decisions and behavior that even his closest friends would not have predicted. This characteristic especially manifested itself at key points in his career, such as in his decision to join the patriot cause or in his utter fearlessness in battle; but it did not mean that he was frivolous or whimsical. On the contrary, once he had decided on a line of action, he was unwavering in his adherence to that commitment.

Stirling's total dedication to an enthusiasm showed itself early in life. From childhood he worked hard to please his talented parents, and he continued to do so into adulthood. For his father, the famous lawyer James Alexander, he studied science, mathematics, surveying, law, politics, and military arts, and for his mother, Mary Alexander, a hard-driving merchant, he mastered trade and commerce while working with her in business. Later, after he had become a man, he defended his mentor, Governor William Shirley (who had opened opportunities for him in the Seven Years' War), against criticisms after the Oswego campaign of 1755–56. His ludicrous yen to claim a lapsed Scots earldom led him to squander a fortune in a futile attempt to become a peer and sit at Westminster. When the House of Lords rejected his claim, he did not abandon his inflated dreams and return to the prosaic life of a New York merchant. Instead, after 1761, he insisted upon being addressed as Lord Stirling, and he adopted the style of a country aristocrat. Thereafter, he confined his business dealings to what he considered more gentlemanly economic pursuits and, in the process, threw his estate into a befuddled financial disorder that still defies understanding or clarification.

Stirling's politics during the unsettled decades just before the outbreak of the revolutionary war reflected his aristocratic pretensions, for they supported, if halfheartedly, the prerogatives claimed by Parliament in America. But Stirling did not take the side of England in 1775, when other colonists of similar political stripe were declaring loyalty to the Crown and empire. On the contrary, he emerged an outspoken advocate of rebellion and republicanism, broke with and persecuted his former highly placed loyalist friends (such as Governor William Franklin of New Jersey), and became over the next few years one of George Washington's bravest and most trusted military commanders.

In his capacity as an officer of the Continental army Stirling made his deepest mark on history. Descriptions of his martial character made by friend and foe alike during the Revolution bear striking similarities. "He is considered," said army surgeon James Thacher, who knew him well, "as a brave, intelligent and judicious officer." Benjamin Rush remembered him as "prudent and wise in council, and brave in the field." Surgeon Albigence Waldo described him as "mild in his private conversation and vociferous in the field." Charles Lee once praised him as a "zealous" officer. And the soldiers on Long Island in 1776 credited him with "the character of as brave a man as ever lived." Washington admired most Stirling's lack of military ambition and his willingness to acquiesce in the judgments of the commander in chief as to where and in what capacity he could do the greatest good for the cause—even when other generals claimed what was Stirling's by right of seniority. Moreover, Stirling remained faithfully in the field during America's darkest hours, never shirking his duty, despite the debilitating ravages of rheumatism and gout.[1]

Heavyset, ruddy-raced, and handsome, Stirling impressed his contemporaries as a "man of very noble presence" with the "most martial Appearance of any General in the service." According to Waldo, "he much resembles the Marquis of Granby—by his bald head—the make of his face, and figure of his Body." "In his personal appearance," said Thacher, "his lordship is venerable and dignified; in his deportment, gentlemanly and graceful; in conversation, pleasing and interesting." An extremely sociable man, Stirling was a lover of good food, good drink, and good conversation, and he was widely reputed to run the most convivial headquarters in the American army. Some people, like the Marquis de Chastellux and Benjamin Rush, thought him "rather dull," because of his tendency, "like Charles II . . . to tire his company with repetition of the same stories." He was never accused of lacking hospitality, and many people were regaled at Lord Stirling's table with "Sumptious and elegant" fare.[2]

Not every contemporary assessment of Stirling's character and abilities is positive, and often the same people who lauded him in some ways found other things about him less than flattering. Perhaps the directness of such summations makes both positive and negative comments more believable. One fault of Stirling's that was often noted by his peers was his pompous vanity. Both Rush and Chastellux alluded to this quality, and James Thacher passed on an anecdote, widely known throughout American army ranks, that summed up the general's reputation in this regard: "[Stirling], being present at the execution of a soldier for desertion, the criminal at the gallows repeatedly cried out, 'The Lord have mercy on me;' his lordship with warmth exclaimed, 'I won't you rascal, I won't have mercy on you.'"[3]

Drinking was another of Stirling's shortcomings, although from the evidence it is impossible to ascertain the degree or severity of his problem. When one considers what everyone called "normal" alcohol consumption in the eighteenth century, Stirling must have been quite a tippler to earn such a reputation. Benjamin Rush, for example, once declared that any commander who drank more than a quart of whisky or got drunk more than once in a twenty-four hour period, should be chastised by his superior officer before his unit. Rush ascribed the cause of Stirling's drinking to "his [financial] misfortunes before the war," which "had led him to seek relief in toddy." Whatever the cause of the problem, it was widely commented upon by Americans and Englishmen alike. Chastellux noted that Stirling liked "the table and bottle full as much as becomes a Lord, but more than becomes a General." Rush once accused Stirling of being "a proud, vain, lazy ignorant drunkard" who gave the commander in chief bad advice. Charles Lee, after a falling-out with Stirling, claimed that the earl was a drunkard who overindulged in liquor as often as he could lay his hands upon a supply.[4]

Not surprisingly, Stirling's reputation for drinking was the butt of numerous, sarcastic gibes from the enemy. A typical satire was produced by Jonathan Odell, a bitter loyalist, who wrote

> What matters what of Stirling may become?
> The quintessence of whisky, soul of rum;

> Fractious at nine, quite gay at twelve o'clock;
> From then till bed-time stupid as a block.

Yet no one ever accused the man of being drunk when duty called, and he never fell into the trouble of Adam Stephen, who was incapacitated by drink during the battle of Germantown and dismissed from service. Perhaps the worst that could be said of Stirling was that "When seated at the head of his own table he did not love 'a lingering bottle / Which with the landlord makes too long a stand / Leaving all claretless the unmoistened throat.'" Hence, when Lord Stirling died during the war, he was accused by some detractors of being full of not only honor but also good liquor.5

Despite the universal acclaim heaped upon Stirling by his fellow officers for his bravery on the battlefield, he was not held in high esteem for his military abilities. Drink was not the problem. The Marquis de Lafayette said the general was *"Plus brave que judicieux"* [More brave than wise], and Chastellux, echoing the sentiment, said he was "brave, but without capacity." It was difficult for Washington or anyone else, perhaps Stirling himself, to understand exactly what went wrong with a military operation under his direction, or why. But something always seemed to happen. Apparently, Stirling's ardor was not matched by his judgment. Nevertheless, said Chastellux, "he had, at least, his zeal and seniority in his favor; thus he will retain the command of the first line . . . but care will be taken not to employ him on special expeditions."6

Stirling's American colleagues did not rate him as harshly as Chastellux, but neither did they expect him to show the strategic acumen of a Nathanael Greene or the battlefield genius of a Benedict Arnold. He was one of a group of officers, the largest in the army, that Washington (if he had his way) would never consider getting rid of or of promoting to more important positions. As far as Stirling himself was concerned, he was a divisional commander and perfectly content to remain in that role. Clearly, he was not as dull witted as some of his colleagues seemed to think he was, for unlike many Continental officers whose reach exceeded their grasp Stirling knew his limitations and kept carefully within them. Moreover, his courage far outweighed his vanity. For these reasons, he was admired and respected by Washington, and his other colleagues treated him with a respect that contained no malice and a great deal of affection.

William Alexander was born into comfortable circumstances and a high social position in New York City on December 25, 1726. His father, James Alexander, by then a prominent citizen in the tightly knit upper class of the colonies of New York and New Jersey, rose in a few years' time to even more notoriety, distinction, and wealth. All these young William could look forward to inheriting at his father's death. James Alexander, a native of Scotland, had been educated in mathematics and Whig politics, and in both he showed a youthful proficiency. His strongest characteristic seemed to be independence of spirit, which got him into trouble early in his life. During the Rebellion of 1715 against George I he supported the House of Stuart, serving as an engineer in the Pretender's army. He fled to New York in 1716 when the rebellion collapsed, and there he immediately began to rise to prominence, assisted by the patronage of his friend John, Duke of Argyle. In the next few years, he was appointed to numerous offices in the provinces of New York and New Jersey: surveyor-general of both colonies, recorder of Perth Amboy, New Jersey (where he resided), deputy secretary of New York, commissioner to survey the boundary between New York and New Jersey, and member of the councils of the two colonies. He studied law and in 1723 was admitted to the bar of New Jersey. Immediately thereafter he became attorney-general of the province.[7]

James Alexander was drawn into the factional politics of New York soon after his arrival in the province. The New York political swirl into which he plunged, and into which his son William would also be lured, was dominated by members of the upper class, which was anything but a monolithic whole in terms of its interests. The main characteristic of New York politics during the first decades of the eighteenth century was its fluidity, with people shifting from one faction to another seemingly at the drop of a hat and with many factions in existence at any one time. The colony's political life was dominated by a conflict between two major interests: the merchant, controlled by the Philips, Van Cortlandt, DeLancey, and Schuyler families, and the landed, overshadowed by the Morris and Livingston families.[8] Neither of these two loose coalitions was motivated by any ideological consistency, and both attempted to use the lower orders of society for their own convenience. By 1732 they were being referred to as the *Court* and the *Country* parties. Although they lacked ideological exactitude, they did have clear-cut programs; the Country party pushed for the development of an indigenous economy, and the Court party advocated a more cosmopolitan economy based upon trade.[9]

James Alexander was in the fray on the side of the Country party (more or less), opposing the "mad measures" Governor William Cosby had taken in some personal financial dealings with him. Consequently, Cosby, with the assistance of Supreme Court Judge James DeLancey, had Alexander removed from the Council of New York. Three years later Alexander also lost his position on the Council of New Jersey and began to rail against the governor's suppression of "free speech" by writing for the *New York Weekly Journal,* a newspaper Alexander had founded in 1733 with the assistance of its editor, John Peter Zenger. Alexander's diatribes against the authorities were so lacking in circumspection that a furor of opposition arose against him and Zenger. George Clarke, president of the council, accused him of flirting with treason in his attempts to "stir up" the people by favorably citing John Trenchard and Thomas Gordon, English opponents of Prime Minister Robert Walpole. Zenger was arrested in 1734 and imprisoned on charges of libel and inciting sedition. Certain copies of his paper, some with articles written by Alexander, were ordered seized and burned by the common hangman. Alexander and his friend William Smith acted as Zenger's counsel when the case came to trial, but both were declared in contempt and disbarred. At that time, the famous Philadelphia lawyer Andrew Hamilton took the case and obtained a verdict in favor of Zenger. Alexander and Smith did not secure reinstatement to the bar until Governor Cosby died two years later; at that time Alexander was also restored to the Councils of New York and New Jersey. Immediately, Alexander asserted his independence on the Council of New York by opposing singlehandedly the appointment of George Clarke as acting governor. But Alexander's political temper began to cool after the demise of his old enemy Cosby, and he lived in considerable tranquility until his death in 1756.[10]

Although the rough and tumble of practical politics absorbed much of James Alexander's attention, he was also deeply involved in many scholarly pursuits, and he taught this eclectic outlook to his son. Because of his interest in science, he helped found the American Philosophical Society and made numerous mathematical calculations on the orbits of comets. He discussed the magnetic declination of New York with the eminent Swedish scientist Peter Kalm, and he corresponded with Edmund Halley and Professor J. Betts of Oxford about astronomy. He took great interest in education, helping the Morris family found a free school in 1732, assisting William Smith five years later in founding Latin High School, becoming a trustee of King's College

(Columbia University) when it was started in 1754, subsidizing the New York Society Library the same year (along with his son, William), and tutoring numerous candidates for the bar (such as William Livingston) in his law office.[11] He was a student of constitutionalism and political theory. In 1754, when Benjamin Franklin visited him while en route to a conference on intercolonial unity at Albany, they discussed Franklin's views on the subject.[12]

In January 1721, James Alexander married an attractive young widow, Mrs. Mary Sprat Provoost, the granddaughter of Johannes DePeyster. Her husband, David Provoost, had been called "Ready-Money," because he had acquired his wealth in illegal trade. But "his more respectable relict" engaged in licit commerce after Provoost's passing and continued to do so until her own death, almost forty years later. The marriage of James and Mary was at first strictly a business arrangement, formalized by a contract in which Mary retained her estate and the right to will it to her six children by Provoost. James and Mary only later discovered affection for each other, laid aside their contract, and wrote wills dividing their property equally among the Alexander and Provoost children. They had seven children over the next few years, five of whom survived into adulthood. The eldest daughter, Mary, later married Peter Van Brugh Livingston, who became William Alexander's business partner and president of the First New York Provincial Congress during the Revolution; Elizabeth married John Stevens, who also later became his brother-in-law's partner and was president of the New York convention that ratified the United States Constitution; Catherine married Elisha Parker III, who died in 1758, then Major Walter Rutherfurd, a regular officer in the British army during the Seven Years' War and the American Revolution; Susanna married Captain John Reid, a regular officer in a Scots regiment, and settled with him in Edinburgh. William Alexander, the only surviving son (a brother, James Alexander, Jr., died in 1731), became in his youth the focus of parental attention, for he was the sole male heir and potential bearer of the family name.[13]

William Alexander, "Billie," as the family members called him, grew up in comfortable circumstances and came to expect these civilities as his due in life. In infancy he lived in his mother's house on Pearl Street in New York City, where James and Mary had settled in 1721. Before long he moved with his parents into their newly built residence, The Mansion House, on the corner of Broad and Beaver Streets. It was here, in a home that he later inherited, that he spent his formative years. The house was centered on a large, fenced-in lot, surrounded by shrubs and gardens in front, fruit trees and a stable in back. The Alexander family was pampered in this elegant mansion by sumptuous furnishings. The dining room contained a mahogany table, marble-top side tables, and a large Holland cupboard filled with china, silver mugs, tankards, a silver tea kettle, and a large silver punch bowl made by Boston silversmith John Coney. It was also graced with sixteen chairs and crimson damask draperies. The other rooms of the house, including two parlors, were equally well furnished with imported rugs, mirrors, tapestries, chairs, and walls lined with blue and gilt leather.[14]

New York City in the early 1700s was an exciting, bustling place for an adventurous boy, and young William no doubt availed himself of opportunities. Opposite the Alexander's house was a path leading to the parade ground, where the militia drilled and where soldiers from nearby Fort George welcomed the arrival of new royal governors with pomp and ceremony. The waterfront, with its constant comings and goings of ships and ferries, was a particular lure for William because of his mother's flourishing mercantile business. From an early age he assisted her in the business and developed an interest in trade that he maintained into his late thirties. Over the years his and his mother's commercial enterprise grew and thrived in the general prosperity of the growing city of New York.[15]

William Alexander's education was not neglected by his prominent father, who knew the value of learning in terms of both personal satisfaction and financial reward. Whether he attended the school begun by his father and the Morrises in 1732 or Latin High School, started four years later, is not known; more likely, he received instruction in basic education, such as reading and mathematics, from private tutors. It is certain, however, that as he grew older, the young man studied under his father, learning higher mathematics, surveying, astronomy, and general science and acquiring an inquisitive mind that served him for the rest of his life. Although he never attended college or stood for the bar, he studied law with his father, receiving instruction along with other law apprentices such as William Livingston, a future brother-in-law and first governor of the state of New Jersey; Peter Van Brugh Livingston, William Livingston's brother and husband of William Alexander's sister Mary, and his own business partner; and Elisha Parker III, who married his sister Catherine and died prematurely.[16]

Young Alexander was overshadowed in his formative years by his rich, powerful, and assertive parents. One might have expected him to have rebelled against them or to have asserted his own personality by being involved in individualism or rejection of his family. He did nothing of the kind. In fact, he slipped amazingly well into the position that his destiny had fated: living as heir apparent of a family that had already established both its reputation and fortune. Part of the ease with which he played this role was due to the stability of his own character, which demanded no rebellion against parental authority for its fulfillment. Part, however, was due to the wisdom of his parents, who to a large degree gave him free rein in business, politics, and society and allowed him to lead the family long before James Alexander was too old and sick to assert such a role. The primary characteristics of William Alexander's personality, as they manifested themselves both in early life and throughout his career as a businessman and soldier, were cheerfulness in outlook, stability in temperament, and willingness to acquiesce to leadership from those whom he thought his superiors in mental endowment or social rank. Consequently, the surviving correspondence between the Alexanders, parents and son, is warm, affectionate, and respectful, reflecting mutual trust and admiration. These letters are filled with news of business, the weather, natural phenomena, wars, and the family's health and typically close with "Your affectionate & Dutifull Son" and "Your affectionate father."[17]

The family to whom the Alexanders alluded in their messages to each other was increasing in numbers after 1748. In that year, William Alexander married Sarah Livingston, daughter of Philip Livingston, heir to the Livingston's wealth, social position, and political power. Sarah's brother, William Livingston, as governor of New Jersey in the Revolution, worked closely with his brother-in-law the general. By 1752, William Alexander and Sarah Livingston Alexander were parents of their only children, two daughters named Mary and Catherine. Mary later married Robert Watts, who was a moderate loyalist during the revolutionary war and caused her patriot father no small amount of embarrassment. Catherine, Lady Kitty as she was usually called, married William Duer, a member of the Continental Congress and a revolutionary. Sarah Alexander, a handsome woman as portrayed by the artist Benjamin West, left little record of her life from which to draw impressions. She retires into the background of her husband's career, rarely appearing by his side, and, if so, little noted by her contemporaries. A letter that she wrote her husband, "Billie," while visiting her family at Manor Livingston in July 1752, gives a hint of her personality and the love she felt for her spouse:

> We arrived here yesterday morning after a very hot but merry passage and found all the family in perfect health, I should not be Sorry to see you here a fortnet hence for your Journey in the woods wil be killing in this excesif hot wether if I had thought it so bed I would not have Stord from home. . . . how very agreeable a line from you will be to me pray let me have it when ever you have an oppertunity for that shall be all my comfort here . . .[18]

Alexander's "journey in the woods" probably was a business trip of some sort, for throughout the third decade of his life he devoted more time and energy to commercial affairs than to any other interest. Gradually, he drifted toward economic independence as he built up a fortune separate from the one his parents already possessed. But he continued to work in his mother's mercantile house, where he was centrally located to take advantage of trade with London and the distribution of English goods. He engaged in partnership with John Stevens in 1748, becoming deeply involved in trading and shipping just as the War of the Austrian Succession was drawing to a close and business conditions were improving. The two men occasionally met at Combs Tavern on Staten Island to transact business, mostly involving speculations on the prices of flour, molasses, and ships' rigging and canvas. Alexander also entered a business deal with his mother involving the iron industry in the Hudson Valley and acted as a broker for the sale of several hogsheads of sugar for a widow who was disposing of her estate. He became a landowner himself when in 1752 his half brother David Provoost died and left him land at Esopus; in addition, he purchased a one-sixteenth share of the vast Hardenbergh Patent and joined with other owners to pay costs of surveying and roadbuilding on the site.[19]

Alexander and his partners sometimes worked through agents in other entrepôts to advance their business and sometimes traveled as their own agents. William Alexander carried on an extensive correspondence with a cousin of the same name and his wife Catherine in Edinburgh that resulted in 1749 in a large sale of beeswax, logwood, and other items in that city.[20] After he and Henry Livingston became partners in the purchase of several ships during the 1740s, Livingston went to Jamaica to assure that the boats did not lie idle. Alexander himself took a business trip in 1753 to New England, attempting to collect some outstanding debts. It is not known if he succeeded in his mission, but the trip was worthwhile for him socially and politically. He was well received by many of the "gentry" of Connecticut such as John Winthrop of New London and Josiah Dwight and John Lyman of Northampton.21

In addition to these financial ventures, Alexander and his business partners were deeply involved in the slave trade for a time in the late 1740s, quitting the business only when it seemed unprofitable. That William Alexander evinced no moral scruples about slavery comes as no surprise, for he reflected in this attitude not only his father's but also practically all white people's ideas (excepting a few Quakers). James Alexander had made known his views on the place of Negroes in society when after the New York slave rebellion of 1741 he had volunteered, along with every other member of the bar of New York City, to prosecute white and black persons implicated in the plot. He had assisted Attorney General Richard Bradley in securing convictions against numerous defendants, twenty-two of whom were hanged and thirteen of whom were burned alive for their offenses. William Alexander and John Stevens were involved in the slave trade by late 1748, buying one-sixth interest in two vessels that were sailing for Africa; Alexander's parents helped him finance the venture. One of the ships returned with a cargo of 40 Negroes in August 1749, and Alexander and Stevens managed to sell all of them, including children and the sick, except "one who burnt himself in the fire and expired." The second ship never arrived, for as Stevens wrote Alexander in January 1750, "bad luck" had struck the previous autumn and the vessel had gone to the bottom of the ocean.22

Alexander, undaunted by this disaster, purchased two slave ships, the *Wolf* and the *Rhode Island,* on his own and in time received 100 more slaves for the auction block. Meanwhile, he acted as a broker or middleman for other slave traders, in his correspondence cold-bloodedly discussing the slaves as though they were cattle. "I shall get as much . . . as I can," he wrote Stevens; "selling them is no trouble to me." Yet, as suddenly as he had begun the slave business, he quit for reasons of unprofitability, and no mention of Negroes ever again occurred in his correspondence. Later on, he used white indentured servants at his estate in Basking Ridge, New Jersey, rather than Negro slaves, but this was due to practicality not principle. Slavery was a question of business to him, and in this attitude he was no more or less enlightened than the vast majority of his eighteenth-century colleagues.[23]

Alexander's business interests consumed the greater part of his time and energy in his early thirties, but he also was involved in public affairs and politics. He followed with interest his father's participation in attempts to evict tenants of John Penn from land in New Jersey claimed by the proprietors of East Jersey (a group that James Alexander served with distinction for thirty years and that William would join when his father died in 1756). His attention was also directed to matters closer to home in New York. He wrote a letter to his half brother John Provoost in London in 1750, jokingly complaining of the paucity of news: "It's not now as it was in Warr Time, when we had every day some Sea or land fight to write of. Oh! Barren peace!" He went on, however, to report that a grand jury in New York was indicting many merchants for shipping bad flour; he approved of these proceedings, for "neither the English, French, Dutch, Spaniards or even Negroes," he complained, "would buy a barrel of N. York flower while Philledelphia flower is to be had." His interest in military matters at this time was also strong, for he was captain of a New York militia company, actively drilling his men on muster days and seeing to their organization and equipment on a regular basis. This duty, while not demanding or even particularly serious, gave him at least a taste of what it was like to command soldiers and partake of a military life.[24]

In 1752, Alexander became involved in the so-called "Whig Club," a society composed of young men who fancied themselves philosophers and a cut above the majority of their peers. The leading lights of this group were William Livingston, John Morin Scott, and William Smith, Jr.; the lesser luminaries included Alexander and William Peartree Smith. They assembled weekly at the King's Arms Tavern, drank toasts to Oliver Cromwell, John Hampden, and "Liberty," and composed manifestoes. They began publishing a weekly paper, *The Independent Reflector*, in November, "to oppose superstition, bigotry, priestcraft, tyranny, servitude, public mismanagement and dishonesty in office." The paper, which was in existence for one year, opposed the founding of King's College under a board of trustees dominated by Anglicans and in general rejected the idea of an Episcopal hierarchy of any kind for America. Some essays by Livingston and Scott also appeared in the "Watch Tower" column of the *New York Mercury,* and five years later one of these men, probably Livingston, wrote *A Review of the Military Operations in North America, 1753–1756,* in defense of Governor William Shirley of Massachusetts. Alexander seems to have taken a peripheral part in these goings on; he may have written one, and perhaps as many as three, essays in *The Independent Reflector,* and he later contributed information to the authors of the *Review,* in Shirley's defense. However, many of the political views expressed by Livingston, Scott, and Smith were more Whiggish than his own, even in the 1750s, and as time went on he tended to become even more politically conservative.[25]

Two

•

Service for Crown and Colony, 1754–1756

In 1754 Alexander took part in events heralding the Seven Years' War, beginning a public career that was to span the next three decades. Since ratification of the Treaty of Aix-la-Chapelle in 1749, which ended the War of the Austrian Succession, England and France had quarreled over territory lying between each of their empires in North America. The British government by 1753 was ordering its colonial governors to repel with force any French attempts to penetrate the vast wilderness bounded by the Allegheny Mountains in the east and the Mississippi River in the west. Governor Robert Dinwiddie of Virginia implemented his instructions in the fall of that year by sending a message of protest in the care of a young Virginian, George Washington, to the commandants of the new French forts at Presqu'Isle, French Creek, and the seized English post of Venango. This mission failed to dislodge the French. Then, in the following year, Dinwiddie ordered an armed expedition against Fort Duquesne, led by Colonel Joshua Fry and Lieutenant Colonel Washington. This undertaking came to grief at Fort Necessity in western Pennsylvania.[1]

Meantime, in June 1754, Alexander attended the Albany Congress as the proxy of his father, who was kept away by the gout. This gathering, composed of commissioners from Pennsylvania, Maryland, New York, and the New England colonies, met at the instigation of the English Crown to negotiate with the Indians of the Six Nations for support in the impending war against the French in Canada. The Albany Congress also made efforts toward intercolonial union, favored by leaders in both England and America. Alexander was involved both privately and publicly in the proceedings of the congress. He made a quick business trip to Philadelphia in March to discuss with Richard Peters, one of the appointed Pennsylvania commissioners, the possibility of selling him Indian goods for use in upcoming negotiations with the Six Nations. At first Peters agreed to a deal, but he later bowed to pressure from Philadelphia merchants and canceled his contract with Alexander. Meanwhile, Alexander arranged accommodations in New York for the four Pennsylvania commissioners who would visit the city while they were en route to Albany and made plans for Benjamin Franklin, one of the commissioners, to talk extensively with his father.[2]

William Alexander's primary task at the Albany Congress was to lay before the commissioners his father's views on the proposed union of colonies. The elder Alexander's ideas were mostly quibbles over minor details that were in Franklin's "Hints . . . for Uniting Northern Colonies," which Franklin had shown to him during his visit to New York City. In any case, the congress unanimously accepted Franklin's plan calling for a federal council of delegates from all the colonies that would have power to legislate, tax, raise armies, and deal with Indian affairs. Franklin's plan was later rejected by the colonial legislatures. William Alexander's sole personal contribution to the plan was designed to satisfy Indian demands in upstate New York. He offered to give up claims to lands that might accrue to him as a part of the estate of his father-in-law, Philip Livingston.[3]

At the Albany Congress Alexander was also to act, in lieu of his father, as attorney for his Pennsylvania friends in countering attempts by Connecticut agents of the Susquehannah Company to buy vast tracts of land in the Wyoming Valley from Indians who lived there. He had warned Richard Peters three months earlier about plans of the Susquehannah Company agents to purchase one hundred square miles of central Pennsylvania land and had urged Peters to have Pennsylvania Governor Robert Hunter Morris scare them off. Peters had complied. At Albany Alexander alerted William Johnson, imperial agent for Indian affairs in the northern colonies, that Connecticut agents, led by Eliphalet Dyer, had made a treaty with the Indians and that, therefore, the goodwill of the Six Nations Indians, so ardently sought by British agents at Albany, was seriously threatened.[4] He failed to mention, however, that at precisely that same time his clients, Richard Peters and John Penn, were attempting to execute orders of their governor and purchase the same Indian titles for Pennsylvania—in equally reckless disregard of imperial policy.

   The results of this intercolonial bickering over Indian lands were twofold. First, British war efforts were impeded in later years because the colonists were venting their spleen on each other rather than the common enemy. Second, Connecticut and Pennsylvania became embroiled in a legal controversy, with Alexander always taking the side of Pennsylvania in the struggle. He gave to Governor Morris of Pennsylvania in 1754 his opinion that Connecticut's putative claims to Pennsylvania lands through charter rights were spurious. Then, in 1760, after Pennsylvania had acquired from the Six Nations Indians the same lands that Connecticut thought it had gotten in 1754, he gave a similar opinion to another Pennsylvania governor, Thomas Penn. Both states claimed the territory during the Revolution, and in 1782 Alexander gave a deposition in a court battle that once again favored Pennsylvania's claims. Finally, late in the war, the Continental Congress awarded the land to Pennsylvania, and in 1790, seven years after Alexander's death, the United States courts finally confirmed Pennsylvania's claim and supported Alexander's contentions.[5]

   During the winter of 1754–55, Alexander had the good fortune to receive an invitation from Governor William Shirley of Massachusetts to join Shirley's personal staff as secretary. He and Elisha Parker had visited Shirley in Boston earlier at the instigation of James Alexander, who was a friend of the governor. It is not hard to surmise that William Alexander's appointment came as a consequence of paternal intervention. Governor Shirley, who had made a military reputation for himself in the previous war by planning and organizing the expedition that in 1745 captured Louisbourg, on Cape Breton Island, was already deeply involved in preparing for the present one. Shirley was an able and convivial man, easy to work for, and Alexander, newly promoted to the rank of major in the New York militia, thought he could hardly be luckier in his choice of commanders. Even George Washington, who was not easily impressed by public office holders, called Shirley a "gentleman and great politician." Major Alexander immediately took up his duties, attending a meeting of the New York Council on March 12, 1755, to discuss the important subject of Indian policy.[6]

   Alexander's first significant assignment was to accompany Governor Shirley southward to Alexandria, Virginia, in April 1755, for a meeting of colonial leaders to formulate strategy for the upcoming campaign season. The council was called by General Edward Braddock, newly appointed commander in chief of North America, and attended by Braddock; Admiral Augustus Keppel; Governors Shirley of Massachusetts, Dinwiddie of Virginia, Horatio Sharpe of Maryland, Morris of Pennsylvania, and DeLancey of New York; and by Indian commissioner William Johnson. The plan of operations, which was agreed upon, had been drawn up by the Duke of Cumberland, son of George II, and contained a number of provisions. First, Braddock, as commander in chief, was to march against Fort Duquesne. Second, Shirley would strengthen Oswego and assault Niagara, using his own regiment, a new one under Sir William Pepperell, two companies of independent regulars in New York, and some provincial troops and allied Indians. Third, and finally, Johnson was to attack Crown Point at the southern end of Lake Champlain. For Alexander, as Shirley's aide, the second part of the plan was most interesting in the long run. For the present, however, he was more concerned with socializing than with military policy. He renewed such old acquaintances as Thomas Pownall, whom he had gotten to know the year before through his father's friendship, and met new people, such as Washington, with whom he would work closely in future military ventures.[7]

Shirley and Alexander returned to New York after the meeting and began organizing the expedition against Niagara, for the campaigning season was drawing near and there was no time to lose. One of the commander's most important decisions was to award the contract for supplying the expedition to Peter Van Brugh Livingston and Lewis Morris, Jr., two prominent and well-connected New York businessmen. Because Alexander was Livingston's partner, and John Erving, Jr., Morris's partner, they were automatically included in this arrangement; and, because the former was Shirley's secretary and the latter his son-in-law, there was no question but that through this contract the commander was taking care of friends and family. Although these arrangements look unethical and are not common practice today, they were not unusual at the time. In fact, Shirley may have been attempting to ensure himself against fraud and incompetence by awarding to his secretary and son-in-law, both of whom he trusted implicitly, the crucial task of supplying the army. His success or failure, after all, would be theirs as well.[8]

When Shirley failed in his mission to capture Niagara, he was severely attacked in both England and America, and his military career came to an end. One of the primary charges laid against him was that he had mishandled the army's contracts and that the contractors themselves had proved to be incompetent and corrupt. The evidence shows that Shirley's inability to fulfill his assignment was due in large part to forces beyond his control and that neither he nor his contractors can be given all the blame for their lack of success. The richness of the commission itself—five percent of all expenses—was enough to arouse jealousy among those not in on the prize, especially when the ones excluded were already predisposed to dislike those rewarded. As William Alexander noted in a letter to John Shirley, the governor's son, in May 1755, criticism of Shirley's financial arrangements was rife primarily among the DeLancey faction, the long-time enemies of the Livingstons. Soon the DeLanceys were spreading rumors widely through whispering campaigns that the contractors were making illegal profits and hiding their embezzlements by falsifying records.[9]

Alexander received a larger share of this criticism than did his business partners because he was more deeply involved than they in organizing and running the campaign. General Shirley's confidence in his secretary was so great that he put the army's administration in Alexander's hands while he was absent, relied upon Stirling for advice when making important decisions, allowed him to order all the army's supplies, and empowered him to ship these war materials over the long route to Oswego. When the expedition failed, therefore, "the *soi-disant* Earl of Stirling," as historian Stanley Pargellis called Alexander, had to accept "much of the responsibility for the wretched condition of Oswego." This assessment rests upon the willingness of Shirley's critics, especially John Campbell, Lord Loudoun, who replaced him in 1756, to listen to the carpings of the DeLancey faction. Such complaints were not disinterested, to say the least, and are therefore highly suspect.[10]

The task facing Alexander and his fellow contractors in fulfilling their obligations was enormous. In his initial instructions, Shirley ordered them to provide the army with supplies for 1,600 men for three months, and he appointed them his agents to construct two ships on Lake Ontario. In addition, he gave them authority to buy all equipment necessary to carry out these instructions, to build five hundred bateaux and four hundred flatboats for transporting goods to Oswego by the Mohawk River, Wood Creek, Lake Oneida, and the Oswego

River, and to provide proper storehouses for provisions at each end of the Carrying Place, between the Mohawk River and Wood Creek. He gave Alexander in particular the assignment of implementing these instructions in the field. Additionally Alexander was charged to engage wagons, horses, oxen, and drivers at the carrying places on the route to Oswego; buy cattle for the soldiers: survey the fort and works at Oswego and make an exact map of them, finding out all he could about the navigation of Lake Ontario; and provide shipping to transport his regiment from Providence, Rhode Island, up the Hudson River to Albany.[11]

These were daunting tasks, but Alexander took them on with gusto, traveling back and forth for the next month between New York City and Albany in order to spur on his subordinates and complete this work. He knew he must act quickly, because Shirley had warned him that the expedition must be launched as early in the summer as possible. Alexander's first concern was to build ships on Lake Ontario. Within days after receiving Shirley's instructions, he sent forward to Oswego rigging for the schooners, ships carpenters, sawyers, one wheelwright, and two blacksmiths. He also purchased numerous necessities, such as nails, oakum, canvas, and pitch. On May 17 Alexander happily announced to Shirley that a sloop, carrying officers for the vessels to be built on Lake Ontario had arrived in New York from Virginia.[12]

Alexander also worked with diligence and success in procuring arms for Shirley's troops. During his stay in Virginia, he had been promised five hundred muskets by Governor Dinwiddie, and he now had Lieutenant Governor James DeLancey and his council agree to purchase them. He also pleaded with the lieutenant governor to sell him eight brass cannon that were available in the city and finally managed to secure seven. Meanwhile, he acquired cannon balls and shot from Robert Livingston, proprietor of Ancram Furnace, and he managed to buy five hundred barrels of gunpowder.[13]

Alexander realized the importance of the construction and use of bateaux in the ultimate outcome of the campaign and spent much time in organizing that work. Early in May he put the building of bateaux under the supervision of James Stevenson at Albany and instructed Joseph Van Eppes and John Fisher at Schenectady to supply him with lumber, pitch, iron, paint, and oars. Stevenson and his aides hired Walter Quackenbush, a shipwright, to build bateaux. Alexander informed Shirley on May 27 that construction was proceeding rapidly and that within three weeks seventy or more bateaux would be launched. Sure enough, seventy vessels, sufficient for the needs of the campaign, were ready weeks before the army arrived. Alexander ordered that the upper Mohawk River and Wood Creek be cleared ahead of time so that the waterways upon which the bateaux would move would be free of obstructions. He also warned the bateaux handlers that they must take care not to submit bateaux to extra wear and tear, especially when they were in portage, or they could be broken apart unnecessarily.[14]

As the army's transport was being completed, Alexander turned his attention to another of the many duties that Shirley had given him in his original instructions, the erecting of two storehouses at either end of the Carrying Place. Shirley had given Alexander precise guidelines as to the size of and materials for these storehouses, but Alexander still asked Captain John Bradstreet for advice on how and where they should be built. He issued orders for their construction on May 27, but a week later William Johnson was protesting that the storehouses should not be built without the consent of the Six Nations Indians. Alexander had his orders, however, and wrote Johnson a polite note saying the project must proceed; hence he directed Captain William Williams to put his soldiers to work on the building.[15]

Alexander and his partners, while carrying out myriad other tasks, also sought to secure the three months' supply of provisions that Shirley had contracted for in April. They succeeded in purchasing the best available provisions at the lowest price, despite what their critics said, and they took care to protect them from wastage in the field. Alexander counteracted profiteering on bread, pork, and beef in New York, by securing large supplies of these items from merchants in Philadelphia, using a grant of ten thousand pounds that the Pennsylvania legislature had contributed to the war effort. (One suspects that Alexander was buying products in Philadelphia for reasons other than wholly market forces. It is likely that the Pennsylvania merchants insisted on this procedure or that Alexander was doing it to stay in their good graces.) He also purchased dried peas and bread in the Albany market, telling his agent, James Stevenson, not to allow prices to be inflated above those of the New York area, and he secured live cattle to be on hand there as troops began to arrive from New York City. In addition, he sent Captain Bradstreet various types of vegetable seeds, with instructions for their planting and care, that fresh produce might be available for the troops that summer. He was confident enough in his preparations by May 10 to inform General Shirley that the commander could expect all provisions for the army of the Niagara expedition to be at Albany within two weeks.[16]

While carrying out his assignments as an army contractor, Alexander also acted as Shirley's military adviser on the scene. The general, busy in Massachusetts attempting to procure artillery for his army, was being delayed in his arrival in New York. Alexander kept Shirley apprised of troop movements by informing him in May that three companies of soldiers were marching from Albany to Schenectady and in June that William Pepperell's regiment was in New York fitting out in preparation to take post. It was Alexander's opinion that two of the companies on their way up the Mohawk ought to be stationed at either end of the Carrying Place to frighten off Indians. He also believed that for greater security in troop movements, all marching soldiers in the wilderness should be sent along in small bodies. In mid-May Alexander made a scouting trip as far as the Carrying Place, surveying potential campsites for the army, obtaining charts of the layout of Oswego, and drawing accurate maps of the entire region. He reported these matters to Shirley on May 27, at the same time urging the general to hurry with his preparations, because Alexander had just learned from local inhabitants that the water in Wood Creek and the Mohawk River became shallow in midsummer and that bateau traffic would be impeded. In the interim, intelligence reports from Canada were excellent. The French, Alexander told Shirley, were off their guard at Niagara (if not in the Ohio Valley and the East, where they expected attacks). They thought the troops moving to Oswego were only a garrison reinforcement and that Johnson's Crown Point expedition was designed merely to strengthen New York's hold on the frontier.[17]

The expedition that Alexander had worked so hard to help organize was launched in early July. Shirley arrived from Boston after a quick voyage and was entertained with his son in Alexander's own home. Shirley spent only two days in New York before sailing with the army toward Albany, leaving behind the cheering of the people and the booming of the cannons. Exultantly, Alexander wrote on July 6, from aboard the sloop *Massachusetts* on his way to Albany, "We left New York in high spirits." A general war seemed inevitable, "and it is like to be a new fashioned one—an army and a prodigious fleet in North

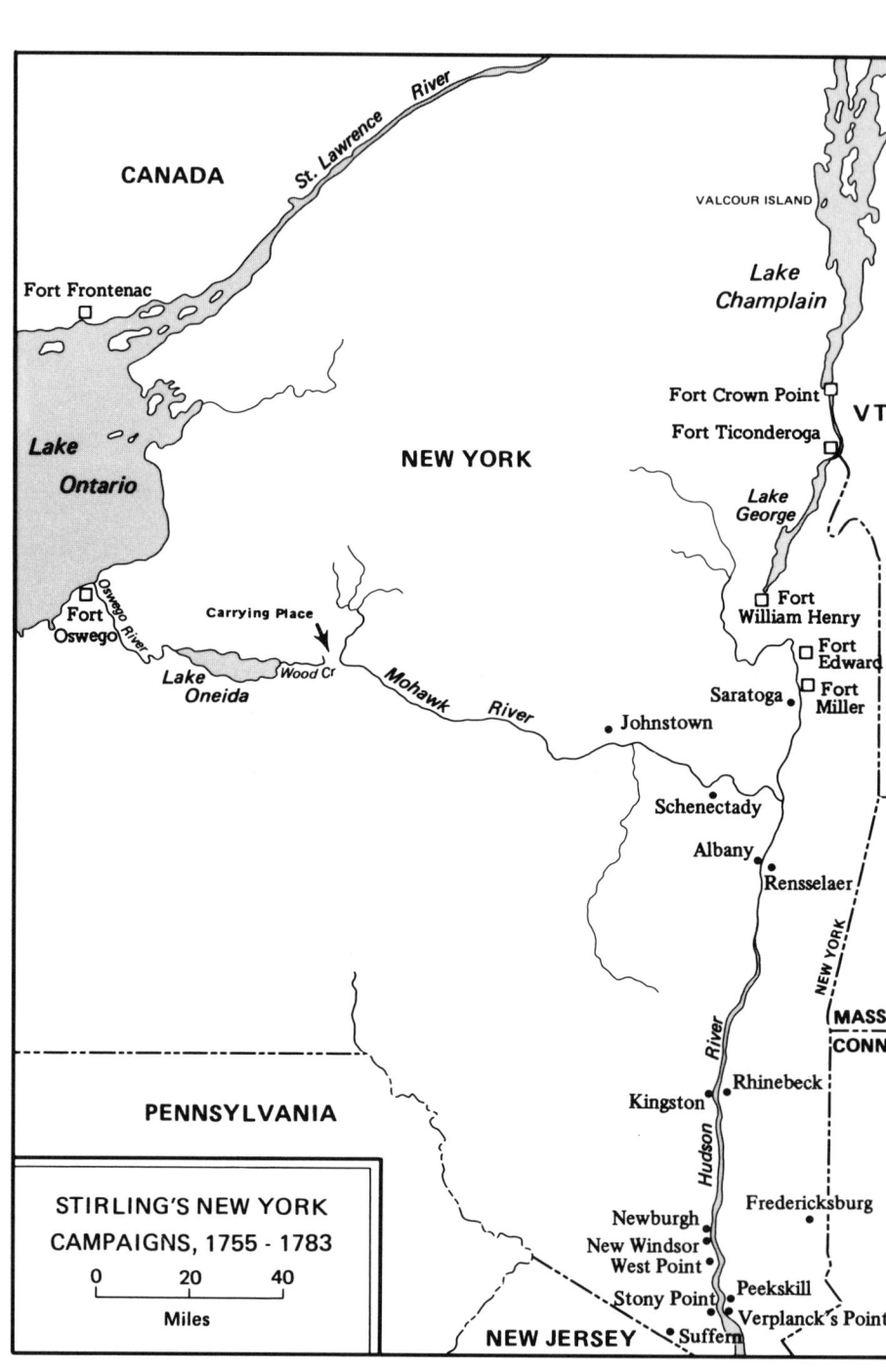

America, and the English nation behaving with spirit enough to terrify all Europe."[18]

Alexander's celebratory mood was quickly dampened by bad news awaiting him at Albany. First, he learned from Peter Van Brugh Livingston that his mother and wife were unwell; the former had fallen on July 7 and the latter had "a pain in her skull." Fortunately, they were on the mend within a short time. Second, Alexander himself fell sick, apparently from overwork; but he too began to recover after about a week. Third, he received word that General Braddock had suffered a resounding defeat near Fort Duquesne in western Pennsylvania and had been killed, along with one of Shirley's sons. It was hoped in Albany that the news might prove false, but unfortunately it was all too true. Fourth, Alexander became embroiled in misunderstandings that had quickly flared up between Generals Shirley and Johnson. Antagonism between the two commanders broke out in part because one was a New Englander and the other a New Yorker, and both were extremely sensitive to perceived sectional slights. Additionally, their armies were fitting out in the same confined territory, and the resources of the region simply were inadequate to the demand. Thus they found themselves competing for scarce campsites, water, and other items. Moreover, they represented the two warring factions of New York politics, the Livingstons and DeLanceys, which was for them sufficient cause for antagonism.[19]

The trouble began when Shirley tried to shift troops from Johnson's expedition to his own, in order to balance the forces more evenly. For Johnson this was bad enough, but his fury reached a new level when Shirley and his aides tried to lure Indians away from his expedition into their own, "without my knowledge or Consent," by "Bribe, to work every possible Artifice in their power." "They spared no money, they spared no reflections upon me," Johnson reported to Thomas Pownall; "every Trick that could be practised, they made use of" and "Billy Alexander [was] as active as any of 'em." As Johnson told James DeLancey, Alexander was even insulting to "two of my own Servants . . . I had sent . . . up for part of my Baggage." Moreover, Alexander tried to lure a faithful interpreter away from Johnson by promising that "he should have a larger salary than he received from the Province." When the agent had complained "That his [present] salary was too small, Mr. Alexander said it was in [Johnson's] power to double it & was surprized [he] did not do it." "These," said Johnson, "are some of the outlines of a Picture wch. I believe has scarce a parralel."[20]

The two armies went their separate ways in late July, much to the relief of their commanders. Shirley had 1,750 men in his expedition, all of them struggling along the difficult Mohawk-Wood Creek-Oswego River water route, with its numerous portages, shallow places, and rapids. Alexander did not find time in this period of "greatest fatigue" to write to anyone in New York City. When he finally did send a letter to Peter Van Brugh Livingston on August 4, the news he conveyed was not good. The army, he said, was on the verge of needing three hundred more barrels of pork, one hundred of rum, and two hundred bushels of salt. The soldiers had bread in abundance, for wheat was easy to procure and grind on the scene, and Stirling had purchased one thousand bushels of peas from nearby suppliers. Many other provisions had been lost or destroyed because they were not tightly packed. He urged that all provisions be stored in good barrels that would not jar apart on the trip toward Oswego. Alexander's letter to Livingston could not alleviate what was becoming a crisis in supply, however, for soon thereafter army provisions were exhausted. Alexander quickly appealed to James Stevenson in Albany to have his bateaumen take more care with the goods in shipment in order to reduce the enormous wastage.[21]

The problem of army supply that now began to plague Shirley's command, and which would continue throughout the rest of the expedition, clearly lay not with Alexander and his business partners but elsewhere. The real reasons for the shortages were low water in the transport streams, a paucity of bateaumen to haul supplies, and the carelessness with which previous stores had been handled on the trip. All these were problems that Alexander had tried to avert beforehand but that he now was powerless to control.[22]

Despite the army's troubles with provisions, General Shirley pushed on toward Oswego, where he arrived with his army on August 18. He discovered that the forts there had serious weaknesses and felt compelled to halt his march toward Niagara in order to avoid leaving behind him an insecure base of operations that was open to French assault from Fort Frontenac. Shirley had learned in any case (as Alexander noted to Livingston on October 4) that the bateaux which he had intended to use for transporting soldiers on Lake Ontario, were worthless for the job and that he must wait throughout the winter while two hundred whaleboats were constructed at Schenectady. He had assigned this task to Alexander and his partners, and the work was commenced immediately. The army with Alexander reluctantly settled into their new surroundings for a long, dull winter sojurn, while Shirley, who had been given command of all British forces in North America after Braddock died on the Monogahela, turned his mind to thwarting French ambitions for the remainder of the year.

The governor of Canada, Pierre de Rigaud de Vaudreuil, had learned from intelligence sources exactly what British plans were for 1755, but luckily for Shirley he decided to attack Johnson's army before turning his attention to the threat at Oswego. Vaudreuil's commander, Baron de Dieskau was defeated and killed at Lake George, and Shirley was given respite at least until the following spring. He took advantage of the lull to have Alexander and Bradstreet draw up plans for rebuilding Fort Ontario. When Alexander presented the plans to George Dimler, who was to build the fort, Dimler argued that they were insufficient: "But Mr. Alexander ordered to have the plan executed according to the draught, and that I had nothing further to do than follow his Orders which the General Confirmed."23

Meanwhile, Alexander and his partners were attempting to deal with yet another problem that had arisen in their role as army contractors—a chronic lack of ready cash. They had been issued crown warrants for forty thousand pounds in early summer, but by September they had been paid only fifteen thousand pounds. In order to see that the demands of men like James Stevenson were met, Livingston was forced to cover bills from his own funds. Even these were not enough to meet all costs, however, and he was forever being hounded by creditors for payments that he could not make until the contractors were reimbursed by the government. In August, Alexander had persuaded the army paymaster to issue Livingston two thousand pounds for emergencies, but this sum was quickly exhausted. Alexander suggested to Livingston on September 17 that perhaps the latter exaggerated his problems, for "I believe such large sums have Seldom been paid with more dispatch." Livingston testily replied that if he did not soon receive another warrant, he would leave home to escape his creditors, "be the consequences what it will." He did not get any money, but neither did he carry out his threat. He, Alexander, and Crown agents handling governmental accounts in Boston and Virginia quibbled for the next few months about payment of a warrant for ten thousand pounds, and at the end of that time the issue still remained unsettled—as it would for years to come.[24]

Before the end of September, Shirley and Alexander were confronted with profound unrest in the army at Oswego. The commander, lacking civilian workmen, employed his soldiers, to their extreme disgust, in constructing the fortifications that had been designed by Alexander and Bradstreet. The troops were already angry because they were on half rations, without rum or pay, and seemingly without prospects of securing these items any time soon. Obviously the crisis of supply had not abated, despite Alexander's every effort to alleviate the problem. He continued into the winter to implore Livingston to rush provisions to the army, and he purchased what he could of peas, cattle, and firewood in the Mohawk country. To no avail. He fell "very ill" in early October for the second time that year, but, as he wrote Livingston on the fourth, "I am well now." He missed his family more than usual during his sickness, and he asked plaintively to be remembered to "my father and mother and all friends."[25] Finally, the men of Shirley's regiment mutinied. A number of bateaux had arrived at Oswego carrying not supplies for the army but private goods for distribution by sutlers. The mutineers, angrily jumping to the conclusion that Alexander was at fault for their plight, stormed to his headquarters and insisted on explanations. Alexander, pushed to the limits of forbearance, just as angrily retorted that he could not be expected to make bread from thin air and sarcastically suggested that they try eating stones. This ugly situation was alleviated only when Shirley promised his soldiers that their grievances would be met. Instead, supply problems lingered throughout the winter.[26]

Was Alexander involved in these private business deals that were obviously detrimental to the public good? Lord Loudoun, who replaced Shirley as commander in chief a few months later, thought so, and told the Duke of Cumberland that Alexander had turned Shirley's expedition into a "Trading Voyage," using a dozen bateaux to ship his goods to Oswego while the army starved. Captain William Williams was sure that the number of bateaux in Alexander's private use was even higher, although he conceded that some of them may have been filled with presents for the Indians. Alexander was not only accused of using bateaux illegally but also, as historian Stanley Pargellis charges, of profiting "in his private capacity as a merchant by using his official powers as a member of Shirley's staff to assign trading privileges."

Robert Livingston, for instance, supposedly advised Charles DeWitt on one occasion to see Alexander about permission to trade within Shirley's army in exchange for one-third interest in the business. Pargellis claimed that Shirley knew nothing of this deviousness until early in 1757, when it was far too late to correct it; nonetheless, "private trading ambitions contended with and took precedence over government needs" while gullible General Shirley was in command. Lord Loudoun at the time did not forgive Shirley, as Pargellis did later; for Loudoun declared that his predecessor had employed Alexander "where he means to have his own nearer friends not appear."[27]

Alexander vehemently denied these charges when they became known to him in September 1756. He said that only on one occasion, when a small amount of privately owned clothing was shipped to Oswego, had he and his partners sold their own stores. The charges, he alleged, were politically motivated by the DeLancey faction and based on hearsay evidence. He did not attempt to refute the fact that publicly owned bateaux had carried private goods to sutlers at Oswego, because that practice was absolutely necessary unless the officers, who had to purchase their own supplies, were to do without. In fact, said Alexander, Oliver DeLancey, one of his most vociferous critics, had taken advantage of the system himself to send thirty bateau loads of goods to Oswego. Moreover, DeLancey had gouged his customers with ridiculously high prices until General Shirley put a stop to it by regulating sutlers' prices. Alexander *did* refute the assertion by his enemies that he and his partners had been involved in the trade.[28]

While he was at it, Alexander also denied that he and his partners had charged too much for their services. He repudiated claims that contractors were allowed additional commissions above the regular five percent, that the bateaux he had ordered constructed had cost too much, that storehouse charges at Albany were too high, or that the cost of provisioning troops was excessive. In fact, declared Alexander, if the total of debits and profits for the contractors were added up, in fifteen months they had made only £5,000 sterling, and even that was contingent on the outstanding charges against government ever being paid. The claims of his political enemies, and those of General Lord Loudoun, he insisted, were patently untrue. He was supported in these assertions by a committee of merchants in New York City, who met with Governor Charles Hardy to go over the contractors' accounts. Try as they might, they found nothing amiss in the partners' claim that the government still owed them an honest debt of £14,378 sterling. However, Shirley and Alexander lost any hope that they might receive quick vindication in London when Shirley's patron, the Duke of Newcastle, was superseded in 1757 by a new ministry. This government, especially Minister William Pitt, paid attention only to charges by Loudoun and others that something was wrong with the contractors' figures and would not let the issue be resolved. A growing conviction now possessed Alexander that his only hope of vindication and payment rested with an appeal in person to the Treasury in London.[29]

The military campaign, meantime, played itself out to its bitter end. William Alexander accompanied General Shirley to Boston in early 1756 in order to expedite plans for upcoming military activities against the French. He and the contractors collected materials and workmen to construct a third sloop for use on Lake Ontario, and also 250 whaleboats for convoying troops. Additionally, Alexander continued to purchase provisions for the army, and by June 18 he confidently reported to Pennsylvania Governor Robert Hunter Morris that John Bradstreet had transported to Oswego three months' supplies for five thousand men. Preparations for an expedition to Crown Point were also well matured, and a number of good ranger companies, including one led by Robert Rogers, were raised and ready to go. In March, he belittled rumors that French and Indian forces were moving against Oswego. Even if the stories were true, he said, the place was strong enough to fend off any attack; he should know, he insisted, for he had helped Bradstreet the previous winter in designing the fortifications.[30]

Hence, Alexander was convinced that if William Shirley were to be relieved of command, as rumor now had it he would be, the general's successor was in a fine situation to expedite the campaign. The new commander's "plenty," he noted gratuitously, would be "owing to Mr. Shirley's care"—a point that Alexander wanted clearly understood. Already he had received word of the "calumnious performance" of a New York newspaper writer, who had criticized with "misrepresentations, and falsehoods" the conduct of the Oswego campaign in the previous year. Now, he told Livingston disgustedly, news from London had arrived in Boston on the warship *Lyn* that DeLancey partisans in England were "very busy and impertinent" in saying "many dirty things of us [Shirley and the contractors]." The record must be set straight, he believed, while there was still time to do so.[31]

Alexander devoted most of his time to public business during his

Boston visit in early 1756, but he still found time—indeed, was forced to by circumstances—to attend to private matters. He wrote Livingston in New York to check with a silversmith there about "The Silver Bread basket & Coffee pot wch. I spoke to him about as a present to Mrs. Alexander with her arms upon it." But his greatest family concern was with his father's health, for Peter Van Brugh Livingston had informed him that James Alexander, while on a trip to Albany, had become bedridden with a severe attack of gout and might not recover. William Alexander replied to Livingston on April 5 that he hoped to get away from Boston within a week, and he expressed grave concern that his father was so ill. When he finally did arrive in New York City late that month he spent only a short time with his family and friends before anxiously departing for Albany aboard a sloop. His progress upriver was halted two days later by a storm from the northwest, and he boarded an open whaleboat for a "very cold & disagreeable" trip, reaching Albany and his dying father's bedside on May 8.[32] Shortly thereafter, James Alexander died.

The death of the patriarch of the Alexander family left William as the sole male heir to both his father's fortune and position. The Board of Proprietors of East Jersey on June 16 appointed him a member and made him surveyor general of the colony, and Governor Jonathan Belcher followed the proprietors' lead a few days later by naming Alexander a member of the New Jersey governor's council. He was also appointed to the governor's council of New York at about the same time and was made a member of the board of trustees of King's College. Other offices and positions would come to him in the 1760s, but they would be based more upon his personal merits than on his being the son of a famous man.[33]

As he dealt with personal affairs attendant upon his father's death and his assumption of family leadership, Alexander continued to act as Shirley's secretary. It was now well known to everyone that Shirley was to be replaced as commander in chief of North America by Lord Loudoun, and about the only military task that remained for Alexander was to act as an intermediary in effecting the transfer of power between two men who thoroughly disliked each other. In August he sent Loudoun copies of the detailed maps he had drawn the year before and asked that the new commander pay him the £145 that he had advanced from his personal funds to pay bateaumen earlier that year. In letters that were polite but guarded, he also explained to Loudoun certain technical details about Shirley's financial accounts. It was probably a relief to both Loudoun and Shirley when in the fall all their correspondence ended. Their relationship by that time had an added strain, because on August 14, Oswego had fallen to the French, and each blamed the other for the debacle.[34]

Alexander decided in July 1756, to accompany General Shirley to England, where Shirley had been summoned by the ministry to give an account of his activities in the Oswego campaign. "It will give me the highest pleasure," said Shirley to Governor Morris of Pennsylvania, "to have that voyage prove of real service to him in the future course of his life." Alexander's recently widowed mother was at first reluctant to part with her only son, but Shirley softened her opposition with soothing words, and soon "the Old Lady" was "perfectly settled to it." Alexander immediately set about to put his affairs in order for an extended absence from home, among other things taking an inventory of his "Wearing Apparrel." He discovered that he possessed seven suits, two red silk waistcoats, one pair of doeskin breeches, and numerous other articles, the quantity of which no doubt eased his mind on the question of whether he was sartorially prepared to venture into the heart of the British Empire. At last, Alexander and Shirley settled all matters of departure, made all good-byes to family and friends, and boarded ship for England.[35]

Three

The Provincial Becomes a Nobleman, 1757–1761

Although Alexander had intended for his sojourn in the British Isles to last only a few months, one thing after the other intervened (not least his own pleasure in living there) to keep him from going home. It was almost five years before he finally returned to America. He was swept into intense governmental activity soon after his arrival, serving the interests of numerous American friends and clients, including the Board of Proprietors of East Jersey, for whom he acted as agent in London. He was called before the Board of Trade as an "expert" on colonial affairs to give his opinions about the situation in America, which he continued to give the board even after his return to New York.

In the spring of 1757, along with Shirley, he became involved in a political maneuver in the House of Commons initiated by his new friend, Charles Townshend. Townshend, the leader of certain dissidents, at that time launched an attack on the Duke of Newcastle, Secretary of State, and Henry Fox, paymaster general of the forces, by questioning the wisdom of some of their military contracts in America. Townshend's claim was that the costs of these contracts had been excessive, and he used figures supplied by Alexander and Shirley to make his argument. He also called these two men before the House to testify, and although both were careful not to insult or disparage Newcastle (Shirley's patron), they did insist that they could have provided the same provisions for 20 percent less cost. The inquiry abruptly ceased when the Duke of Argyle and other friends of Lord Loudoun intervened in his defense.[1]

Alexander was by no means stilled, however, in his search for the justice that he and his political supporters in New York believed General Shirley was owed by the DeLanceys and their "dupes" in England. He had in his luggage a manuscript, entitled "Review of the Military Operations in North America . . . ," which had been written, most likely, by William Livingston, Alexander's old Whig Club colleague. This article, designed for publication in London in defense of Shirley, was a scathing attack on Massachusetts governor Thomas Pownall, whom Shirley's supporters believed had deliberately plotted with New York Governor DeLancey and William Johnson to get Shirley relieved of command. When the pamphlet appeared on the streets of London, it created quite a stir, especially among supporters of Loudoun, who thought the entire performance a scandal. However, John Pownall, secretary to the Board of Trade and brother of Governor Pownall, was even more disturbed. When he met Alexander, as he later told Alexander Colden, he angrily charged that Alexander was responsible for writing these "false . . . reflections upon my Brothers character." Taken aback, Alexander replied, "'Sir I am not the author I assure you upon my honor,'" but he did admit that his "particular friend at New York" had written it and that he had conveyed it to the printers. At that point, as Pownall told the story, Pownall broke off the conversation and departed. Shortly thereafter, at Vauxhall Gardens, a famous amusement ground of eighteenth-century London, Colden met with Alexander and Staats Morris, another American friend, to discuss this matter. "We went into an Alcove & drank a bottle of wine," said Colden, and Alexander confirmed Pownall's account of their conversation. But Alexander insisted that it was incomplete. In fact, Alexander said, he told Pownall that although he had not written the essay, he could "prove every article charged to be true & a great deal more," as could hundreds of other witnesses. He concluded the conversation with Pownall, he said, by telling him that his brother, Governor Pownall, "is a man not fitt to be intrusted, he is void even of common honesty, & capable of any thing." Colden, in relating these hard words, conveyed a tone of distinct skepticism that Pownall would tolerate such abuse of his brother from Alexander.[2]

A year later critics on both sides of the ocean had not stopped carping against the general's administration, and Alexander was still defending Shirley against abusive attacks. "Those who appear'd . . . his first friends and Counsellors," noted Alexander, "I always supported." However, these same people "now most ungratefully appear with the

The Provincial Becomes a Nobleman 33

first open mouths against him; such are the attendants on a Great Man's fall." Not a single one of these erstwhile friends, fumed Alexander, was "possess'd of Virtue enough to defend the Man and Measures they had just before approved and advis'd." Therefore, it was they who "deserve the Ignomyny which I am afraid his Lordship alone will foot." Clearly, however, it was not from lack of effort on Alexander's part that his mentor's reputation continued to suffer.[3]

Alexander spent considerable time defending Shirley, but he did not in any way neglect his purpose for going to England—to secure payment on the contractors' claims for the Oswego campaign. He talked to various people in his attempt to discover the best tactics to follow, and in July 1757, he presented a petition from himself and his business partners to the Treasury, asking that the £14,378 still owed them be paid. He also had General Shirley submit an affidavit in support of the memorial. The lords of the Treasury politely accepted these documents and immediately fowarded them to Henry Fox and William Wildman, Viscount Barrington, respectively paymaster general and secretary at war, for their opinions. Fox, after keeping the records three months (to revenge himself for Alexander's support of Townshend in the House) and after conferring with Barrington, suggested to the lords commissioners that the accounts ought to go to the king's Auditor of the Imprests for a decision. Consequently, the documents were sent to that officer in January 1758, where they languished for months without action, while Alexander produced document upon document in support of his claim.[4]

Finally, the Treasury decided that it must procure more evidence on the matter from Loudoun, and in August 1760, Loudoun recommended against Alexander's claim. Once again proceedings came to a halt. The case was renewed in January 1761, when Alexander was asked to recast the accounts, which he and a Treasury clerk did over a period of two months. At this point, as Alexander himself later explained, writing in the third person, "On finding his applications ineffectual, [Alexander] by the influence of his friends at Court was so fortunate as to be able to communicate his case to the Royal Ear, and did accordingly mention the same to the king himself." The consequence of this "application to his Majesty" was that the "business was ordered to be dispatched. A special meeting was summoned for the purpose and an order obtained to Sir Jeffery Amherst [now commander in chief in America] to cause the accounts to be liquidated and the Balance forthwith paid." Thus Alexander, after five years of frustration and expense had gotten the claims verified. Angrily he noted that most of this money was payment for private cash outlays and that the interest on it for five years would have amounted to more than the "profit"—five thousand pounds sterling—that the contractors had made. Indeed, the entire venture had proved to be a financial, and a political, nightmare for Alexander and his partners.[5]

While he pursued his business affairs, Alexander at the same time followed the unfolding of events in the Seven Years' War. He was delighted with the victories of the British army, under William Pitt's able administration, which, by 1759, had captured or recaptured Forts Frontenac, Duquesne, Niagara, Oswego, Ticonderoga, and Crown Point, and the city of Quebec. On the whole, he said, "Our Successes in the Material parts of North America have been sufficient to content us for our Campaigns," and it appeared that France must soon sue for peace. British triumphs in Europe, he said, bolstered this viewpoint, for "Success has not been confined to America." The only slightly worrisome matter was that the French might be planning an invasion of the home islands—they were collecting troops and flat-bottomed boats in the Bay of Biscay—"but I don't think they're mad enough to try it."[6]

Alexander was occupied with war and mindless bureaucratic ineptitude, but he did not allow either of these to make him angry or despondent. His natural ebullience and gregarious personality exerted themselves in his search for friendships and "connections" among well-placed Britons. The life led by this class had charms to entice men stronger and more level-headed than William Alexander, so it is not surprising to discover in him an almost embarrassing overfondness for the attentions of the social and political leadership of the British Empire. One English newspaper account reported of Alexander's doings in London, "Great respect was shown, and court paid to him, by the Scotch, particularly by Mr. Alexander Wedderburne, Drummonds the bankers, Lord Aberdeen, and others of Scotland." But "many other considerable people on this side of the Tweed" also were paying him attention. He became friends with Charles Townshend, the Duke of Argyle, William Pitt, Lord Chatham, George Grenville, and George Germain, Lord Sackville, whose trial for cowardice in battle he witnessed in 1760.[7]

Other highly placed Britons were also in his circle of acquaintance.

Three of these, the Earl of Bute, Henry Clinton, and Lord Shelburne, became such close friends that even after Alexander returned to America he continued to give them advice on matters of colonial policy. He also came to know and respect Patrick Graeme, his father's friend and protector of the Penn family's interests against the antiproprietor faction in Pennsylvania. In a letter to Graeme in 1758, Alexander took a distinctly anti-Franklin position, declaring that Franklin, as an opponent of the Penns in the Pennsylvania legislature, had for years demanded "unreasonable concessions" and created "anarchy, confusion & great mischief there." Now the legislature was sending Mr. Franklin over to represent "what they call their grievances," and he hoped the Penns could "turn 'em back." In light of the foregoing, it comes as no surprise that Alexander was a firm friend of John and Thomas Penn, grandsons of William Penn and proprietors of the Pennsylvania colony. He also made close acquaintance with a number of Americans who were residing in England, such as New Yorkers Philip Schuyler and Staats Morris. He returned to American in 1761 on board the same ship as Schuyler and later served with him in the Continental army as a rebel general.[8]

Alexander's transparent attempts to rub elbows with the British aristocracy and to make a place for himself in this society were at times almost ludicrous. He was frequently visiting someone's country estate or maneuvering to be introduced to this proud lord and lady or that prominent duke and duchess. In early 1758, he was at Gordon Castle in Scotland, wringing promises from the Duchess of Gordon to send him puppies from the litters of Thisby and Chloe, two of her favorite bitches. He was breathlessly announcing a few months later to Andrew Stuart, his Scots solicitor, that one acquaintance had invited him to make a "jaunt" to the Isle of Wight, and another, the Duke of Argyle, had promised to introduce him to the king. He was invited by Charles Townshend to visit Adderbury, Townshend's estate in Oxfordshire, during the autumn to "go chasing the hare & hounds," to admire the fine seats in the surrounding countryside, and to read in the mansion's extensive library. Alexander gladly availed himself of Townshend's invitation, and he spent a number of weeks in October 1758, taking advantage of the sumptuous pleasures of Adderbury, including riding. On one of his gallops, he fell from a horse and injured his shoulder. While "your humble servant" broke nothing, he could not use his arm for a few days and had to ask someone to write for him.[9]

Alexander's quest to become prominent in British society continued in 1759. In a letter to Robert Hunter Morris in November, he listed the "new & valuable acquaintances" that he had made during the previous months in England. His "first excursion from town was with Lord Gage into Sussex, where I continued almost a month & had the good luck to lay the fdn. of a good acquaintance with the Duke of Newcastle and several other people of consequence particularly with Lord Northampton, with whom I have lived almost ever since." He had also met Lord Halifax at the house of one of these new friends. (He might also have noted, although he did not, that the meeting with Newcastle was no accident; it had been carefully arranged by William Shirley, the duke's esteemed acquaintance, as a formal presentation on the morning of June 9.) Thus did Alexander get ahead in the world of the British upper classes, a world that he, colonial merchant *cum* Scots aristocrat, had embraced as his own.[10]

The seriousness of Alexander's embrace was made clear when he decided, early in his visit to England, to seek title to a lapsed Scots earldom that had earlier belonged to some Alexanders whom he believed (hoped? wished?) were his father's direct ancestors. A number of his new British friends, including Northampton, Wedderburne, Aberdeen, the Penn brothers, Townshend, Bute, and Argyle, urged him to lay claim to the title, and he needed little urging. For Alexander there was more involved in this matter than vanity, although for him that would have been motive enough. In 1621 and 1625, Charles I had granted to William Alexander, first Earl Stirling, fabulous tracts of land in North America. These lands encompassed much of Maine and all of Nova Scotia, New Brunswick, Long Island, Martha's Vineyard, and Nantucket, more than ten million acres in all. In addition, Alexander learned, the Duke of York, later James II, had bought back Long Island for seven thousand pounds but had never paid the debt. Therefore, if Alexander could prove right to the title of Stirling, he would automatically lay claim not only to vast areas of land that had never legally been lost to the Stirling heirs but also to James II's debt, with accrued interest. It was unclear exactly what financial rewards would fall to a successful claimant, for many of the Stirling lands had been ceded to France or returned to the Crown. Moreover, the first Earl Stirling had never upheld his end of the bargain with Charles I, to settle in his vast domain. Hence, a claim to ownership of this land by the Stirling heirs would be anything but assured after the passage of more than 130 years since the original grant. But none of these things gave Alexander pause, for the promises of princely profits and a life of ease as a landed nobleman were too much for him to renounce.[11]

Perhaps Alexander's British friends took all this business about titles seriously, but his rustic American acquaintances thought their colleague's claim was not only a bit daft but also more than slightly ridiculous. Alexander Colden in London could hardly wait to tell his New York friends about Alexander's quest when word of it began to spread in 1757. "The title of Earl of Stirling," he said in a letter to Cadwallader Colden, was "at present in one James Alexander a miller in some part of Scotland," who was persuaded by his friends not to take it, "least it might hurt him the Miller in which he lived very well but would make a very poor Lord Indeed." But, "Pray who do you think is about to Assume the Title why truly (for I have it from his own mouth) Mr. Alexr." Colden declared that when Alexander first told him about it, he almost burst into laughter, for he thought Alexander was joking. When he realized that his friend was serious, he could hardly contain his incredulity. Neither could a large number of other Americans.[12]

Alexander, undeterred by the scarcely veiled disbelief of his provincial friends, set out for Edinburgh in the summer of 1757 with letters of introduction from Alexander Wedderburne to a number of learned Scots solicitors, including Andrew Stuart, whom he chose as his councilor. There he remained for a considerable time, working with Stuart to establish his claim. His major difficulty, which appeared early on in his and Stuart's research and continued to bedevil him to the end of his quest, was that no clearly provable link could be found between his known ancestors and the last possessor of the title, the fifth Earl Stirling. Stuart dared not "venture the *service*," that is, allow the case to be taken to a jury of Scots peers who would ascertain whether Alexander had a right to claim the title, until this link could be made and it was shown that William Alexander was the surviving male heir.

Month after month passed, while Stuart struggled to overcome one problem after another in his research. First, he believed that Alexander's family possessed too many known generations to "quadrate" into the time since the last Earl Stirling lived; but that matter was cleared up to his satisfaction, and he drew a neat family tree to show all connections. Second, however, there remained the problem that no documentary proof could be found to show that William Alexander's great-grandfather, Alexander Alexander, was (as Alexander believed) son of a John Alexander, who himself was a brother of the first Earl of Stirling. In trying to find that proof, Stuart and his assistants spent hundreds of hours (and thousands of pounds of Alexander's fortune) searching through repositories of the Dukes of Atholl and Argyle, the chancery, the Laigh Parliament, and many other places to find the missing evidence. Finally, after six months' work Stuart admitted that no such brotherly connection existed. But he thought he could prove that John Alexander *was* Alexander Alexander's father and that the said John Alexander might be an *uncle* of the first Earl Stirling. If so, he believed a jury would accept such findings as definitive. Alexander told him to proceed along this line of research but seemed pessimistic about its outcome. In any case, Alexander said, "the state of uncertainty and expectation is awkward. My friends will be asking impertinent questions of me."[13]

At this point, however, Stuart decided to "test the waters" by asking certain of his legal colleagues whether they thought he had a case. The outcome of this conference, as Stuart wrote Alexander, "was a difference about the sufficiency of our proof . . . viz., John Alexander's relation to the (first) Earl of Stirling." Thus, he was forced to consume even more time (and money) in "searches for some written evidence on that point." Finding none, he decided that his only recourse was to use as evidence "the common fame of the country, about your branch being relations of the Earl of Stirling, from witnesses who were in no ways related to the family." So he scrounged up "two very old men," by using a council arranged by the sheriff of Edinburgh to examine witnesses, who remembered that in the gossip of the countryside many years ago, there was a story to the effect that the branches of the Alexander family were connected. With only this shaky proof to support his client's case, Stuart reluctantly set about to compose a jury "of the most creditable gentlemen in the country," for "an improper choice of a jury [that is, one containing members not friendly to Alexander] would have given a bad aspect to the whole." At last, this carefully selected and pliable panel of citizens met on March 24, 1759, in Edinburgh and unanimously found Alexander "the nearest male-heir to the last Earl of Stirling," Henry Alexander, who had died without leaving a male-heir *"of the body."* Stuart then regaled the gentlemen of the jury with an elegant entertainment—paid for, of course, by William Alexander—and dismissed the drunken Scotsmen with grateful thanks from both himself and his client.[14]

Alexander's relationship to the Earl of Stirling had now been "established," but legally he still was not a peer, for neither the Scots nor English House of Lords had confirmed the title. It was the sage advice of Stuart that Alexander should at this point petition only the Scots lords. Under the laws of Scotland, Stuart explained, patents "not confirmed to the heirs-male *of the body* would go to the heirs collateral, but . . . the case is otherwise in England." The Scots laws and customs regulating peerages were different from those in England because they had existed before the Act of Union and had been altered neither by this nor any subsequent act of the English Parliament. Therefore, laws of Scotland in this case would take precedence, for a preexisting Scots peerage was at issue. Moreover, the Scots lords were much more likely to be disposed toward accepting Alexander's evidence, for some of it, Stuart admitted, was weak. Hence, Alexander simply would have to accept such confirmation from the Scots lords, incomplete though it might be considered by the uninformed, if he wanted any confirmation at all. Alexander, seeming to bow to the logic of this argument, agreed with his solicitor and allowed the claim to be laid before the House of Lords of Scotland. There his title was confirmed.[15]

One fact of the case, however, made it absolutely necessary for Alexander to have his peerage accepted by the English House of Lords: his ambition to lay firm claim to the vast properties that had been granted the first Lord Stirling. Consequently, he instructed Stuart in late 1759 that he intended to petition the English lords. Nonplussed, Stuart strongly urged his client to forbear. Alexander's title was already on the Scots rolls; he might raise dormant suspicions by doubters of his present title; he would assuredly anger Scots peers "whose situation is similar to yours." Alexander, without mentioning his real reasons for his course of action, wrote Stuart a letter declaring that he agreed with his lawyer and that he really did not like pursuing the matter. "What must I petition for? . . . It is hard to petition when I have nothing to ask for. . . . This was my language to certain great men." But, he said, "Petition I must, and . . . let it be, that His Majesty would *declare & Establish*" his title.[16]

Alexander commenced his campaign by having the Earl of Holdernesse present to the English House of Lords on May 2, 1760, a memorial outlining his claim and making his request. The petition was immediately referred for examination to the Lords Committee for Privileges, and there it languished for nine months before Lord Willoughby recommended to the House that Alexander and three other applicants for Scots peerages be ordered to appear on the second Monday of the first session of the next Parliament, "to shew by what Authority, and upon what Grounds, they take upon themselves such Titles." The Lords agreed, and after hearing the claimants' testimony at the appointed time, waited ten more months before again examining the matter of Alexander and the other Scots petitioners. At last, the business came before the Lords on December 14, 1761, and Lord Bute, "by the King's order," again presented Alexander's claim, only to have it once more referred to the Committee of Privileges. Alexander's petition finally came up for what turned out to be final consideration on March 10, 1762. At that session, Lord Willoughby reported that Alexander's agent was asking for more time to prepare his case, whereupon the Lords tabled any more proceedings on the claim until the next parliamentary session. In the meantime, they asserted, Alexander "ought . . . to be considered as having no Right to the said Title." There the case rested. Although Alexander was furious at the House of Lords for its obvious reluctance to certify his title, he pursued his claim no further, because it was clear that it would not be accepted. Lawyer Stuart had been correct in his advice.[17]

While Alexander pursued his peerage, he did not neglect his land claims. He had employed Stuart as early as 1758 to search for copies of the grants that Charles I had awarded to his illustrious "ancestor," the first Earl Stirling. Word of his intentions had gotten around, and two other claimants had come forward to assert their rights. They were William Philipps Lee and Mary Trumbull, grandchildren of the fifth Earl Stirling by two daughters. Alexander and they agreed to petition the Crown on an equal basis for those lands and emoluments of Stirling's grant that might be still within their reach. By Alexander's calculations, they could at least claim seven thousand pounds sterling in payment for Long Island, plus the entire province of Nova Scotia and the territory between the St. Croix (Saghadoc) and Kennebec Rivers in Maine. Realistically, Alexander told his partners, title to the Saghadoc lands was all that was likely to be confirmed, since those territories alone of all the original Stirling grant were yet unsettled.

But just those properties could prove to be worth a small fortune to them.[18]

With this hope to sustain them, Alexander, Lee, and Trumbull on June 12, 1760 (only a month after Alexander had asked the Lords to confirm his title), laid their petition before the Privy Council. The document caused quite a stir, especially with William Bollan, the agent of Massachusetts Bay in London, who immediately perceived its threat to his colony's Maine lands. Therefore, he and others prevailed upon the Privy Council in July and August of that year to send the petition to the Board of Trade and to the attorney and solicitors general for opinions on its legality. At that point, business upon the Alexander-Lee-Trumbull memorial came to a grinding halt and was not started up again for almost eight years. But Alexander was assured by someone in the labyrinthine governmental bureaucracy that his and his copetitioners' rights to the Maine lands would sooner or later be confirmed. The proof for this assertion is that eight years later, as we shall see, Alexander was attempting to sell the tract, one hundred thousand acres at a time, as though his title were clear.[19]

By 1759 Alexander had been in Britain for four years and was enjoying his life in the islands immensely. In fact, he was flirting with the idea of purchasing an estate in Scotland and living there permanently, returning to America only long enough to collect his family and settle his affairs. One of Alexander's close friends in Scotland, the Reverend James Porteous, was inspecting property for him, especially the house of the first Earl of Stirling, located in the village of Stirling and belonging to the Duke of Argyle. The estate, reported the reverend, was "in a fine situation, and has a grand prospect over the most beautiful country and river in the kingdom," and "a perfect trifle would furnish therein a small lodging" until "a grand house" could be erected. In addition, "here are two small estates, viz., Newton, and Pleam, in the County of Stirling" which Alexander could purchase on a twenty-five year mortgage without risk, for "land is improving with us." If Alexander wished to pursue the matter, his lawyer could handle the details, "as you go soon to America."[20]

This situation greatly appealed to Alexander. He was tempted to settle as the sixth Earl of Stirling on the family's ancestral estate and elevate the Stirling name to its former grandeur. Such was not to be. The hard realities of rejection by the House of Lords and inability to lay immediate claim to the Stirling lands in America made Alexander's dream impossible. In any case, by 1761 he was anxious to return to America. His mother had died the previous year, and he needed to be in New York personally to settle her estate. He also desperately missed his family and friends after a five-year absence, and he wrote Lewis Morris, "I am pushing every point in my power to release me from this Country." Finally, in October 1761, he found passage on the ship *Alcide*, outbound for New York, and after bringing on board with him a vast quantity of presents, furnishings, and other items that he would need to ease his existence in the provinces, he sailed for home.[21]

Four

The Whig as Royalist, 1761–1775

William Alexander received a rousing welcome home from his family and friends. From the moment he came ashore they addressed him as Lord Stirling, despite the shakiness of his claim to the title. He was called by that title for the rest of his life, even in the years of the American Revolution and even by such perfectly respectable republicans as George Washington. In fact, Washington got into political trouble after the revolutionary war for having called Stirling "my Lord" and Stirling's daughter, Catherine, "Lady Kitty." Washington's opponents accused him of aristocratic leanings because of this practice.[1] Stirling himself certainly never did anything to discourage being addressed as a lord. It was clear from the moment of his arrival in New York that he intended in the new world to support the pretensions of the English landed aristocracy. He would no longer work in the countinghouse or on the dank and smelly waterfront. These may have been fine pursuits for his mother, but they were too mean for her titled offspring. In any case Stirling had allowed the family's mercantile business to run down almost to nothing while in England.

Instead, Lord Stirling would take the property that he had inherited, the estates of his and his wife's parents, estimated to be worth more than one hundred thousand pounds, convert most of them into land, build himself a splendid seat in the countryside, maintain his mansion in New York City, and emulate in every way possible the life of an English country gentleman. He had, in fact, already put his plans into action while in England, for he brought with him to America a splendid coach, six horses, and a "neat and handsome" harness, which he and his lady rode through the muddy streets of New York on special occasions. The coach was painted crimson, and all its trim, including the Stirling coat of arms on each door, was silver. The frame and springs were gilded, and the interior was finished in mahogany, brass, and light colored upholstery. No vehicle in the province, not even the governor's, could be even remotely compared with Stirling's for sumptuousness and vulgarity.[2]

Stirling began construction of his country mansion shortly after his return to America, on a tract of 584 acres near Basking Ridge, New Jersey. This tract, part of his inheritance from his parents, was valued at £1,380 and was secured from his sisters and brothers-in-law in three indentures. The house was begun in 1761 and was envisioned on such a grand scale that when the American Revolution began in 1775 it was still incomplete. The edifice and grounds were described in the mid-nineteenth century by Mrs. Eliza Susan Morton Quincy, who had grown up nearby at her father's house:

> The seat of Lord Stirling, called by the country people "The Buildings," was two miles distant. Designed to emulate the residence of an English nobleman, . . . the stables, coach-houses, and other offices, ornamented with cupolas and gilded vanes, were built round a large paved court behind the mansion. The front, with piazzas, opened on a fine lawn, descending to a considerable stream called "The Black River." A large hall extended through the centre of the house. On one side was a drawing room, with painted walls and a stuccoed ceiling. Being taken there when a child, my imagination was struck with a style and splendor so different from all around.

The hallway ended in a transept at the back of the house, and stairs wound up both sides to meet in an upper hall. The upper and lower hallways were of the same dimensions, and large rooms, furnished with carpets and elegant furniture imported from England, opened off each. The floors were of oak, and each door had a silver plate upon it denoting its use or occupant. The lawn had many trees, and Stirling saw that a deer park was kept stocked to one side. In addition, he maintained a rose garden, an Italian vineyard, and an orchard full of various fruit trees, including six cherry trees imported from England. Stirling maintained the entire establishment with skilled indentured servants whom he imported especially for this purpose. Nearby were the homes of Elias Boudinot, Dr. Samuel Sutherland, and Mrs. Quincy's father,

RESIDENCE OF LORD STIRLING
(Courtesy of Perkins Library, Duke University,
Durham, North Carolina)

John Morton. But the social life of the region centered on Basking Ridge, where Stirling's daughters, Mary and Kitty, cavorted with the Livingston girls and entertained the younger Eliza Morton. Reflecting his formal but not deeply spiritual approach to religion, Stirling in 1763 appointed the Reverend Richard Peters to be his chaplain and at the same time enrolled with the local Presbyterian congregation of his friend the Reverend Dr. Samuel Kennedy. The earl also continued to be a member of Trinity Parish in New York and a subscriber to St. Thomas' Church in Alexandria, New Jersey.[3]

Stirling enjoyed his country seat immensely, spending his summers there with his family throughout the 1760s. As befitted a landed gentleman, he collected a library of more than two hundred volumes, including Smollet's and Hume's histories of England, Montesquieu's *Spirit of the Laws*, Johnson's dictionary, Sully's *Britain*, Cato's *Letters*, various histories of France and Italy, books on horsemanship, a garden dictionary, a military dictionary, a volume on the laws of New York, and all sorts of pamphlets. He continued to dress well from his wardrobe of 31 coats, 58 vests, 43 pairs of breeches, 6 powdering gowns, 2 pairs of trousers, 30 shirts, 17 handkerchiefs, 27 stocks, 27 cravats, 8 razor cloths, 119 pairs of hose, 6 pairs of socks, 15 nightcaps, 5 pairs of drawers, 2 pairs of gloves, 14 pairs of shoes, and 4 pairs of boots. His interest in agriculture was keen during these years, and with the help of his friend James Read he was constantly experimenting with new farming techniques, especially viniculture. He wrote the Earl of Shelburne, president of the Board of Trade in 1763, encouraging the British government to support the planting of vines in America. He had just planted twenty varieties himself, he said, in order to see which ones would grow in New Jersey, and he expected to reject nine-tenths of them after ten years. He entered a contest sponsored by the Royal Society of Arts in 1767 to see who could grow the most grapes in America. Although he did not win first prize, he received a gold medal "for having planted 2100 vines. . . ."[4]

Stirling mixed his own business interests with concern for England's imperial greatness by presuming in the 1760s to give various British officials advice on how to run colonial affairs. In his letters to these men, he emerges as an imperialist who generally supported England's laws for regulating American commerce. He wrote to Lord Bute in 1762, nominating himself for the post of collector of customs in New York. The position, which he said was then held by "an elderly gentleman" who could be persuaded "to resign in my favor," was not being efficiently run and therefore was bringing in "little or nothing to the Crown; yet with care and proper Management I am persuaded the Income might be increased so as to be in a few years Sufficient to pay all the officers of Government within this province; & for which they at present depend on the will of the people, who sometimes take it into their heads to refuse them any Support but on Certain Conditions." Stirling concluded to Bute that "if his Majesty will be pleased to honor me with the Commission . . . I will take care that it be faithfully executed."[5]

A year later, he instructed Lord Shelburne and the Board of Trade on policies to encourage the growth of industries and to regulate seaborne commerce in the colonies. The production of iron and hemp, he said, should be assisted. New Jersey was becoming active in iron production; great amounts of capital were needed to get started in the business, and government should stimulate such activities. "As to hemp, our farmers have got into a beaten track of raising grain and grazing cattle, and there is no persuading them out of it, unless by examples and premiums; and these it would be well for Government to try." He closed by pointing out to Shelburne that smuggling in the colonies was hurting British trade, especially with the Dutch, and the problem was increasing daily. Although customs house officials sometimes made feeble efforts to stop the practice, they were "generally in Vain from the Great Number of Small Harbours our beaches abound with, where they leave the Cargoes unnoticed." There was only one way to suppress this criminal activity, said Stirling sternly, "& that is by small Cruising Ships Stationed at the great Inlets from the Sea, such as the Mouth of the Chesapeake Bay," with orders to stop and board all ships, both leaving and arriving. These policies would be palatable to the most ardent of supporters of parliamentary prerogative in America.6

Stirling's attention to public business after he returned to America was by no means confined to advising ministers at the seat of the Empire. He also assumed his place in various positions that had fallen to him at his father's death and in others that he earned by his own labors. He rejoined the Councils of New York and New Jersey and the Board of Proprietors at East Jersey, and he immediately assumed, along with James Read, Peter Kemble, and others, special duties on a New Jersey commission for trying pirates. In addition, the governor of New York appointed him commandant of the Independent Company of Grenadiers, a militia unit in the city. This unit was called to arms twice in 1762, once in February when the governor suspected that some criminals might try to escape from jail and two months later when word arrived in the province that Britain had declared war on Spain. Historian William Smith, Jr., said that the citizenry was so aroused on the last occasion that a celebration was held, and "the grenadiers, led by Lord Stirling," took part in a martial procession of gentry from Fort George to the town hall. For a short time during this war fever, Stirling actually commanded a few British regulars that had been detached to him from the army of Jeffery Amherst, British commander in chief in North America, but he had to return them to Amherst's command in June.7

Council business in both New York and New Jersey occupied much of Stirling's time in the 1760s. Twice during the decade he exerted his influence to have colonial agents dismissed from their posts and his own friends installed in their stead. The New York Council acted in

1762 to remove Robert Charles, whom Stirling described as good but without influence. His recommendation for the post, Thomas Harley, an English acquaintance, was accepted. Stirling took advantage four years later of Joseph Sherwood's political difficulties in his position as agent for New Jersey to recommend to the council his friend Henry Wilmot. Earlier in England, Stirling had snubbed Sherwood (by the latter's account), because Stirling had wanted his own man in the post. In any case, the council, over the opposition of Governor William Franklin, went along with Stirling's recommendation. Wilmot fortunately turned out to be a more competent agent than Sherwood. Stirling also used his leverage to recommend new members of the councils from time to time. He prevailed upon the governor of New Jersey in 1764 to appoint his friend Charles Read to that colony's council, and four years later he won a seat on the council of New York (which was later rejected by the Privy Council in London) for his compatriot Robert R. Livingston. Stirling was not above using the councils for his own advancement as well, and on at least one occasion, in 1764, he introduced a petition in the Council of New York for a grant of land on the upper side of the Batten Kill to twenty-five agents, including himself and James Duane. The outcome of his petition is not recorded.[8]

A tremendous stir took place in the politics of the New Jersey Council when, in 1762, William Franklin, the illegitimate son of Benjamin Franklin, received a Crown commission as governor of that province. Many persons were opposed to this appointment, and apparently they assumed Stirling was included among their number. John Penn in England wrote Stirling that, because of "the Character & principles of this gentleman," it was a "shamefull affair," an "indignity," a "Dishonour," and a "disgrace" to New Jersey. Stirling, however, was not inimical to the man, and his opinion of Franklin—at least until the outbreak of the Revolution in 1775—remained good. In fact, the new governor and Lord Stirling were fast friends over the next few years—belying, at least for a while, Peter Collison's observation to Benjamin Franklin in 1762 that his son William would have a hard time in New Jersey with Stirling's "unruly Spirit."[9]

In 1765 the councils of New York and New Jersey faced the Stamp Act crisis, the worst political storm confronting them while Stirling was a member. When word of Parliament's attempt to tax the colonies reached America, a wave of outrage from the citizenry overwhelmed governmental officials from Massachusetts to South Carolina, and stamp agents quickly resigned their positions, either willingly or by force. Colonial governors in a very short time were unable to enforce the law and turned to their councils for advice. Cadwallader Colden, acting governor of New York, called a meeting of his council on September 4 to ask its opinion on three matters. First, he wished to know whether the council favored inviting Thomas Gage, army commander in North America who had replaced Amherst, to assist the civil authority in quelling disorders in New York City. Second, he wondered if editors and printers of papers filled with "maliciousness" and "treason" ought to be prosecuted. Third, he needed advice on whether to appoint a new stamp distributor in the place of the original one, James McEvers, who had just resigned. The council members, in this and subsequent meetings, encouraged the governor to remain calm, leave the newspapermen alone, handle the disorders without military interference, and by no means make any attempt to appoint a new stamp agent or in any other way try to peddle the stamps. Lord Stirling had nothing to do with these decisions. He remained discreetly at home, not committing himself in any way.[10]

Meanwhile, Governor Franklin in New Jersey was also having problems brought on by Britain's colonial tax policies. Already, the economy of New Jersey was in disarray because of rumors that the British ministry planned taxes, and Stirling for the first time in May 1765, had publicly opposed ministerial checks on foreign trade. The Navigation Acts, he declared (in contradiction to both his previous and subsequent positions), were detrimental to American commerce and ought to be abolished outright. Bounties, he said, should be offered in their place to stimulate and encourage American agriculture and commerce. However, Stirling made no attempt to use the stamp crisis six months later in New Jersey, any more than he had in New York, to crystallize his opposition to British policy. When Governor Franklin called a council meeting on November 6 to deal with the stamp problem, Stirling, along with three other members, stayed away. It is not clear what his absence meant in terms of his position on Parliament's right to tax Americans, for even though he wrote Governor Franklin a letter to "explain" himself, most of his arguments were couched in practicalities rather than principles and explained nothing. He understood, he said, the critical nature of the council meeting he had missed, but he was in bed at Basking Ridge, racked by "Rheumatick Pains in every limb and joint," and simply could not attend. As to advice, he urged Franklin to do nothing at all while awaiting news from London on whether the law had been repealed, as Americans expected it would be. Since the New Jersey collector had resigned, a new one certainly was not needed, for such an appointment would only be "raising up an Object to the resentment of an enraged, and, as they think, an injured People." Any step that might "irritate" should be avoided, as witness the missteps of Governor Colden in New York. So, since the stamped paper was on board a ship and not yet unloaded, keep it there "& avoid anything that might lead to altercation with the people."[11]

After the Stamp Act was repealed and the political crisis in the empire receded, Stirling remained on good terms with all factions of that quarrel, and in the councils of New York and New Jersey he tried to keep a low profile over the next few years on imperial problems. Although he continued to advocate abolition of the laws regulating trade with England, he supported London's insistence in 1767 that New York conform to Parliamentary legislation on quartering of troops. He was upset when the DeLancey faction won key elections in New York—such as in 1769 when various Livingstons and John Morin Scott were swept from office—but he entertained the governors and councilmen of the two provinces in his home on many occasions with no thought for their political leanings and generally favored the counsels of prerogative when a political issue arose that pitted appointees of the Crown against "the people." At a time when interest in the Church of England in New Jersey was considered tantamount to favoring constituted authority, he, with his friend Governor Franklin, was a member of the Society for the Propagation of the Gospel. In sum, his political stance right up to the time of American rebellion in 1775 gave no hint of disloyalty to, and every indication that he still supported, empire and Crown.[12]

Lord Stirling, as befitted a man of his eminence in colonial America, was on friendly terms with a large circle of people, both young and old. Acquaintances leaving for England wanted his recommendation to meet his noble friends there, and others in America and Britain sought him out for various kinds of patronage. Stirling successfully recommended Lieutenant Walter Barland to Thomas Gage in 1767 for a commission in a regiment that had not been reduced after the Treaty of Paris in 1763, and he was responsible for Philip Livingston's being accepted to study law at the Inns of Court. He received a request from

Henry Clinton, his old friend in England, addressed to "one of the first friends I ever made," for assistance in selling some land in New York that was part of the estate of Clinton's deceased father.[13] In 1763, Stirling welcomed William Amherst, brother of Jeffery Amherst, to New York, and in the same year he lavishly entertained Benjamin Franklin when he came to the city on a post office inspection trip. Stirling's relationship with his near neighbors at Basking Ridge was also close. A Masonic lodge was organized there in 1767, and he became the grand master. Additionally, he took charge of keeping neighborhood roads in repair, even spending his own money to maintain them.[14]

Stirling's social ties and acquaintances in America during the 1760s, while centering in the colonies of New York and New Jersey, were not confined to these two provinces. His affairs before and during the Seven Years' War had taken him to Pennsylvania, Maryland, and Virginia, and he strengthened the associations he had made in those places in the decade after he returned from England. He met Anthony Wayne for the first time in 1766, when he went to Philadelphia on a business trip; later, as American army generals, these two men would become fast friends. During the same year, perhaps while on the same journey, Stirling joined the Philadelphia Jockey Club, a society formed to promote the breeding and racing of good horses. Many prominent Philadelphians were members, including Governor Richard Penn and John Cadwalader, and many other men of note visited there from time to time. One such individual was George Washington, who stopped in Philadelphia in May 1773, while on his way to enroll his stepson, John Parke Custis, in King's College. "Spent the Evening at the Jocky Club," wrote the Virginian in his diary on the 17th, at Michael Duff's Tavern in the company of Stirling, Governor Robert Eden of Maryland, and others. A few days later, Washington and Custis journeyed on toward New York in the company of Stirling, pausing on their way to dine with Governor Franklin at Burlington, and for a two-day visit at Stirling's home in Basking Ridge. Stirling declared to Joseph Chew after his company had departed that the time he spent with Washington had proceeded "Very Happily."[15]

As a landed gentleman, Stirling had time to do more than play at farming and socialize with friends. He pursued educational and scientific interests like his father before him, for they had animated his attention since he was a young man. A decade earlier he had helped found the New York Society Library and had taken an interest in King's

College. He now became more deeply involved with the college. On April 15, 1762, he was unanimously elected by the corporation of King's College to its Board of Governors, and he immediately set about to solicit money from his wealthy friends in Britain to support the institution. He wrote letters of introduction for James Jay, whom the college was sending to England as an agent, and Stirling deserved the credit when Lord Bute and Henry Drumond gave Jay contributions.[16] He kept up scientific interests by pursuing practical mathematics in the form of surveying and also by observing astronomical phenomena. He had brought with him from England a surveyor's quadrant for the New Jersey proprietors, and he took great delight in explaining its operation to anyone who would listen. Another surveying instrument, the compass, drew his attention in 1765, when he became aware of improvements in its design by Aaron Miller. He excitedly reported these to the Royal Society of Arts in a paper that he submitted under the sponsorship of Benjamin Franklin, who was a member. Stirling also remained active in the American Philosophical Society, where he was associated with other provincial men of science such as Franklin, John Bartram, William Logan, Charles Read, and John Witherspoon. He read two scientific papers to this learned company, one in 1769 on "The Transit of Venus," the other four years later on "The Variations of the Compass."[17]

Problems with money began to plague Stirling in the years following his succession to the peerage, and no matter how he tried to act as though financial concerns were unimportant to him, the inexorable laws of economics proved not to be suspended even for a man of his caliber. Consequently, his business affairs by the time of the American Revolution were in such a perplexing snarl that his attorney, William Paterson, struggled valiantly but without success to make sense of his "monumental legal difficulties." What had gone wrong? Simply put, Stirling's fortune after 1761 had been invested primarily in vast landholdings and capital-intensive ventures such as flax milling, timber cutting, and iron production, which generated little ready cash for payment of business and living expenses. When he attempted to collect money that was owed him, his clients pleaded the same excuse as his own: their money was tied up and could not be shaken loose to pay debts. Likewise, he could not collect rents from his tenants, for they had no money to give him, and thus in a typical year, 1769, he received from them only a pittance of twenty-seven pounds. Stirling's response to his lack of money was to live ridiculously beyond his means, running up larger and larger debts while at the same time mishandling his fortune by investing in worse and worse business deals. The final consequence of his remarkably bad business sense was his total economic ruin.[18]

The details of Stirling's financial perambulations are lost in documents that today make little sense, but the broad outlines of his schemes may be traced. From 1761 to 1775, Stirling transacted deal after deal with family, neighbors, and partners to buy or sell tracts of land. All these ventures, taken together, left him bereft of liquid capital and with total mortgage debts in excess of ten thousand pounds. Before long, he was incapable of covering either tradesmen's bills or mortgage payments and was being hounded day and night to meet these obligations. Even while in England, he had been careless of paying his bills, and his agent, Henry Drummond, wrote him in April 1762, that his "name [in England was] treated as an adventurer from N. America who had come here and assumed a title you had no right to, and then went away without any body's knowing of it or paying [your bills]. I'm sure, my Dr. Lord, you must remember how cautious I told you you . . . should be in owing Trades people." Stirling may have recalled these words of admonition when, in April 1769, Job Stockton, sheriff of Somerset County, advertised his "goods, chattels, house & lands" for sale "at public vendue" in order to settle the claim of three debtors. Somehow Stirling staved off the crisis, and the sale was not held. But he received within the next six months (as typical examples of his problems in the fourteen years after his return to America from England) bills large and small for debts or interest from ten persons. He could pay none of these, although he figured in 1772 that debtors owed him more than nineteen hundred pounds, enough money to liquidate many of his debts, if he could but collect it.[19]

In 1768, Stirling's financial difficulties were compounded when his former business partners, Peter Van Brugh Livingston and Lewis Morris, brought a lawsuit against him. The cause of the litigation was that Livingston and Morris had not received from Stirling after his return to America in 1761 the amount they had anticipated for their expenses as army contractors during the Oswego campaign. It was Stirling's contention, however, that he had been forced to expend "large sums to support himself in a manner suitable to those connections which he made" as a necessary prerequisite to the facilitation of "the business he was transacting for such Agents." Hence, his claim of living expenses of "not less than five thousand guineas," which he had deducted before distributing the remaining funds, was not excessive. The outcome of this lawsuit remained in doubt for the next few years, and it finally terminated when the courts dropped it at the outbreak of the Revolution. However, Peter Van Brugh Livingston after the war foreclosed one or two of Stirling's mortgages (which, incidentally, by that time were worthless) in order to recoup what he considered his financial loss to his former partner.[20]

In the first of many attempts to collect money and get back on his feet financially, Stirling in 1768 decided to sell off 150 thousand acres of land in Maine on the Penobscot and Castine Rivers. This tract was part of the Stirling grant of 1631, which Lord Stirling had claimed with two partners in a Crown petition in 1760 but which (as he well knew) had never been affirmed to him by any ruling of the Privy Council. In fact, Jasper Mauduit, who replaced William Bollan as agent of Massachusetts Bay in London, worked assiduously to see that no such ruling was ever forthcoming, for it would have been detrimental to the interests of his colony. To complicate matters, the General Court of Massachusetts in 1762 had granted Mount Desert Island, which was a part of the original Stirling grant, to Governor Francis Bernard, and Bernard could not gain title to it as long as the present Lord Stirling claimed it. There was every reason, then, for Governor Bernard to be upset when in August 1768, he received a letter from Stirling, enclosing an advertisement to sell the Maine lands "belonging to me, scituate in the eastern part of your Goverment." Nor was the governor put at ease over the matter when he learned that Stirling had engaged the services of a precocious Connecticut lawyer, Jared Ingersoll, to argue his claims in Massachusetts.[21]

Governor Bernard laid Stirling's letter before the Council of Massachusetts in September 1768, and the Council immediately agreed with him that the Stirling-Lee-Trumbull claim was invalid. The Massachusetts General Court had already settled families in the region covered by the advertisement, and the council believed "That it is inconsistent with his Majesty's Interest that the said Grantees should be disrested." The members hoped Stirling would understand, and they were convinced that once he analyzed their arguments he would "desist from his pretensions." More to the point, however, they and the governor sent copies of these proceedings to the Privy Council, and this body, on December 19, 1769, finally concluded the matter by declaring that no territory in the old Stirling grants of 1631 and 1635 could be claimed by the putative earl, his friends, or his descendants. Hence, Stirling's grand dream of wealth based upon the land grants of Charles I, which would have splendidly supported his American earldom, disappeared. Surely, it was no more than he had ever expected.[22]

Stirling was undaunted by this economic setback and immediately began pursuing another path to riches—speculation in the New Jersey iron industry. As early as 1754, he had thought about buying into the Rocky Hill mine, and he had been interested in iron production for some years; in 1763 he encouraged Lord Shelburne to have the Board of Trade stimulate "the making of pig and bar iron" in America. In 1767 he entered the business of iron manufacture, by purchasing with James Anderson and Benjamin Cooper one-third interest in the Hibernia Iron Works, which was located in the finest ore district of New Jersey. The cost of running Hibernia was very high, with prodigious expense involved in damming streams, procuring timber for operating the forge, hiring workers and supplying them and their families with free food and housing (which had to be constructed at the forge site), and meeting the workers' payroll. Therefore, Stirling was very quickly in debt to his supplier William Neilson for the sum of £125. But he believed these conditions were temporary and that as soon as iron could be produced and sold plenty of money would be available.[23]

Even after selling his first year's share of Hibernia's production, however, Stirling was far from breaking even. Although his debts were refinanced by Neilson, in subsequent years his economic picture became worse. By 1771, he was obligated in his iron production venture for £3,500, a year later for £5,500, and he continued losing money on his investments because of too little output and too low prices for finished goods. This situation prevailed despite the fact that the Hibernia operation was constantly improving production methods and that, in 1769, the New Jersey Assembly freed Hibernia Iron Works of taxation for seven years.[24]

Stirling and his partners by 1773 had hopes for better times at Hibernia. They had made arrangements with Daniel Cooper and his son, Benjamin, for financial backing. Moreover, a new forge supervisor, Joseph Hoff, had been employed, and Stirling and Neilson had worked out plans to supply the workers with provisions for a year. But Daniel Cooper became impatient to have his loan repaid, and when

Stirling informed him that no cash was available, Cooper arrived one day at Hibernia with the sheriff, seized all the coal, ore, and wood, and stopped the shipment of pig iron. At this point, Neilson also began to complain to Stirling, and the latter retaliated by stopping payments to him for goods supplied. Cooper informed Stirling that he "wanted no rupture" and would not seek legal redress if this affair "were compromised amicably," but Stirling had no money to pay Cooper's loan. Therefore, Cooper and the sheriff in early 1774 began selling movable items, the furnace, and lands at Hibernia.[25]

Stirling was unwilling even at this late date to give up the idea that there was money to be made in iron production, and he wrote Cooper asking for a meeting to rearrange the financing of Hibernia. Consequently, Cooper halted the sale of Hibernia's assets, and he, Stirling, and Neilson agreed essentially to the same scheme that they had followed a few months before for running the iron works (thus raising the question of what Cooper thought he had gained by his recent activities). A week later, Stirling became sole owner of the operation, although the details of the new arrangement are not clear. He launched the new deal in a golden glow of optimism, but within weeks he was suffering the same problems as before. Creditors pressed him for cash, workers were uneasy about pay, and delays of all sorts sprang up in running the works. Samuel Ogden, another person to whom Stirling owed money, appeared on the scene in June and began causing trouble. He had decided to take a pile of ore for another of his furnaces in partial payment for his loan. Ogden's activity, however, was due to more than unpaid debts. He was also angry with Stirling because the latter had been making disparaging comments about Ogden's rapaciousness as a creditor in New Jersey council meetings, and now Ogden wanted revenge.[26]

When Ogden and his men came for the ore on June 2, 1774, Hoff quickly notified Stirling of his dilemma, and two days later Stirling arrived at Hibernia to protect his interests. He confronted Ogden's men (but not Ogden, who had departed the scene by this time), drew his pistol, and threatened to blow out the brains of anyone molesting his property. He also struck one man with a horsewhip. Although Stirling thus temporarily fended off Ogden's men, the creditor finally had his way, and the ore was hauled away. Trouble between Stirling and Ogden continued to build after these incidents, and Stirling finally pressed charges of business malpractice against Ogden in the New

Jersey Council. Governor Franklin intervened and tried to mollify the two men, but with little luck. Ogden counterattacked against Stirling's charges by continuing to cause trouble for Hoff at Hibernia and by threatening to have his lawyer, Jonathan D. Sergeant, bring suit against his opponent in court. The council chided Stirling for persisting in his quarrel with Ogden, implying that much of this dispute was his fault, which it was, and the angry earl let the matter drop.[27] (Stirling did not forget the council's censure, however, for a short time later it helped him decide to join the American rebellion against England.)

At this point, Lord Stirling at last was convinced that he must withdraw from active participation in the iron business. For a time in October 1774, he flirted with the idea of improving management of the forge by consolidating his dispersed system of supply and sales, but he reluctantly gave up the plan when growing colonial tensions with Britain made business prospects uncertain. He reasonably concluded that if he could not make the mine pay when economic conditions were in his favor, he certainly had little hope of profit in unsettled times. Therefore, he sold most of his interest in Hibernia furnace, after protracted negotiations with Robert and John Murray, wealthy dry goods merchants in New York. But Stirling was not completely out of the iron business. He continued throughout the Revolution to take an interest in Hibernia, and he used his status in the Continental army on occasion to assist the Murrays with deals. As late as July 5, 1780, he signed a lease to rent the furnace to John Jacob Faesh, indicating that although he no longer ran the business he still contained certain controlling rights on how others would run it.[28]

Stirling's continuing need for ready cash over an entire decade finally made him decide in early 1772 to dispose of part of his land in a lottery. This was a fine idea, if it could be made to work. But lotteries in the past had rarely paid off the prizes they advertised, and potential ticket buyers were highly skeptical of Stirling's. Lotteries were allowed in New Jersey only by special permission of Crown officials, and six had been held before, usually for financing institutions such as the College of New Jersey. Since Stirling's was the first lottery to be designed purely for the benefit of an individual, some people protested against the colony's allowing it. But Stirling had friends such as Governor Franklin backing him, and he ran into no trouble in getting governmental approval of his scheme. Thereupon, he persuaded a number of prominent persons to act as "managers" of the lottery, in order to take the affair out of his own hands, and he began to distribute tickets. It was Stirling's plan to print 12,275 tickets, each to be sold for £4, from which he would realize gross sales of £49,100. He would offer 1,518 cash payments and 894 land parcels as prizes with a total value of £34,998. Hence, if he could sell all the tickets he would make enough money to recoup at least some of his business losses of a decade and pay all expenses of the lottery.29

Stirling worked for a year on the details of his lottery, vigorously advertising it to stimulate interest up and down the Atlantic seaboard. He sent letter after letter to friends in all parts of America and Britain, including Samuel Allinson in New Jersey, James Hamilton in Pennsylvania, John Penn and William Kelly in London, and Henry Cruger in Bristol, asking them to advertise or sell lottery tickets, or do both.30 He had every newspaper that he could persuade to do so run free advertisements for the lottery, including the *New York Journal,* the *New York Gazette,* and *Rivington's New York Gazeteer.* Finally, he made a special trip in the winter of 1772–73 through Pennsylvania, Maryland, and Virginia to promote sales. He enjoyed himself thoroughly, observing country he had never seen before, commenting on the growing town of Lancaster, Pennsylvania, and ending up at the home of his Virginia friend George Washington. After a two-day visit at Mount Vernon, during which time he persuaded Washington to take sixty lottery tickets, he returned home, accompanied as far as Alexandria by Washington and Edward Foy, secretary to Governor Dunmore.31

Unfortunately for Stirling's financial solvency, his well-laid lottery plan brought him no relief from debt. Stirling's blandishments to people to snap up his tickets before they were all sold out were resisted by skeptical and chronically money-short consumers. Therefore, too few tickets had been sold when it came time for the drawing on November 1, 1773. No one had seemed overly impressed when Stirling reminded them that Washingtons, Randolphs, Harrisons, Tryons, Beekmans, Livingstons, Boudinots, Gages, and Duanes had purchased tickets. It was "absolutely necessary," announced newspapers such as the *New York Gazette,* that the drawing be delayed until the end of December. When that time came around and the drawing was again postponed, the public became more skeptical. The managers of the lottery themselves intervened to announce that unless Stirling's agents were immediately forthcoming with at least six thousand paid tickets, it would "be imprudent to draw the lottery and make ourselves lyable," for Stirling had so muddied the waters by distributing four thousand pounds' worth of tickets to his creditors to help cancel his debts that not enough money was on hand to cover the prizes offered.[32]

Stirling now took over management of the lottery himself, declaring to the public on August 22, 1774, that he would assume the risk of covering the cash prizes, "and make up the deficit, if any, out of my other estates." Moreover, the land prizes would be adjusted in number and based on the more likely potential sale of 5,400 tickets. Under these new auspices, Stirling finally had his drawing in late August on Burlington Island, under the watchful eye of a number of "respectable gentlemen" such as Daniel Coxe, John Lawrence, and Charles Pettit. A list of prize winners was published about two weeks later, and Stirling wrote letters to his many ticket salesmen—including Washington, who himself had been "fortunate" with two tickets—informing them of the lottery's results. He was, however, wasting ink and paper, for he knew full well that the lottery had been an utter disaster financially. Only 4,510 tickets had been sold, and when the final results of the lottery were tallied, Stirling had lost £3,938 on his venture. Hence, he was compelled ("after the manner of lotteries," as one cynic put it) to repudiate its results and return all the money to those who had purchased tickets.[33]

Lord Stirling was now in a worse financial muddle than he had been when the lottery business had commenced three years earlier. His accumulated debts by 1774 totaled an estimated half of his entire fortune, or fifty thousand pounds, and one writer has suggested, probably with exaggeration, that they had reached eighty thousand pounds. Moreover, his credit was at an end. When William Neilson insisted in October 1775, that Stirling pay Hibernia encumbrances of one thousand pounds that were left over from the earl's iron business, Stirling could find no one to lend him money. Hugh Wallace, his friend and financial counselor, suggested that if Stirling intended to preserve even a shred of his estate "for your Family, you must pursue the Scheme proposed some time ago & make out the whole Estate to Trustees to sell & pay off the Creditors according to their priority." Although Stirling would not heed this advice in 1775, he would be compelled to four years later.[34]

Hence, Lord Stirling suffered the indignity of having creditors seize all his household goods and sell them in a long drawn-out series of public auctions. Even worse, these creditors were so anxious to grab his property that they sometimes widely advertised sales without so much as notifying him. He accidentally came upon one of these notices, he told Philip Livingston with acute embarrassment, while "lately traveling through Hunterdon County, at a Country Tavern door." When the sales were completed in April 1776, Stirling had lost a considerable amount of his elegant, imported furniture, all his books, and other valuable items, which were sold for a pittance and replaced with cheaper substitutes. The earl was rankled when neighbors such as Elias and Elisha Boudinot, Philip Livingston, and Jacob Foord took advantage of this situation to walk away with marvelous bargains rather than bidding in his property and protecting it until he could reimburse them. He was almost relieved under these conditions to embrace the political diversion offered by the roiling quarrel that was now going on between Great Britain and its American colonies.[35]

Five

The Republican Earl, 1775–1776

The momentous political events within the British Empire over the decade following the Stamp Act crisis of 1765 had hardly touched William Alexander, Lord Stirling. He was mired in economic distress, straining in every way except thrift to extricate himself from his difficulties and barely noticed the growing colonial resentments against such parliamentary measures as the Declaratory Act and Townshend Duties. If he was upset by the Boston tea crisis in 1773 or by Parliament's retaliation against Massachusetts with the "Coercive Acts" a year later, he left no record of his chagrin. His silence on these great proceedings, his record of support for Crown prerogatives, his friendships with men of similar views, and his assumed great wealth, caused many Americans in 1774 and 1775 to believe that on the question of colonial resistance to Parliament Lord Stirling would side with London and become a loyalist.

Exactly the opposite occurred. By 1775, Stirling was listed as a member of the extralegal New Jersey Council of Safety, which had been formed in defiance of the Crown's authority in the province, and thereafter he never wavered in support of America's republican revolution. In fact, some of the Council of Safety's earliest business in New Jersey was intervention in an altercation between Stirling and James Murdock, a surgeon in Perth Amboy who had challenged Stirling to a duel because Stirling had expressed the justice of the American cause too strongly for Murdock's tastes. The council declared that Murdock's "audacious insult" of a member was "a daring contempt of the authority, and a manifest violation of the rights and privileges of this house." Murdock was forced to apologize to both his lordship and the council.[1]

Why did Stirling declare for the Whigs? The most often asserted and also least likely reason is that Stirling was so badly in debt by the outbreak of the Revolution that he joined the rebels in order to escape his financial obligations. Thomas Jones, the Tory historian, makes this claim, as does Ambrose Serle, secretary to Admiral Richard Lord Howe. Stirling, declared Serle, was "a thousand times worse than nothing in his Circumstances" and "made desperate push to get rid of the Inconvenience of his legal Obligations." No evidence supports this argument, for Stirling never attempted to use the Revolution to squirm out of his financial plight. It is true that in 1779 he prevailed upon the New Jersey Legislature to put the remains of his estate into a trust, but "to sell the same . . . for the Discharge of his debts," not to hide his property from creditors. In fact, his service to America may very well have had an adverse affect on his financial condition, for had he taken the side of the Crown he might have been compensated after the war by the British government.[2]

Numerous other reasons for Stirling's joining the rebellion have been asserted by scholars over the years, and although they do not give a complete explanation of the earl's motives, whether taken collectively or singly, they do offer a partial understanding. Stirling's disgust with the House of Lords for its rejection of his petition for a title had rankled him for years, and both he and his colonial friends, seeing themselves spurned by their counterparts in England, viewed the matter as a slap in the face. (In fact, ironically enough, Stirling's republican colleagues during the Revolution insisted that he retain his title, precisely because it had been denied to "their" earl by "arrogant" Britons.) This treatment of Stirling by the House of Lords was coupled in the earl's mind with the failure of highly placed London officials to take seriously his copious advice during the past decade, and he was led to wonder if he really had much of a future as a supporter of British prerogatives. Stirling was also angry with Governor Franklin and the Council of New Jersey for its recent censure of his business dealings with Samuel Ogden, for until that incident he had regarded both the governor and council members as his friends. It did no good for Governor Franklin to point out to him that the weight of evidence was on Ogden's side and that Stirling was in fact not upholding his part in a binding business contract. In addition, Stirling was led into rebellion by his need simply to quench his eternal and vainglorious thirst for recognition and renown.[3] With his nature, he would be inexorably drawn to the showy trappings of military command, and he reasonably could expect to receive much higher rank and more psychic gratification from joining the harried and therefore grateful rebels than by declaring loyalty to a king who seemed altogether too self-sufficient and not a little arrogant toward his colonial subjects.

Lord Stirling was also led into rebellion by two other factors, which have not been considered by historians but were in fact more weighty than all the others combined. First was Stirling's disgust in 1775 with the way the British government had reacted to colonial protestations about constitutional rights during the previous few months. Writing to Governor Franklin in September of that year, Stirling flatly stated that his ultimate reasons for taking up arms for America were "the rejection [by the king of America's] most humble, dutiful, and respectful, petitions to the Throne . . . the battles of Lexington and Bunker's Hill . . . the wanton and cruel destruction of Charlestown, and . . . the design of the Ministry to bring indiscriminate ruin on the Colonies of this Continent."[4] Second were Stirling's basic personality, character, and intellectual traits, all of which drew him to the side of the Whigs. In truth, he simply did not have the attitude toward human nature that a genuine conservative possesses. He, no more than Thomas Paine or Thomas Jefferson, could in the last analysis be comfortable with the world view of loyalists such as Thomas Hutchinson and Jonathan Sewall. To be sure, Stirling *appeared* to be a natural supporter of the status quo in the 1760s, but his posture during that decade was based more upon a childlike ebullience with his exalted status than upon principle. When he finally was forced by events to make a stand on basic issues, his earlier Whiggism, in which he had been nurtured by his father, reasserted itself. His vanity remained intact, and he reveled in the title "lord," but both he and his American colleagues understood that the use of such address was whimsical.

Certainly the rebels never doubted for an instant the genuineness of Stirling's conversion to the republican cause, and they welcomed his defection with open arms. There can also be no doubt that Stirling's support of the Whig position bolstered the party of protest in the middle colonies. "The Jerseys appear spirited," wrote Eliphalet Dyer to Samuel Adams in early 1776, "animated principally by Ld. Stirling."[5] This assessment was overly generous, for there were many prominent men in that part of colonial America assisting Stirling in mobilizing people in favor of rebellion. But there is no question that Stirling's pronouncement of support for the patriot cause in 1775, despite his financial difficulties, helped rally sentiment behind it. There is also no question that his steadfast devotion to the Revolution through all the difficult times until his death in 1783 continued to be an asset to the Americans.

Practically the first result of Stirling's declaration for the rebels was his rupture with Governor Franklin and an end to their long but already strained friendship. The governor was deeply hurt when rumors reached him that his colleague had accepted a colonelcy in the New Jersey militia from the Provincial Congress, an extralegal body. To find out if the rumors were true, Franklin on September 7, 1775, had Charles Pettit, clerk of the council, write Stirling a polite note summoning him to a meeting of the council for September 14, and inquiring about the status of his rebel military commission. Stirling, in a letter of reply sent directly to Franklin, expressed "astonishment" at the manner in which the question of his commission had been put. Considering their long friendship, said Stirling, Franklin might have asked this delicate question "through some more elevated Channel" than a letter written by a "mere Clerk." But since the governor was curious about his rank, he was glad to inform him "that the good people of this Country have *unanimously* chosen me a Coll. of a Regiment of Militia."[6]

Franklin's reply to Stirling, on September 15, was not conciliatory. He countercharged that it was Stirling who was abusing their friendship and that Stirling had not "the least excuse for the style and manner" of his last letter. The governor then went on to remind Stirling of the latter's supposed frequent declarations "that a man ought to be damned who would take up arms against his sovereign on the present occasion." In any case, "was there no other means now left in your power, which might have a chance of effecting your desired purpose, but disrespectful treatment of a Governor?" Stirling, in rebutting this letter, adamantly denied that he had said anything negative about opponents of the Crown "since the present occasion occurred"—meaning events that had taken place after the adjournment of the First Continental Congress in 1774. True, he had been critical of the Whigs until that time, but his recent reversal of opinion was in no way unethical or dishonest, for it was based upon his disgust with British policy toward America since then. In closing, Stirling sardonically chided Franklin for "descending to the language of a certain place in the environs of London," meaning, of course, Billingsgate. He thereupon sent off to the Provincial Congress copies of all recent correspondence between himself and the governor, in order to guard against the possibility that members of that body might be misinformed about the recent altercation. Governor Franklin retaliated by expelling Stirling from the Council of New Jersey and from the New Jersey Royal Militia, and he also had Governor William Tryon of New York follow suit for the council of that province.[7]

Stirling's appointment to high command in New Jersey's revolutionary militia forces in the fall of 1775 seemed for all concerned to be a foregone conclusion; neither he nor anyone else even considered that he might serve in any capacity but military in the struggle against Britain. He entered his new assignment with zest, dredging from his memory details of military organization and supply that had lain dormant since his service under General Shirley in the Seven Years' War twenty years before. Also, he began like many of his amateur colleagues in the patriot officer corps to read and reread every book or pamphlet pertaining to military matters that he could find, while the troops of his province were being embodied by the Provincial Congress into two batallions, or regiments (the terms were often used interchangeably during the revolutionary war). The Eastern Batallion was placed under Lord Stirling's command and the Western under Colonel William Maxwell. The organizational chart of these battalions had hardly been drawn up before the New Jersey legislature was recommending to the Continental Congress that they, along with their present officers, be enrolled as New Jersey's contribution to the Continental army, voted into existence five months before under George Washington, the commander in chief. Without hesitation, Congress accepted this arrangement on November 7. At the same time, Stirling's supporters in Congress had all New Jersey Continental army commissions except Stirling's postdated to November 8, in order that Stirling's rank, according to the custom of the day, be superior to Maxwell's in terms of tenure. Thenceforth, Lord Stirling was considered by Congress, and the New Jersey legislature, to be overall commander of New Jersey troops and the conduit through which all orders pertaining to the armed forces of the province should pass.[8]

Colonel Lord Stirling of the Continental army now began to put the New Jersey forces on a sound military footing, receiving in the process a much more thorough military education than he had gotten from his experiences under Shirley or from the printed word. He left his regiment in mid-November under the charge of Lieutenant Colonel William Winds, his second in command, and traveled to Philadelphia for conferences with members of Congress about military matters. Pursuant to congressional orders, he instructed Maxwell and Winds a few days later to detach three companies from each of the New Jersey regiments and march them to New Windsor, New York, where they were to take station in fortifications being constructed to guard the Hudson River. He left Philadelphia on the 22d, and proceeded to Burlington, where he conferred with the Jersey Committee of Safety about making arms purchases for the New Jersey troops a priority. A day later, he rode to Trenton and from there dispatched orders to the captains of his regiments (except those ordered to New Windsor) to muster their companies by December 1, according to congressional command, and march into barracks "as contiguous to New York as may be." From Trenton he proceeded to New Brunswick, where he examined barracks that he intended to use for his troops, only to discover that they were occupied by refugees from New York. The following day, a Saturday, the weary forty-nine-year-old colonel wended his way to Basking Ridge, where he spent the weekend recuperating from his exhausting labors of the previous two weeks.[9]

Stirling continued during the following weeks to maintain his hectic military pace, traveling from town to town inspecting his companies, advising their captains about qualities and deficiencies in their men, and listening to the complaints of officers and soldiers alike. One recurring problem, he discovered, was that troops were running up debts and being thrown in jail by angry justices of the peace "on the slightest pretext." He complained to Congress that if this practice continued all his men would soon be incarcerated, and he suggested that soldiers not be taken from the army by civil authorities for debts of less than 15 shillings. He was also having trouble getting barracks for his men. "Assembly, Committee of Safety, county committee, and Barrackmaster," he complained, "refer me from one to the other whenever I apply for the possession or repair of any of 'em." But he was hoping soon to have the barracks at Burlington "cleared out & repaired" for occupancy by at least three of his companies, and he was applying to the barrackmaster at Perth Amboy for five hundred blankets for his troops. His regiment, as of December 2, numbered 333 soldiers, with 268 more soon to be mustered, and for the entire number, he told Congress, only sixty-eight muskets and ninety-five blankets were on hand. Obviously, he must do something about supplying his troops, and he wondered to Congress what the normal "footing" for a regiment was in the Continental service.[10]

Stirling continued to spend most of his time during December in simply trying to get his battalion organized and supplied with arms, and both he and the state of New Jersey were fortunate that the British were focusing their primary attention at this time on Boston. He followed orders of the Continental Congress and opened a correspondence with the New York Provincial Congress in an attempt to requisition muskets that that colony possessed. However, he had managed after a month of writing New York leaders only to secure a promise that one hundred firelocks would be given his men. Even this offer was repudiated after the colony was ordered by Congress to raise and arm four battalions more than it already had in the field. However, Stirling learned some good news from the New Yorkers when he was told (and so informed Congress) that the Hudson River Fort at New Windsor was adequately manned and that he need not detach six of his companies to reinforce it. Both he and Colonel Maxwell were relieved, because they knew that the New Jersey troops were in no way ready for active service.[11] Meanwhile, both the New Jersey government and Congress continued to support Stirling's troops, by constructing new barracks at Perth Amboy, purchasing arms, blankets and other supplies, and furnishing his regiment with a surgeon, an adjutant, and a quartermaster. Stirling himself remained in close contact with the officers of his regiment, sympathizing with their complaint that they could not adequately supply their men and prodding them constantly to keep their troops trained, alert, and ready for immediate action should the need arise. His only slight indiscretion during this time was to pass on to Congress on December 6 a false rumor that Benedict Arnold had captured the city of Quebec. Despite Stirling's blunder, Congress continued to be impressed with his "zeal and attachment to the cause," and the legislators expressed "the firmest confidence" that he would continue in the future to uphold those same high standards.[12]

With the New Jersey regiments embodied and at least partially armed by the beginning of 1776, Stirling, Washington, and Congress began to put them to military use. In fact, Stirling had already notified Congress two weeks earlier from his headquarters at Elizabethtown that his regiment was protecting the New Jersey coast from the "ravages of the enemy." (The only problem with this vainglorious boast was that the enemies, Englishmen on British naval vessels, were not doing any "ravaging.") Stirling's first real military action began on January 2, when he was ordered by Congress to seize all arms and ammunition of loyalists in the province, a task he commenced with such zeal that Crown officials like Governor Franklin and Attorney General Cortlandt Skinner were soon furious at him. Congress also instructed him to give every aid and assistance within his power to "friends of America" who were importing ammunition and other stores of war not prohibited by a congressional boycott of British goods. While he carried out these duties, he and his troops were under discussion for a larger role in the defense of America. General Charles Lee was strongly urging Washington to pay more attention to fortifying New York, for both he and the commander in chief had become convinced that this city would be a vital area in future British military operations. Lee envisioned that Stirling's regiment would play a dual role in securing New York, by defending New Jersey's shores and by eliminating "that dangerous banditti of Tories, who have appeared on Long Island, with the professed intention of acting against the authority of Congress." Washington, immediately grasping the merits of Lee's arguments, appointed Lee commander of New York and ordered Stirling to serve under him, affording Lee "every Assistance in your Power, for facilitating this Business."[13]

Before he could effect Washington's orders, however, Stirling became embroiled in a nasty confrontation with the enraged William Franklin, his former friend. Some of Stirling's soldiers on patrol in eastern New Jersey on January 6, 1776, seized Henry Kelly, a courier bound for New York with dispatches from Franklin to the Earl of Dartmouth and with a letter from Cortlandt Skinner to his brother in England. Stirling on the same day sent Congress the entire lot of these papers, after having examined Skinner's message and discovering the man to be "most dangerous" because of his scurrilous attacks on a number of American "rebels." The colonel declared in his cover letter to Congress, that he would await that body's pleasure before taking any further action, but around noon the next day he ordered Lieutenant Colonel Winds into Perth Amboy with a military detachment to guard Franklin's house. Stirling told Congress on the eighth that he took this unilateral action for fear that Franklin might flee to the British in New York, because Skinner had just eluded his clutches by escaping to the British ship *Asia*.14

Whether by ill timing or Stirling's deliberate design, Winds waited until 2:00 A.M. on January 8 to post his guard, then roused Franklin and his terrified wife from their bed to deliver an ultimatum from Stirling not to leave New Jersey unless Congress approved. The governor was enraged by this treatment, but he had no recourse except to agree to Stirling's terms. Just the day before, he had mailed a letter to Dartmouth (which had gotten through) warning that some of his messages had been intercepted and that there would be the "devil to pay" because of their contents. Nevertheless, he adamantly declared his intention not to yield an inch to the rebels, especially to Stirling, in his prerogatives as royal governor. Given Franklin's defiant attitude, Stirling's behavior toward him appears less vindictive than it otherwise might. Yet there is no reason to doubt that Stirling by this time thoroughly disliked Franklin and may have been avenging himself for past slights, imagined or real, by making the governor's life uncomfortable. Franklin, in fact, swore that Winds had told him this was Stirling's design, and he declared, "We have been most abominably ill-used by a most abominable _____."15

Although Stirling had now forced Franklin to promise that he would not emulate Skinner's dash for freedom, the colonel still would not lift the governor's guard while he awaited instructions from Congress. Franklin indignantly insisted to Winds on January 9 that the American soldiers be removed from his gate, but Winds refused to comply. When Franklin continued to protest, Stirling ordered him arrested and brought to Elizabethtown. As Stirling told Congress, it was plain that the governor had no intention of desisting from attempts to escape, and Stirling wanted him near his headquarters where he could keep an eye on him. Franklin refused at first to obey Stirling's "invitation to dine with me," as Stirling sarcastically called his order, but seeing that he had no choice, he called out his coach and steeled himself to be hauled off under guard like a common criminal. Just then, New Jersey's rebel chief justice, Frederick Smyth, intervened, prevailing upon Winds to delay his march for one hour while Smyth rode to Elizabethtown and conferred with Stirling about allowing the governor to remain at his home in Perth Amboy. Consequently, said Stirling, "The Chief Justice came *Chargé d'affaires,* to negotiate the business here," and an agreement was reached to lift the guard and leave Franklin alone, if he would stay in his house. Congress, which had no wish to see Franklin under any sort of physical constraint, much less military arrest, gladly gave its approval to this arrangement. Thus, Stirling had deliberately injected his personal feelings into his affair with Franklin, who was admittedly a hard man to deal with, and overstepped the bounds of the policy that he knew his civilian superiors would have him follow.16

Returning his attention to military matters, Stirling continued his war against New Jersey loyalists near New York City and vigorously enforced the American embargo against trade with Britain. On January 12, under orders from General Lee, he began to plan an attack on friends of the king on Long Island, opposite Oyster Bay. He decided as well to disarm Tories on Staten Island and wrote the New York Committee of Safety about his intentions. The committee had received no instructions from Congress as yet on what to do about the Staten Island loyalists and dissuaded him from attempting the second part of his program. Finally, his other expedition had to be suspended as well, because the troops assigned to that duty, as Lee explained to Washington on January 16, were disbanded before they could attack. However, Stirling did provide three companies of troops to Colonel Nathaniel Heard for a successful operation against loyalists in Queens County. Closer to home, he chided officials in Elizabethtown for being too lax in their enforcement of import and export restrictions and ordered them in the future to make sure that all ships clearing port had proper certification from Congress. He also asked the New Jersey Committee of Safety to examine this matter, and the committee resolved to do so immediately.17

Stirling received news at his headquarters in Elizabethtown on January 21 that set off greater activity in his command than any event for the past six months. A British transport ship laden with stores for the King's army in Boston had gotten into trouble off Sandy Hook and might be seized if prompt action were taken. Immediately, Stirling made his way to Perth Amboy, where early in the morning of the 22d he and 120 civilian volunteers boarded the enemy ship without opposition. The vessel was the *Blue Mountain Valley,* commanded by Captain James Hamilton Dempster, laden with 107 tons of coal, 100 butts of porter, 15 tons of potatoes, 112 bushels of beans, 10 casks of "sour Krout," and 8 hogs. Although Stirling was disappointed that the vessel was not burdened with arms and ammunition, "as I expected," still he was pleased with his prize and proudly reported to Congress that it would make a fine warship. On January 25, Stirling got the ship into port and wrote Congress, "The cold and fatigue I have been exposed to for the last fortnight has almost got the better of me; it is with difficulty I can sit up to write this." The members of Congress were as enthusiastic about Stirling's prize as he was, and on January 29 they ordered that both ship and cargo be sold under the colonel's guidance. They also commended Stirling for "the alertness, activity and good conduct" he had shown in the entire operation. Stirling, as always, was pleased to have the approbation of Congress, and he quickly arranged with Cornelius Blanchard, a merchant in Elizabethtown, to oversee sale of the *Blue Mountain Valley* and its cargo.[18]

Stirling recovered quickly from the debilitating rigors he had undergone while seizing the ship, and in early February 1776, he received orders from Charles Lee to march to New York with his regiment immediately. On February 6, he took advantage of a break in the ice on the Hudson River and ferried his five hundred men across to the city. General Lee received him warmly and immediately drew him into the work of fortifying New York. Soon these two men, so unlike each other in many ways, became fast friends and mutual admirers. Stirling wrote that Lee manifested "Vigilance and judgment," and Lee declared to Washington that Stirling was "a great acquisition. He is a most zealous, active, and accurate officer."[19]

The city of New York that Stirling had known for a lifetime was shocking to him in its wartime disarray. Streets were deserted, shops were closed, loyalists' houses were boarded and deserted, and every part of the place was under the threatening muzzles of British men-of-war. In fact, New York had gotten grimmer in only three months since artillerist Henry Knox had visited there on his way from Boston to Fort Ticonderoga in quest of cannon. At that time he had written his wife, Lucy, "The people, why the people are magnificent; in their equipages, which are numerous; in their house furniture, which is fine; in their pride and conceit, which are inimitable; in their profaneness, which is intolerable; in their want of principle, which is prevalent; in their Toryism, which is insufferable, and for which they must repent—in dust and ashes." Knox's prophecy seemed hollow in early 1776, for it appeared that atonement was about to be visited on the patriots rather than the loyalists. Lee then had too few men to carry out the vast task that he had been assigned, and even with the addition of Stirling's regiment, his numbers did not exceed fifteen hundred. Frederick Rhinelander, an inhabitant, bravely asserted on February 23, that "Troops are daily coming in," but the statistics that Lee and Stirling saw belied this statement.[20]

The proximity of General Lee's military forces to the civilian population of New York City created perfect conditions for civil-military tensions, and sure enough, there was grumbling from both camps. However, the relationship of the army with New York's citizens was on the whole remarkably harmonious, made possible by a willingness of all parties to bend over backward to advance the common good. Alexander McDougall, a member of the New York Committee of Safety and the New York Provincial Congress, was of great assistance to Lee and Stirling in this effort, for he persuaded army officers to confer with civilians on matters of mutual concern and thereby reduced possibilities for misunderstanding. Also he helped soften military demands made by Lee and Stirling on "skittish members of Congress," who feared that overzealous officers might provoke the British navy into destroying the town. Finally, he helped stimulate civilians to greater military efforts, for he sympathized with, and understood the plight of, officers who must overcome manifold problems of command with too few resources. Stirling's difficulties were particularly acute. In transferring his operations to New York, he had lost his supply sources in New Jersey and could find no new ones to replace them. Immediately, he discovered himself deficient in ammunition (New York muskets were of a different caliber than his, and their cartridges were worthless for his use), provisions, and money. The New York Provincial Congress, to which he appealed for relief, soon resolved some of his problems, but the one of supply was chronic. In addition, the financial embarrassment of the colony made it impossible for the Provincial Congress to give Stirling the cash he needed.[21]

Stirling's fortunes took an upward turn in early March 1776, when the Continental Congress ordered Charles Lee to Charleston, South Carolina, and appointed Philip Schuyler to command in Lee's place. Lord Stirling, whom Congressman John Adams now referred to as "a very good officer," remained second in command at New York. Since Lee quickly set out for his new post, and since Schuyler decided to remain at his headquarters in Albany, Stirling became the de facto commander at New York until March 20, when he was superseded by the arrival of Brigadier General William Thompson. Lee expressed great confidence in Stirling as he departed for the South, noting to Washington that "His Lordship is active and distinct. . . . He will acquit himself well." Congress thought equally highly of Stirling; on March 1 it promoted him, on recommendation of Congressman James Duane, Stirling's friend and supporter, to the rank of brigadier general in the Continental army. Stirling was delighted with this "high Honor" and assured Congress that he would do all within his power to continue meriting the approbation of his countrymen.[22]

In a letter to Schuyler on March 10, General Lord Stirling did not sound very optimistic about his chances of getting New York into a state of reasonable defense any time soon. Lee's departure, he said, "has left me in a situation not a little perplexing, especially to a young beginner, as I now may call myself, after twenty years retirement from the busy scenes of life." He needed eight thousand men, he told Schuyler, to construct and defend the many posts that Lee had laid out before departing for Charleston, but he had only eighteen hundred effectives. Of these one thousand Connecticut troops were to go home on the 25th, and three hundred of the remainder were New York "minutemen" with no arms. He recited the same dismaying statistics to Congress, and pleaded with the legislators for reinforcements. Intelligence reports from New England, he said, indicated that while most British troops leaving England at present were destined for South Carolina under Charles, Lord Cornwallis, the ministry in London was attempting to engage twenty thousand German and Russian mercenaries, and all of these would probably be on their way to New York by autumn. At the same time, however, he was noting to Washington, "I am in hopes we shall have an easy summer's work to secure the whole Continent." Also, he was trying to scare the New Jersey Provincial Congress into action by asserting on March 3 that the "ministerial Army" in Boston was already embarked and on its way toward New York City. While the threat of such a maneuver was real, Stirling knew that any intelligence along those lines that he might receive at such an early date was practically worthless. He was desperate for troops, however, and if civilians would not act without such prodding, then he would provide the spur to get them into action.[23]

Despite occasional lapses into hyperbole, Stirling continued to work more or less amicably with the authorities of New Jersey and New York. Both he and the Jerseyite revolutionaries realized that while the patriot boycott was failing to halt trade between British sailors on two warships, the *Asia* and *Phoenix,* on station in the Narrows and Gravesend Bay, at the same time rebel shipping was being bedeviled by these two vessels. Stirling's response to this double barreled crisis was twofold. First, he requested the New Jersey Provincial Congress to stop all shipping in and out of New Jersey ports while the ships of war remained on station. Second, he asked that the colony send New Jersey troops to garrison Staten Island, suppress loyalists there, and halt any comings and goings with the two enemy vessels. The New Jersey legislature complied with Stirling's first proposal, but despite his numerous requests would not go along with the second. To Stirling's great surprise, the Provincial Congress informed him on March 9 that it did not have the manpower to carry out his sound military proposal because it was attempting to embody two companies of artillery. Consequently, Stirling had to sit idly by while contacts between the citizenry of Staten Island and British sailors continued.[24]

Meanwhile, Stirling and New York's civilian authorities hastily prepared an agreement outlining how they could work together to defend the city. These proceedings were conducted in an atmosphere of increasing urgency, because Stirling saw growing indications that New York's defenses might be put to the test very shortly. On March 13, he relayed a message to Congress from Washington in Boston that the British were evacuating that town. Since the enemy army might be headed for New York, Lord Stirling immediately urged the New York Provincial Congress to form a committee to meet with him and draw up a mutually acceptable manifesto on defense. The committee reached quick agreement, and on the same day presented a resolution calling for the citizens to help with building the fortifications and for a draft of men from a number of New York militia units to serve in the extremely dangerous, therefore highly unpopular, artillery corps. Both the Provincial Congress and Stirling were pleased with these harmonious proceedings, and the general over the next few days praised the legislators and the people for "cheerfully turning out" in the cause.[25]

Stirling also began putting into effect other programs designed to defend the city. On March 13, he sent out calls to county committees of safety in New Jersey to enroll their militia, and he halted at New York a battalion of Pennsylvania troops on its way to reinforce the patriot army in Canada. He also took possession of seven tons of gunpowder that were being shipped to Washington at Boston, on the assumption that it would be needed more by him than by the commander in chief. He then informed Congress of his actions, offering to amend any of them if so ordered. Congress responded to Stirling's extensive preparations with general approval. John Hancock, the president of Congress, informed him on March 15 that eight thousand more men were to be raised for New York's defense. This number of troops, said Hancock, would make the city invulnerable to assault by land. But since the enemy was not likely to attack New York any time soon, Stirling ought to send the gunpowder on to Washington, for the commander in chief could use it immediately. Moreover, Stirling should release all troops destined for Canadian service, since the patriot forces in Canada were in greater need of soldiers than was Stirling.[26]

In the midst of this activity, Stirling received a letter from Washington, confirming that Boston was being evacuated and that General William Howe's redcoats might descend on New York in a short time. The commander in chief was sending reinforcements of six regiments and a rifle company. He also was urging Governor Jonathan Trumbull of Connecticut to provide two thousand militiamen, and he wanted Stirling to call in one thousand citizen soldiers from New Jersey to reinforce New York's defenses. With these soldiers, Washington solemnly told Lord Stirling, the New York commander must hold the city until the main body of the army could join him. Indeed, the entire fate of America might rest with Stirling's fortitude in this venture, for if Britain gained control of the Hudson River–Lake Champlain waterway, the contest for American liberties would be in danger of collapse. These were words that might have shaken a seasoned military veteran, much less a "young beginner," but Stirling remained unruffled. He notified Washington that he was doing all within his power to see that the enemy made no lodgement, although he had only four thousand men in his command and half of these were untrained militia. He did betray a slight uneasiness by suggesting to the commander in chief that once the British finally departed Boston he should lose no time in getting himself and the American army to New York.[27]

Stirling continued for the next few days to oversee work on New York's fortifications and to receive reinforcements from various places. On March 17, he gave Congress a detailed outline of activities in his department, reporting that troops from upstate New York were coming in. He also noted that as soon as things got a little quieter around New York City he would turn his attention to fortifying Staten Island

and Bergen Neck on the New Jersey side. He continued to work closely with the Continental Congress and New York Provincial Congress to overcome deficiencies in army supply, to organize artillery units, and to control loyalists. Following Washington's orders (in spite of congressional instructions to the contrary) he retained in New York all shipments of gunpowder, pending discovery of the direction in which Howe intended to move after the evacuation of Boston. He kept up a lively correspondence with General Schuyler in Albany, and he opened an exchange of letters with Governor Trumbull about Connecticut militia forces for his defenses. Praising the Connecticut troops already on hand, Stirling urged Trumbull to allow these men to stay beyond the expiration of their enlistments, and he prodded the governor to send on the two thousand extra soldiers that Washington had asked for earlier. Trumbull willingly complied with all these requests in a spirit of cooperation that made Stirling wish other civilians understood his military predicament half as well. General Washington, who expressed "vast Satisfaction" at Stirling's activities, was delighted at the way Lord Stirling was developing as a general officer and was already turning over in his mind the possibility of making the earl a divisional commander in his own army.[28]

Ironically, Lord Stirling was having problems with political leaders in his own province of New Jersey as he followed Washington's order to enroll militia to defend New York. Although the committees of safety of some New Jersey counties complied immediately with his request for soldiers, others raised a number of questions about Stirling's requisition. It was pointed out that New Jersey law forbade its militia to leave the province; that sending soldiers to New York would leave New Jersey defenseless in case of attack; that if troops were so badly needed then regulars from New Jersey's Continental regiments "swarming around the country" on furlough should be called in. Stirling patiently addressed all these complaints with sound military logic. New Jersey law in this case, he declared, was overridden by congressional orders, and, even if not, civil law should be suspended temporarily in the face of grave danger to the state. As for the people's fears about New Jersey being undefended, Congress was working to redress that problem, and so was he. Finally, if any regulars were roaming the countryside they were away from camp without leave, for all furloughs for Continental soldiers had been canceled. He hoped, therefore, that he would hear no more objections about his calling the New Jersey militia to arms. (Even if he did, however, Stirling was not prepared to take the advice of his friend Elias Boudinot and bypass the committees with a personal appeal to the citizenry. That sort of behavior, he believed, smacked of military tyranny and showed no regard for civil control of military affairs. It was better, he believed, to suffer military inefficiency than to introduce contempt for law into New Jersey's political life.)[29]

Lord Stirling's independent command came to an end on March 20, when General William Thompson, who preceded him in appointment to rank, arrived on the scene. Stirling willingly handed over the burdens of command to Thompson and with his new superior's approval turned his attention solely to preparing the defenses of New Jersey. He had already employed some of the New Jersey militia that was trickling in to build roads in eastern New Jersey, and he was meeting with various county committees of safety to discuss his plans and coordinate his activities. In wretched weather on March 22, he reconnoitered the ground that needed to be defended and decided that works ought to be constructed at Perth Amboy, Elizabethtown Point, Paulus Hook, and on those parts of Bergen Neck and Staten Island that dominated the Kills. He explained his defensive plans to the New Jersey Committee of Safety and to Governor William Livingston, urging them "for God's sake . . . at this critical moment" not to delay calling in more militia to assist him in his work.[30]

Despite his efforts, Stirling had little success in improving New Jersey's defenses. He wrote Washington on March 27 to congratulate the commander in chief upon Howe's evacuation of Boston and to inform him that surveying by engineers was still going on. Stirling was telling Washington five days later that although General William Heath's five regiments, a rifle company, and the Connecticut militia had arrived in New York, Staten Island was "still open to invasion." He hoped soon to get the approval of William Heath, who had superseded Thompson in command at New York, to start work on fortifications in New Jersey. Eleven days later, he finally received orders from yet another new commander, Israel Putnam, to move his own New Jersey regiments to Staten Island. The defenses of New York now looked so promising to him that he wrote Washington, with considerable bombast, "I could wish General Howe would come here in preference to any other spot in America, as I believe it would not be of least detriment to the American cause." Additionally, he fawned to Washington, "then I should have the honor of serving under your immediate command." Stirling now knew it was safe to boast, for he had learned that Howe had evacuated his army to Halifax and would not be ready to carry out an assault against New York for at least three or four months. But the earl also knew that the day of reckoning had merely been postponed.[31]

Six

Lord Stirling at Bay: Long Island to Trenton, 1776

Stirling got his wish to serve under Washington, for on April 13, 1776, the commander in chief arrived in New York and took personal command of the city's defenses. Thus Lord Stirling began his long, devoted, and sometimes illustrious tenure as one of Washington's generals in the Continental army. Almost immediately, Stirling was given his first important duty, for on April 24 Washington reorganized his forces and announced in orders that for the moment the American army would consist of five brigades, commanded by Brigadier Generals Heath, Joseph Spencer, John Sullivan, Nathanael Greene, and Lord Stirling. (In this case, Washington used the term "brigade" in its traditional military sense of meaning a collection of regiments acting together under one officer.) Not long afterward, Washington again reorganized his troops, this time into four brigades, with a reshuffling of regiments. Stirling then became commander of the 4th Brigade, which continued constantly to change size and character because of additions and subtractions of regimental units or detachments by the commander in chief.[1]

General Washington kept Stirling busy in the next few weeks, not only with his duties as a brigade commander but also with special assignments. Stirling served on a committee with Greene and Sullivan on the 27th to organize a system of signals in the American army to convey notice of the British fleet's arrival at the mouth of New York's harbor. A little later, Stirling, Putnam, and Spencer looked into the problem of where to locate regimental alarm posts. Stirling proceeded at Washington's behest in late May to the Highlands on the Hudson River north of New York City to examine the forts there, and he presented the commander in chief with a detailed report on how to improve their military readiness. Washington immediately sent Stirling's suggestions to the commanders in the Highlands with orders that they be followed to the letter. Next, Stirling volunteered to accompany a committee of the New York Provincial Congress on an expedition to sound the channels of New York harbor, in order to determine exactly where British ships might be able to sail.[2]

Stirling also had the duty as a general officer under Washington's command to serve on officers' councils, for it was the practice of the commander in chief to ask his subordinates' advice from time to time. On June 27, Washington presented a council composed of Heath, Spencer, Greene, Stirling, Thomas Mifflin, and John Morin Scott with the especially perplexing problem of whether to uphold a court-martial recommendation that a certain Thomas Hickey be shot. Hickey, a loyalist, had been convicted of sedition, mutiny, and enlisting Continental soldiers into British service. The dilemma was that David Matthews, New York's loyalist mayor, had been implicated in the plot, which supposedly called for an uprising of loyalists in the city when Howe's army appeared in the harbor. The evidence for this scheme, as Washington knew, was skimpy and showed Hickey to be more ignorant than dangerous. Washington also knew that tension in the civilian population of the city was high because a large number of Tories lived there, and rumors were flying that Hickey intended to kill Washington. The general's problem, then, was that he needed to act swiftly to avert the slightest sign of patriot weakness, but at the same time to avoid the appearance of being personally frightened or vindictive. The unanimous recommendation of the council was that the sentence be carried out, and on the 28th it was, without serious repercussion.[3]

Washington and Stirling, both humane men, had a vexing problem in attempting to deal with the New York loyalists. On the one hand, they understood the military necessity of controlling them, but, on the other hand, they were reluctant to play the harsh role that their duty dictated. Stirling's problem was personal as well, for two of his sisters, Catherine and Susanna, were married to British army officers, and his eldest daughter, Mary, was married to a New York loyalist, Robert Watts. In the last analysis, neither Washington nor Stirling allowed public or private scruple to stand in the way of duty to the cause, for the commander in chief decided to control New York's Tory population by appointing a board of officers, consisting of Stirling, Scott, and McDougall (who was now in the army) to act as judges in determining the fate of individual loyalists. Although Washington confined the board's maximum authority to ordering loyalists banished from the city for the duration of the military crisis, the king's friends, whose only "crime" was devotion to George III and their country, found this humiliation almost unbearable.

Thomas Jones, the Tory historian of New York, described the situation: "The Loyalists were pursued like wolves and bears.... Numbers were taken, some were wounded, and a few murdered. The prisoners were conducted under a guard of rebels to New York, insulted and abused on the road." Then they were "ordered by a Board of officers . . . to be transported into a different part of New England." Jones and his family experienced these difficulties. A female cousin of his, whom he declared Stirling had known for years, was treated disrespectfully by Stirling and even told to "*be damned*." Jones himself was seized by a "parcel of riflemen" on August 11, and although he was under parole at the time, "I was told that the parole was dissolved . . . that I was a prisoner of the American Army." Consequently, he was brought before the board upon which Stirling sat and unceremoniously ordered out of New York, along with a number of other loyalists.[4] At least one American revolutionary, Henry Brockholst Livingston, found patriot persecution of loyalist "wretches" a "tyrannical exercise of power," and he declared that men like Stirling and Washington had "no right" to sit in judgment on fellow citizens whose only fault was to be on the wrong side in a political quarrel.[5] Stirling, however, insisted that the critical situation facing the revolutionaries in August 1776, warranted his assisting the patriots to suppress Tories.

Indeed, Washington's army was in grave danger by midsummer of that year. Thousands of British regulars under General William Howe had arrived in New York harbor from Halifax on July 1 and landed on undefended Staten Island (Stirling's troops, sent there earlier by Putnam, had been withdrawn). Howe was joined a few days later by his brother, Admiral Lord Howe, who sailed into New York harbor with a vast armada, and by early August, Washington faced a formidable force of thirty-two thousand men, supported by five hundred warships and transports—the largest concentration of military power ever seen on the North American continent. To oppose this mighty host, Washington could muster no more than twenty thousand troops, and while his army was bolstered by the knowledge that since July 4 it was fighting for the newly created United States of America, all the morale in the world could not turn aside British shot and steel. In order to formulate a reasonable plan of defense against his foes, Washington called a council of war, at which he proposed, to Stirling's delight, an assault on Howe's Staten Island positions. Since Stirling for some time had been drafting plans for a Staten Island operation, he immediately presented the council with a full-blown scheme of attack. However, Putnam, Heath, Spencer, and Greene pointed out the obvious difficulties with the plan, not least that water communication with the island was now endangered by British warships, and the idea was dropped.6

While events in New York during July and August built inexorably toward a contest of arms, Stirling was plagued with a petty court-martial case within his own command. He had been having trouble for a month with the ineptitude of Colonel Rudolphus Ritzema, one of his regimental commanders, who allowed his men to laze about while Stirling's other commanders, Colonels John Nixon, Samuel Blatchley Webb, and Alexander McDougall kept their troops in fighting trim. This situation reached a crisis on July 1, when Stirling called for his brigade to parade at 5:00 A.M. and Ritzema's regiment arrived two hours late. For this offense, the general placed his subordinate on report, whereupon Ritzema went about camp "using disrespectful expressions of Brigadier Genl. Lord Stirling." Washington thereupon ordered a court-martial of Ritzema for his conduct, and it reported on July 17 that since Stirling was "generously overlooking the personal affront offered him," Ritzema was cleared of charges. Some months later, Colonel Ritzema abandoned the American cause and deserted to the British.7

It was apparent to Washington and his general officers by the middle of August 1776 that their military peril in New York was becoming greater with every day that passed. Having already lost Staten Island, their numbers were still too few and their fortifications too weak to carry out their assigned task of occupying terrain on both lower Manhattan and Brooklyn Heights on Long Island. Indeed, by dividing their forces between these two places they were inviting disaster. The American generals also knew, however, that Congress for political reasons had strongly urged them to defend New York if at all possible, and Washington had bowed to this pressure by posting part of his army there. The Howe brothers consequently were offered numerous military opportunities. The most obvious one was to flank Washington's entire position by landing forces on northern Manhattan, but another was to assault the American forces on Long Island and to entrap the rebels against the East River, which was dominated by the Royal Navy. General Howe decided on the latter, more cautious, course of action, and on August 22, he began ferrying twenty thousand soldiers and forty cannon from Staten Island to Gravesend Bay on Long Island. For the next three days, he continued this operation, extending his front to Flatbush and beyond, probing the American army's defenses, and collecting intelligence about his enemy's strength and dispositions.[8]

Washington's strategy for countering the British on Long Island was uncomplicated. Essentially, he would hold Brooklyn Heights, a position that dominated New York City and was, therefore, crucial to its defense. For this purpose, the patriots had constructed a powerful line of fortifications on the heights, trending from northeast to southwest for about a mile between Wallabout Bay and Gowanus Creek, and thought to be impregnable. Washington considered these works, however, to be a fallback line of defense. About a mile and a half in front of Brooklyn Heights to the south and east was a wooded ridge, which stretched for about five miles parallel to the patriots' man-made defenses. It was on this line of hills that Washington would place the great majority of his eight thousand soldiers on Long Island, to guard three roads over which the British must march if they would penetrate to the first line of patriot defense. These roads were the Gowanus, farthest west and near Gowanus Bay, the Flatbush, in the center of the American position, and the Jamaica, on the extreme eastern end of the ridge.[9]

Washington was concerned that Howe might attempt an assault on Manhattan while conducting his Long Island operation, so the American commander was forced to remain in New York City. Therefore, he delegated command of patriot troops on Long Island to a subordinate. This position was held until August 20 by Nathanael Greene, whom Washington trusted implicitly. But that day Washington temporarily appointed John Sullivan in Greene's stead, because Greene had been suffering since the 15th with a high fever. Three days later, Washington decided to send Israel Putnam to oversee the defenses on Brooklyn Heights, and since Putnam outranked Sullivan he automatically took command on Long Island. Putnam, however, promptly ordered Sullivan to take charge of American troops outside the fortified line, while

Putnam commanded the main defensive line. Sullivan therefore began making dispositions on August 25 for a line of battle, ordering Lord Stirling immediately to Long Island to command the right and reserve while Sullivan himself retained control of the center and left. (A month later, Sullivan would insist that he had given Stirling charge of all troops beyond Putnam's lines, but the wording of his orders of August 25 regarding Stirling's duties makes it clear that Sullivan retained overall leadership of the outer forces himself.)[10]

It was obvious to everyone in the American army by August 25 that Sullivan's dispositions perilously exposed the left wing of his line, for it was "in the air" and vulnerable to an enemy strike from that direction. Yet no American commander did anything to counteract the danger. Colonel Samuel Miles, whose Pennsylvania regiment was posted on the extreme left of the American line, was under Sullivan's orders to patrol toward Jamaica Road, the only invasion route left unprotected by the Americans, but he had no cavalry forces for the task and consequently did not follow instructions. Sullivan on his own, or so he said later, sent out five junior officers during the night of the 26th to patrol the Jamaica Road and to give warning of any untoward enemy activity in that direction, but these preparations were woefully inadequate. Putnam and Sullivan as well as Washington, who approved the preparations, must share the responsibility for what happened as a result of patriot military shortcomings. The rebel generals, it seems, had made the fundamental military mistake of believing that the enemy would do as they expected and attack along the axis of Flatbush Road. Howe, of course, had other ideas.[11]

When Stirling received his orders from Sullivan on August 25, he immediately crossed over to Brooklyn Heights and took command of the troops composing his right wing. He worked all day on the 26th to prepare them as completely as he could for battle and that evening retired to his bed in Putnam's headquarters. Next morning at 3:00, he was awakened by a herald from Putnam and informed that the British were advancing toward his positions on the patriot right. Immediately, he marched out under Putnam's orders with the regiments of Colonels John Haslet and William Smallwood to meet the enemy. The battle of Long Island, Stirling's first encounter with combat, had begun. As daybreak came on, Stirling proceeded along Gowanus Road toward the Narrows, and half a mile before reaching the Red Lion Tavern met Colonel Samuel J. Atlee, who commanded a regiment that had been guarding the road. Atlee informed Stirling that the enemy force, eight regiments under General James Grant, was within sight. "Indeed," wrote Stirling to Washington later, "I saw their front between us and the Red Lion."

Stirling now went into action. He ordered Atlee to place his regiment in a masking position facing the enemy on the left of the road while he brought up Haslet's and Smallwood's men and formed them "on very advantageous ground." He then had Atlee withdraw in good order into the protection of a copse of trees on Stirling's left. At that point, General Grant pushed forward his own light infantry to within 150 yards of Stirling's right and left flanks, started a fire fight that lasted about two hours, and then retired to his lines. Meantime, Grant had positioned two field pieces about three hundred yards from Stirling's flanks that kept up a steady cannonade all morning. Beyond these measures, Grant did nothing, although he did keep his main body of troops deployed in menacing lines facing the Americans at about six hundred yards' distance. Hence, Stirling began to suspect as the morning progressed that Grant's object was to keep him "amused" while Howe accomplished some larger proposal on another part of the battlefield.[12]

That larger purpose was not long in becoming clear to Stirling and all the Americans. While Hessian General Philip Von Heister applied just enough pressure on Sullivan at Flatbush to tie him down (as Stirling was tied down on the right), General Howe flanked the patriot line on the left by advancing westward around the hills. Undetected and in place with his troops at 9:00 A.M., Howe fired two cannon as a prearranged signal to Von Heister, and both generals fell upon Sullivan's hapless men, front and rear, with unrelenting fury. Straightaway, the American center crumpled, and patriot soldiers fled toward the defenses on Brooklyn Heights. Some managed to reach the shelter of these lines without difficulty, but others drifted to the left and became mired in the salt marshes of Gowanus Creek. General Sullivan had disappeared in the confusion and was believed by Washington to be dead or a captive of the enemy.[13]

The disintegration of Sullivan's lines and the consequent thrust of Howe westward along the Jamaica Road toward Brooklyn Heights had put Stirling and his men in mortal peril. Not only was their line of retreat, the Gowanus Road, occupied or under heavy fire by British and Hessian troops but also General Grant was now unleashing a

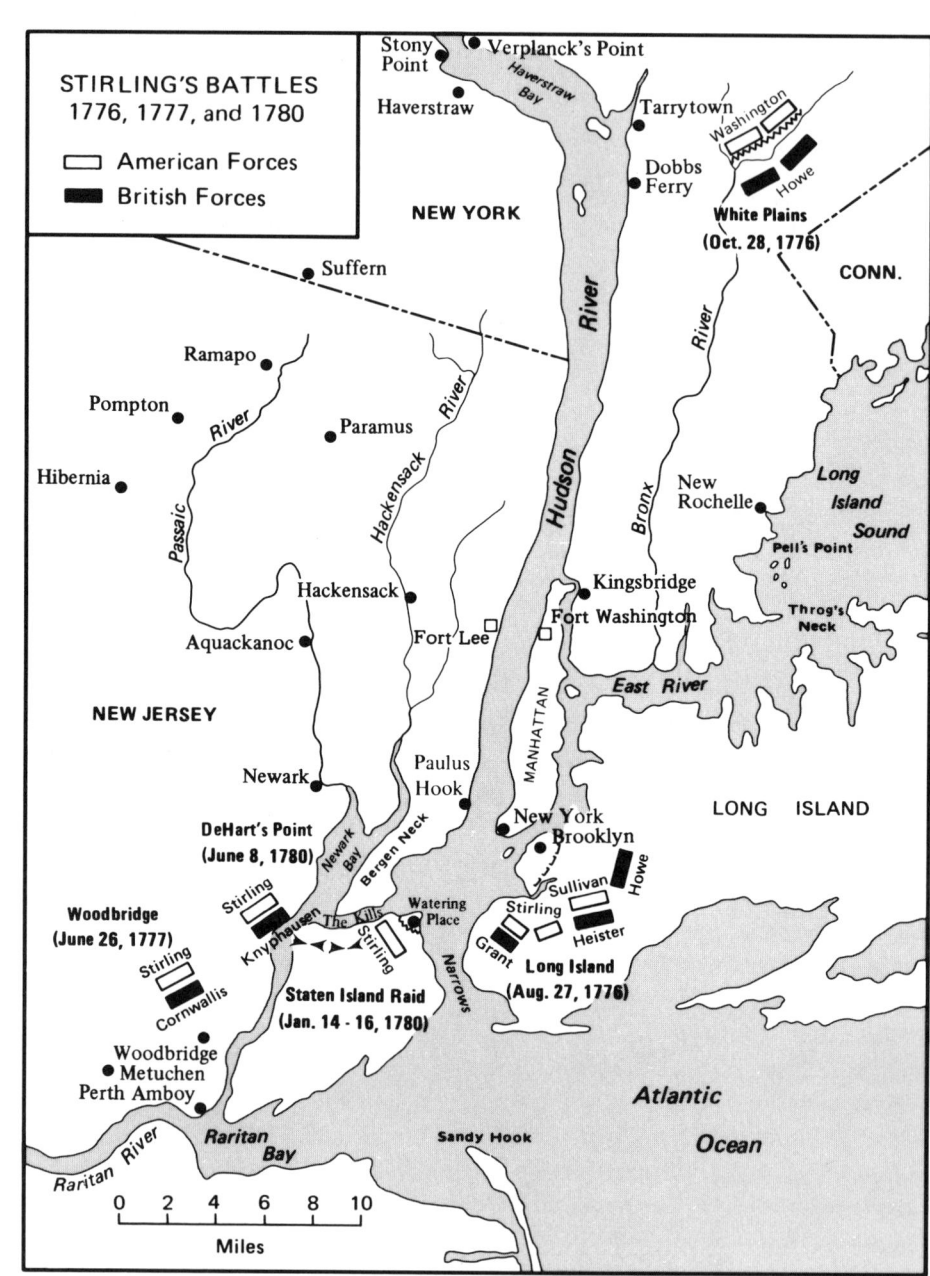

vicious attack in their front. By 11:00 A.M., Stirling's only chance of escaping this trap was to send the main body of his men through the swampy morass of Gowanus Creek, while he rallied about half of Smallwood's Marylanders to cover their retreat. These brave men stood, wrote an observer, Philip Vickers Fithian, "more than four Hours . . . on three Sides of them were the Enemy—on the other Side . . . [the] broad March, & a Creek." Washington, who had come over to Long Island to take personal command of the battle, viewed this unequal contest from the Brooklyn lines and cried, "Good God, what brave fellows I must this day lose!" Indeed, the Marylanders did lose heavily, for by the end of that fatal day, 259 of Smallwood's 684 men were killed, captured, or wounded.[14]

Stirling finally realized that the battle was hopeless and that it was "impossible to do more than to provide for safety." Hence, he made a dash for the American lines along a narrow corridor of dry land between a mill and Fort Box, the southern terminus of the works on Brooklyn Heights. However, "a considerable body of troops [appeared] in my front," and other enemy soldiers "in pursuit of me on right and left" kept up "a constant firing on me." So the general could only gallop to cover behind "the point of a hill," and although he "was soon out of reach" of his pursuers, it became evident "that it would be in vain to attempt to make my escape." At that point, his only consideration was to avoid surrendering to Grant, who had incensed the patriots earlier by declaring in Parliament that Americans "could not fight, and that he would undertake to march from one end of the continent to the other with 5,000 men." Therefore, Stirling sought out the Hessian commander, Von Heister, handed over his sword, and became a prisoner of war. The Germans, it turned out, were hardly more respectful of Stirling than Grant might have been, for shortly after his surrender, Hessian Colonel Von Herringen wrote contemptuously, "My Lord Stirling himself is only an *échappé de famille,* and does not pass for a Lord in England." Given this attitude on the part of his enemies, it did not surprise Stirling to learn after the battle that his personal baggage had not been kept intact and that he had been "plundered" of camp furniture valued at more than five hundred pounds and two valuable horses.[15]

Because Stirling had been removed from the battle, he did not discover that Sullivan was a coprisoner until the two Americans met at Howe's headquarters. Moreover, he was not aware that the patriots, after withdrawing behind their fortified lines, had stood firm and discourgaed further British assaults that afternoon. The battle scene uppermost in his mind was the wild confusion surrounding the collapse of the advanced American line and the travail of his own troops. These facts may account for his wildly exaggerated statement shortly after his capture to his old friend Henry Clinton, "that out of thirty battalions which [the Americans] had in front of their works most of their generals, cannon, and colors fell into [British] hands; and a great number of other officers, with about four thousand men, were either killed, drowned, or taken." He probably gave General Howe similar figures, for the British commander reported them to Lord George Germain on September 3, while listing his own losses as 66 killed, 268 wounded, and 21 missing. Washington, however, who had a clearer picture of the situation, put the patriot casualties at somewhere between 700 and 1000.[16]

Given time after the battle to review his performance against the enemy, Stirling mused upon an age-old question that fighting men who successfully endure their first exposure to enemy fire ask themselves: Why was I able to stand bravely in the face of death without flinching or losing my self-possession? This question was especially perplexing in Stirling's case, for neither he nor anyone else could have predicted that this overweight, rheumatic, vain, pompous, gluttonous inebriate would be so ardent in battle. The answer to the question, as both he and others now realized, was that he possessed at the core of his personality, beneath all superficial trappings, a rock-hard integrity and devotion to duty. It was true that Stirling's boyish enthusiasms sometimes masked this essential substance, but after the horror he had endured with such élan at Long Island, neither he nor anyone else ever again doubted that his courage was his strongest personality trait.

In captivity, both Stirling and Sullivan were treated with civility by the British, at least to their faces. One obvious reason for the Howes's kindness was to convince the two Americans and, through them, Congress and Washington as well of the sincerity of their peace mission. Hence, the Howes "tampered" with Stirling and Sullivan, as one American quaintly put it, wining and dining the two men on board the admiral's flagship, the *Eagle*. The brothers Howe declared (incorrectly) to the two patriot generals that the Americans misunderstood their peace commission, for it was not limited as the patriots believed to dispensing pardons and receiving surrenders. Indeed, it was possible for the Howes to end the bloodshed on a basis mutually acceptable to all parties, and Parliament, the ministry guaranteed, would ratify the agreement. Stirling and Sullivan were reminded by the Howes of the Britons' close connections to America (a brother had been killed at Crown Point during the Seven Years' War), and they were told that Parliament had no right to tax colonists or regulate their internal affairs. Ambrose Serle, the admiral's secretary, also "labored to convince [Stirling and Sullivan] of their error," and soon both "came down vastly in their Style & air." Finally, Sullivan agreed to go to Philadelphia on parole and ask Congress to send an unofficial delegation to the Howes to talk peace.[17]

Taking advantage of Sullivan's departure to send a report to Washington, Stirling on August 29 composed a lengthy but incomplete narrative of his conduct on Long Island. Washington, two days later, when notifying Congress that the two generals had been captured was mildly critical of Stirling's battle account, saying, "It is not so full and certain as I could wish"; however, he correctly noted that Stirling "was hurried most probably, as his Letter was unfinished." Some Americans found things to censure in Stirling's tactics during the battle. "There can be do Doubt but Lord Stirling behaved bravely," said John Morin Scott, "but I wish that he had retreated sooner; he refused . . . for Want of orders. We miss him much; he was a very fine officer." Colonel Joseph Reed, Washington's adjutant, remarked, "My Lord, who loved discipline, made a mistake which probably affected us a great deal. He would not suffer his regiment to break, but kept them in lines and on open ground. The enemy, on the other hand, possessed themselves of the woods and fences. His personal bravery was conspicuous."[18]

While his comrades discussed his military qualities and faults, Stirling whiled away his time in captivity. He visited with the deceitful Serle, who talked directly to Stirling in "the softest Words and manner I could," but sneered behind his back that he was a "despicable" example of "the Want of real officers or valuable Men among the Rebels." Stirling also continued to hobnob with the Howes and other British notables, including John Murray, Earl of Dunmore, recently deposed governor of Virginia, who had achieved notoriety in patriot circles by enlisting slaves in Crown service against their rebel masters. Stirling later enjoyed telling his American comrades about the first time he met Dunmore, at which time the governor remarked to the rebel earl, "So, how do you do; I am sorry to see you in such damn black company." Stirling replied in a manner that the Americans found devastatingly amusing, that the earl "had not of late been so familiar with the Black Company as his Lordship."[19]

Military operations did not cease with Stirling's capture, and the general watched with helpless dismay as both his own fortunes and those of his cause were threatened with destruction. Directly after the battle of Long Island, Washington evacuated all posts on Brooklyn Heights and withdrew in good order to Manhattan. However, he refused (because of Congressional orders) to heed the sound advice of Nathanael Greene, proffered on September 5, to evacuate and burn New York City. Seven days later, he did begin to withdraw from lower Manhattan, but before he completed this evacuation, General Howe landed part of his army at Kip's Bay on the eastern side of the island and came near to cutting Washington off. For the Americans the only good thing to come out of all this maneuvering and fighting was that the British army was finally checked on September 16, after a series of spirited skirmishes with the enemy on Harlem Heights. Since New York was now in British hands, Stirling learned from his captors that his magnificent Mansion House, a legacy of his beloved parents, had been looted earlier by soldiers of his own army. The deed had been perpetrated on August 30, and Washington in general orders one day later had warned "the Plunderers . . . to restore to the Quartermaster General, what they have taken, in failure whereof they will certainly be hanged." Within a few days, the "Scoundrels" were caught and given thirty-nine lashes, so most of the stolen goods must have been recovered.[20]

As the campaign progressed, General Howe found Lord Stirling's attendance at his headquarters to be less and less indispensable. It is entirely possible that he recognized in Stirling the prisoner a greater threat to his supply of vintage than Stirling the soldier would be to British operations. Whatever the case, in early September he began negotiating an exchange for Stirling, and also for Sullivan, by informing Washington that he would be in favor of exchanging Sullivan for Major General Richard Prescott and "Brig.—Gen. Alexander, commonly called Lord Stirling" for any English brigadier whom the Americans held captive. Washington and Congress found this arrangement satisfactory, so the commander in chief suggested on September 6 that Stirling be exchanged for Brigadier General Donald McDonald, who had been captured in North Carolina. Thirteen days later, Washington notified Howe that Prescott and McDonald were at Elizabethtown, New Jersey, awaiting his pleasure. At this time, Howe proceeded with Sullivan's exchange, but he balked at accepting McDonald, "as he has only the rank of major by my commission." However, if Washington were amenable, Howe would exchange Stirling for Montfort Brown, governor of Providence Island in the West Indies, recently taken prisoner by patriot Commodore Esek Hopkins. General Washington and Congress agreed to this proposal. Therefore, on October 6 Lord Stirling and Governor Brown were formally exchanged on board a British ship of war anchored in the Hudson River, and the earl, ever popular in the American army, was welcomed back to headquarters by Washington and other acquaintances among the general officers. The following day, Washington put Stirling in charge of a brigade recently left leaderless when its former commander, Thomas Mifflin, became quartermaster general.[21]

Lord Stirling had hardly assumed his new position before he was given an opportunity to see more action, for on October 9, the British recommenced offensive maneuvers by sailing warships up the Hudson River past Forts Washington and Lee. Three days later, General Howe ferried a strong force to Throg's Point in Westchester County and immediately threatened the Americans' only practical line of retreat from Manhattan. The British commander soon discovered that he had blundered into a position that the rebels could easily defend, for he was on a peninsula that connected to the mainland by a narrow neck of land. Washington quickly rushed two regiments to contain Howe in his confined position, while he spent time he had gained by the enemy's blunder to rethink his options. On October 16, he called an urgent council of war, which was attended by Stirling and the other general officers, including Charles Lee, who had just rejoined the American army after repelling the enemy at Charleston. The question on Washington's mind was whether he could hold his present position and prevent Howe from encircling him or whether he should push his army northward out of Manhattan with all speed. The council's advice was to get off Manhattan and fall back to White Plains in order to avoid either surrender or battle at a disadvantage. At the same time, the Americans would continue to garrison Fort Washington on Manhattan as a counter to British shipping on the Hudson River. Washington immediately began to execute this plan by ordering two regiments to join Stirling's brigade as a reinforcement and by sending the earl's two thousand troops forward without baggage as the army's vanguard, with orders to secure a new encampment on high ground at White Plains.[22]

Flattered that Washington found him competent to lead this semi-independent detachment, Stirling marched his brigade swiftly northward, covering the eighteen miles to his destination in only a few hours. As he moved forward, he was aware that General Howe was landing the British army at Pell's Point, near New Rochelle, in order to extricate himself from his earlier cul-de-sac. Moreover, Stirling realized that the British commander was being delayed in advancing toward his own position only by the less than confident Colonel John Glover and a mere 750 men, who blocked Howe at Pelham Bay. As it turned out, Stirling had nothing to fear from the British army, for Glover's men delayed Howe for twenty-four hours, and then Howe delayed himself by adhering to what was becoming his typical pattern of slowing his movements just at the most auspicious moment for the patriots. Hence, during the next few days the British commander probed forward with extreme caution, in doing so allowing Stirling at least partially to turn the tables against Howe by going on the offensive. Stirling had learned that loyalist officer Robert Rogers, "the old Indian hunter in the last French War" (as William Heath described him), was encamped ten miles away on Heathcote Hill near Mamaroneck. Consequently, Stirling ordered Colonel John Haslet to lead a detachment of 750 men in an attempt to capture Rogers, whom Stirling in March had run out of New York City as a Tory troublemaker. On the night of October 21, Haslet carried out an assault on Rogers's position, capturing 36 prisoners, a pair of colors, and sixty muskets—but no Rogers. Stirling nevertheless was pleased at Haslet's work and praised the colonel before his brigade the following day. Stirling also conducted other business, according to a soldier's cryptic diary entry: "Tue 22 . . . there was a gallows ordered by Genl Starling to hang three of the prisoners at 12 o'clock."[23]

Stirling's skirmish against the enemy, significant as it may have been for American morale, was a mere pinprick as far as affecting Howe's operations. The British commander continued to inch forward, allowing Washington to march with his fourteen thousand men, baggage, ammunition, and forage out of Manhattan. Washington rejoined Stirling at White Plains on October 23, but units of his army were still plodding northward, and both he and the earl were worried that Howe might still attempt to cut off the American rear guard. That possibility ceased to vex them when on the 26th General Charles Lee came marching in with the last of the Continentals. Washington now disposed his army at White Plains in a generally northeasterly to southwesterly direction for three miles along naturally fortified heights, and set his troops to augmenting the defenses with man-made works.24

Washington was certain that these new American lines would shortly be challenged by Howe's army, and he prepared for the fight. On October 27, he rode out with his generals, Stirling among them, to reconnoiter the ground. On the right of the patriot line, and slightly in front of it, he found an eminence named Chatterton's Hill, which was secured only by a few militiamen stationed behind stone fences. The officers were not disturbed by the weakness of this position, for as Lee pointed out the lines the army already occupied were secure from assault. Even as they discussed the issue, a courier notified them that enemy forces were skirmishing with American pickets farther eastward. Immediately, they dispersed to their respective commands, but they discovered that there was no cause for alarm, for the British intended no general assault that day. During the respite, Washington reconsidered the weakness of his position on Chatterton's Hill and decided to reinforce it on the morning of the 28th with Haslet's regiment and McDougall's brigade. His change of heart was none too soon, for on that day Howe deployed his army before the Americans, commenced a general cannonade along the entire line, and stormed Chatterton's Hill on the patriot right wing. After a hot fight the British secured the position by first driving off the Massachusetts militia and then the Continentals, and the battle of White Plains was finished. Washington, his right no longer tenable, was forced that night to retreat a short distance northward to a rugged and defensible position called North Castle.25

Stirling, whose brigade took no direct part in the fighting at White Plains, was now ordered by Washington to march with his troops to a post about three miles on the right of the new American line and delay any attempted enemy turning movements in that direction. Pleased with this responsibility, he was particularly attentive to duty, and so on November 1, at about 6:00 A.M., he raised an alarm at headquarters by announcing that two British columns were advancing in his direction. Washington and his aides immediately rode out to determine if Howe was really attempting to flank the American line, a possibility that all patriot officers dreaded. It turned out that Stirling's alarm was premature: the marching men were actually columns sent out from Washington's main lines to reinforce Stirling. The earl was particularly delighted to secure the additional soldiers; his brigade now consisted of 7 regiments, numbering 2,863 men, the largest body of troops that he had ever commanded and, in fact, the largest in the entire army.[26]

Stirling had nothing to fear from Howe at this time, because the British general had other things on his mind than attacking Washington. On November 5, he abandoned his camp at White Plains and marched southwest, to assault Fort Washington on Manhattan and then to proceed into New Jersey. In reaction to this stunning development, Washington on the 6th held a council of war with Stirling and his general officers to determine a course of action. The officers were forced to conclude that they must divide their pitifully small army, which now numbered only 13,123 fit for duty, into three contingents. Lee would remain at White Plains with 7,000 men to cover New England against attack; Heath would post 4,000 in the Highlands at Peekskill; Washington would retain the remaining 2,000, under Stirling's immediate command, and would march into New Jersey to blunt Howe's advance in that direction. Washington hoped to be reinforced in New Jersey with 5,000 militiamen plus other soldiers, but he was soon to learn from Greene, who commanded Fort Lee, that these troops did not exist. He could depend only upon Greene's garrison of 3,500 to augment his tiny army.[27]

Commencing these operations on November 10, Stirling ferried the men across the Hudson River at King's Ferry, scouted the terrain on the west bank, secured roads and passes that his army must use on its march south, and sent out blocking parties along the river to oppose enemy landings should they be attempted. The next day he was joined by Washington, and these two men, plus Generals Heath, Mifflin, and James and George Clinton, inspected the Highlands fortifications as far north as West Point. Then, Stirling and Washington moved southward with their army, reaching Greene's headquarters at Fort Lee on November 13. At that place Stirling parted company with the commander in chief and marched his brigade to New Brunswick, where he established his headquarters on the 16th of November and began cutting communications between the enemy and the large number of Tories that had suddenly declared themselves in the state since patriot defeats in New York. He also began writing the New Jersey state government and Congress in Philadelphia to assure rebel civilians that they need have no fear of being left prey to the advancing British army. Stirling was vague, however, about how he and General Washington intended to delay the enemy advance, as no doubt citizens of New Jersey and Pennsylvania were quick to note.[28]

On the same day that Stirling arrived in New Brunswick, a terrible disaster befell the patriot cause. Fort Washington and its garrison of 4,500 men were lost to the British. Washington despondently wrote on the 19th, "I am wearied almost to death with the retrograde motion of things," but he refused to give up hope. The next day, as the British poured across the Hudson River and began marching toward Fort Lee, the commander ordered that post abandoned and a general American retreat across the Hackensack and Passaic Rivers. Finally, he established his headquarters at Newark. Stirling was aware of Washington's problems and knew that the commander might need his assistance at a moment's notice. Therefore, he ordered his brigade into a state of alert and sent out an urgent call to Governor William Livingston, his brother-in-law, to help him mobilize the state's militia. "A fright seems to have seized the whole country," he declared, but "We will make the best stand we can." Meanwhile, he attempted with little success to mitigate the harshness with which his soldiers treated loyalists. "Notwithstanding General Stirling deprecates severity to the infernal Tories we catch," one soldier wrote on December 2, "they get absolution often." Although Stirling had proved often enough to hold no love for the king's friends, this sort of lawlessness against them was more than even he could tolerate.[29]

Stirling's preparations for an advance toward Washington were unnecessary. On November 28, the commander in chief had to abandon Newark and fall back to New Brunswick when the British crossed the Passaic River and threatened to force a landing at Perth Amboy. Washington had hoped to hold the Newark line with the assistance of Lee, whom he ordered on November 20 and 21 to join him, but Lee did not arrive in time. Stirling welcomed the commander in chief to his headquarters at New Brunswick, but under the circumstances there was no celebrating. In fact, Washington hardly paused in his retreat, for on December 1, he moved his army of 3,400 men (now including Stirling and his brigade) across the Raritan River. The American generals had had no time to spare, because less than two hours later a British force of at least 6,000 soldiers under Lord Cornwallis marched into New Brunswick. Washington now fell back to Trenton, where he could

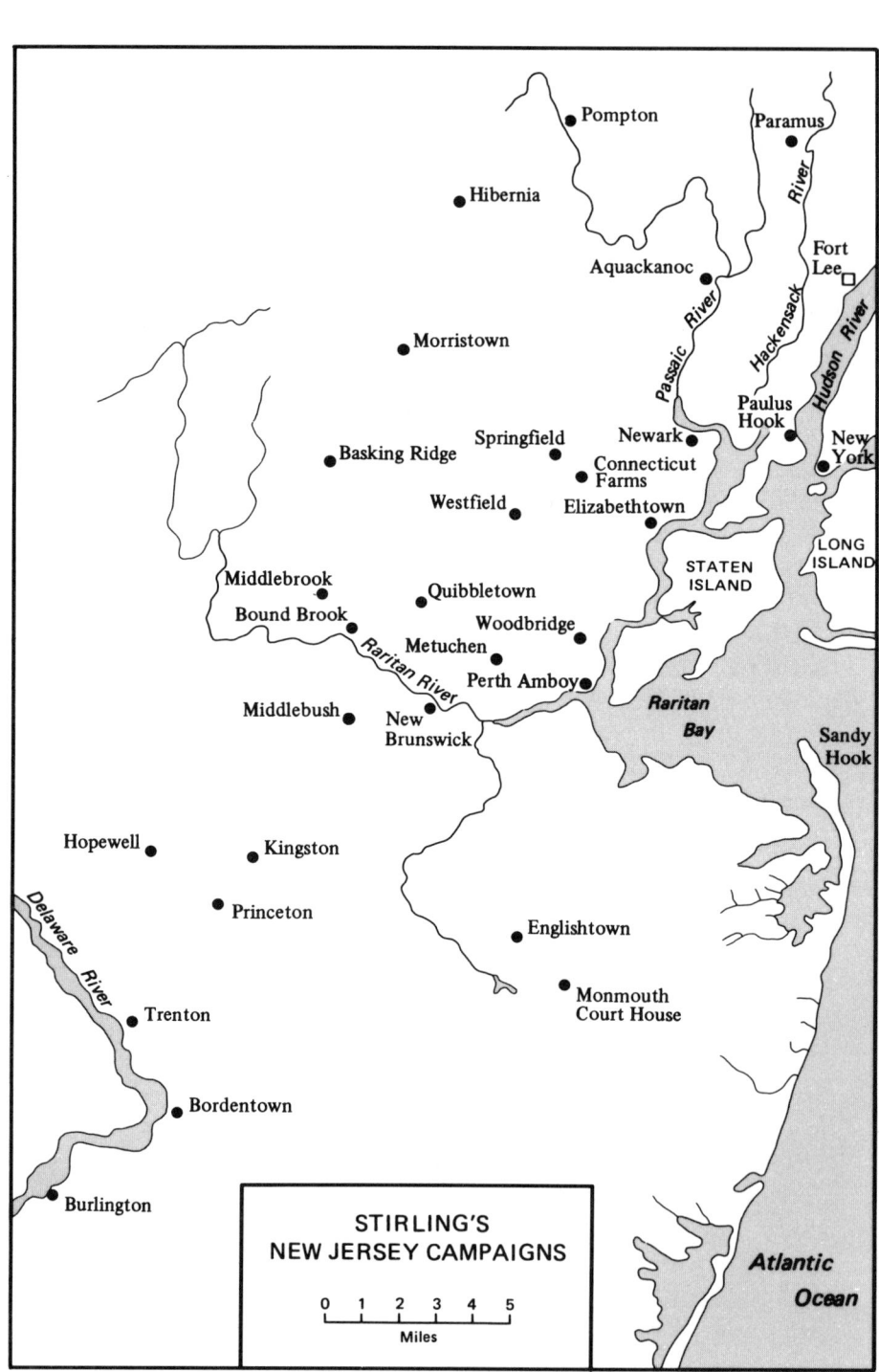

cross the Delaware River if need be with the "main body" of the army, and detached Stirling to Princeton with two brigades, about 1,200 men, to shadow the enemy. However, Washington learned on December 6 that Cornwallis was closing in on him, and he quickly ordered Stirling to rejoin him. At the same time, he began ferrying his army across the Delaware River to Pennsylvania, completing the operation two days later, just as the enemy rode into Trenton.[30]

At this point, Stirling and Washington (although they were not aware of the fact) had reached the end of their harrowing retreat, for General Howe had decided to go into winter quarters in New Jersey rather than chase the Continental army any farther. Since the American generals were not privy to Howe's plans, they continued to do all within their power to thwart the enemy's advance. Washington, in detailed and carefully worded orders, instructed Stirling and other generals to post their brigades along the west bank of the Delaware at various landing places as a guard against surprise enemy incursions. Stirling found this duty easy, and so for the first time in weeks he had a chance to rest and think. He wrote Washington on December 12 that Cornwallis was at Pennytown, ensconsed in a camp that the British considered so impregnable that they were lulled into a sense of the "utmost security." This situation, mused Stirling, was tailor-made for a surprise attack, and if his troops were so not exhausted by their long retreat, he would "gladly try the experiment" of leading 1,200 handpicked men across the Delaware to fall upon Cornwallis from the north. If he could depend upon General Lee's bringing on his forces (Lee was at last reported to be on the march) Cornwallis's rear could be simultaneously assaulted.[31]

By the time he received Stirling's letter, Washington was already contemplating a patriot counterstroke across the Delaware. But in order to effect anything, he must know how many troops he could rely on. He had already instructed Lee to join him with his detachment, and Philip Schuyler was forwarding a body of men from Fort Ticonderoga under the command of General Horatio Gates. Since none of these troops had arrived, Washington ordered Stirling northward with orders to form a junction with Lee and to dispatch trusted emissaries to Heath and Gates to find out how many soldiers they had. "Reposing the most implicit confidence in you and the Officers before mentioned," the commander in chief said, "I do not mean to tie you down to any rule but leave you to the free exercise of your own judgments."

These words together with Stirling's later comments on the commander's verbal orders show that Washington was empowering Stirling to carry out Stirling's proposed foray if it were possible with the reinforcements he would receive from Lee and Gates.[32]

In the early morning hours of December 15, Stirling rode out with his aides toward Easton, anticipating that he might soon be able to retaliate against the British who had so recently humiliated the American army. His party reached Bethlehem by early afternoon, and there he heard for the first time the staggering news that Charles Lee had been captured by the enemy near Stirling's home at Basking Ridge. Spurred by this intelligence, the earl rode quickly on toward Easton, where he was glad to learn that both Gates and Sullivan (Lee's second in command) had ferried their troops across the Delaware, "far above enemy lines," and were safe. Stirling was saddened to know, however, that it was now too late to attempt anything against the British. Under the new circumstances, it would be far too risky, he noted to Heath on the 16th, to cross back to New Jersey. All that was left for him to do was return to Washington's headquarters and report these things, which the commander in chief already had learned from dispatches sent by courier. Sullivan and Gates finally did march into the main camp on December 20, but they brought with them a disappointingly small 2,600 men, fewer than half the number Washington had expected. With the addition of this meager reinforcement, the American army on December 22 numbered 4,707 regulars and 2,000 New Jersey and Pennsylvania militia. Stirling's brigade, consisting of four regiments, could muster only 505 soldiers.[33]

In spite of these discouraging numbers, Washington and his officers felt compelled to attempt a surprise attack against the enemy across the Delaware. The term of enlistment for the Continentals would be up on the last day of the year, and the generals believed something must be done with the army before it melted away. Moreover, there was a tempting target for assault, a Hessian garrison of about two or three thousand men at Trenton, relatively isolated from other British and German outposts. Although General James Grant, Stirling's old nemesis, was warning Colonel Johann Rall, commander at Trenton, that Washington and Stirling might attack him, Rall was not careful to guard against surprise. Hence, Washington devised a plan, with the assistance of Greene, Stirling, Sullivan, and some of the other American general officers, by a roaring fire in the Thompson-Neely house, near McKonkey's Ferry on the Delaware. The commander decided upon a three-pronged assault against Trenton, designed to encircle the town and force Rall's surrender. With a force of twenty-four hundred Continentals, he would cross the river at McKonkey's Ferry, nine miles above Trenton, on Christmas night, march down and cut off the Hessians from the north. Meantime, General James Ewing would pass the river directly opposite the town with his New Jersey and Pennsylvania militia, seize Assunpink Bridge, and prevent the garrison from fleeing southward to Bordentown, where Colonel Carl, Count Von Donlop commanded two thousand men. Finally, Colonel John Cadwalader would cross the Delaware at Bristol with one thousand troops and cause Von Donlop even more difficulty. It was Washington's intention, after forcing the surrender of Rall, either to converge upon Von Donlop at Bordentown from both north and south, he hoped with similar result, or to march against Princeton.[34]

With plans completed and troops prepared, Stirling and his officer colleagues paraded their Continental regiments at McKonkey's Ferry on Christmas evening, December 25. In high expectations and mounting suspense, both officers and privates, under the watchful eye and guiding hand of Henry Knox, boarded the Durham boats of Glover's Marblehead mariners and pushed out into the icy water of the Delaware. The ferrying operation, which Washington had hoped to have finished by midnight, took until 3:00 A.M., and not until an hour later could the regiments be ordered and the march begin. But the Americans adhered to their plan with firm resolve. Through light snow, sleet, and freezing rain, the small army pushed along Pennington Road to Birmingham, where by prearrangement Sullivan moved to the right with half the men and cannon down River Road, to maneuver by Rall's left and get onto his line of retreat (just in case Ewing's men did not make it into position). Stirling, whose tiny brigade, along with Hugh Mercer's made up Greene's command, remained on Pennington Road with General Washington. At about 8:00 A.M., the column ran into an advanced Hessian picket, which it dispersed, and the battle of Trenton commenced.

Washington now quickly ordered Stirling's brigade and Knox's artillery to form a line of battle from east to west on high ground just to the north of Trenton at the head of King and Queen Streets and to open a cannonade along both thoroughfares. As Stirling carried out this maneuver in the midst of blowing snow, Mercer filed his men to the right, behind the houses of King Street, and formed a line from north to south. Both brigades then opened a shattering fire on the confused Hessians in the town, and Stirling's 3d Virginia Regiment charged forward to seize some enemy cannon. Meanwhile the Germans attempted to form for battle or retreat into an open field east of the village. Their only possible avenue of escape was northeastward along the Princeton Road, for Sullivan's men (Ewing had not crossed the river because of ice) had successfully blocked all roads to Bordentown. Soon, Washington closed this last line of retreat. He had observed the Hessians in the field and promptly ordered Colonel Edward Hand's regiment and the Philadelphia German Battalion to block the road. Consequently, the Hessians were trapped and had no choice but to surrender. In two separate contingents, they grounded arms at about 10:00 A.M.[35]

Stirling and his colleagues were delighted with the outcome of the Trenton operation. Without the death of a single patriot soldier (only four were slightly wounded), the Americans had mortally wounded Colonel Rall and captured most of the men of three Hessian regiments; about five hundred hardy individuals had waded icy Assunpink Creek and escaped to Bordentown. After the battle, Stirling thawed out from the bitter cold by entertaining the Hessian captains and lieutenants while Washington saw to the colonels and majors. Exclaimed the earl with delight, "I had the honor to . . . treat [the Germans] in such style as will make the rest of them more willing to surrender than to fight." He made their captivity even less burdensome by ordering a Lutheran minister, who had appeared from somewhere and was nagging them in German about theology and the iniquities of George III, to cease and desist.[36]

Stirling and Washington wished for more victories after the Trenton triumph, but they were compelled to look to the reality of their situation. Although Cadwalader had gotten across the Delaware on the 26th and might support the Continental regiments in a push against Bordentown, Washington feared that the British would move against him in force from New Brunswick. Some of his soldiers had gotten into Hessian liquor supplies and were drunk. The weather was terrible and the low temperatures might freeze the Delaware River just enough to cut off his supplies. He decided after weighing these factors, to recross the river, and by December 28 he was safely ensconsed with his veterans on the west side at Newtown. From his new camp Stirling

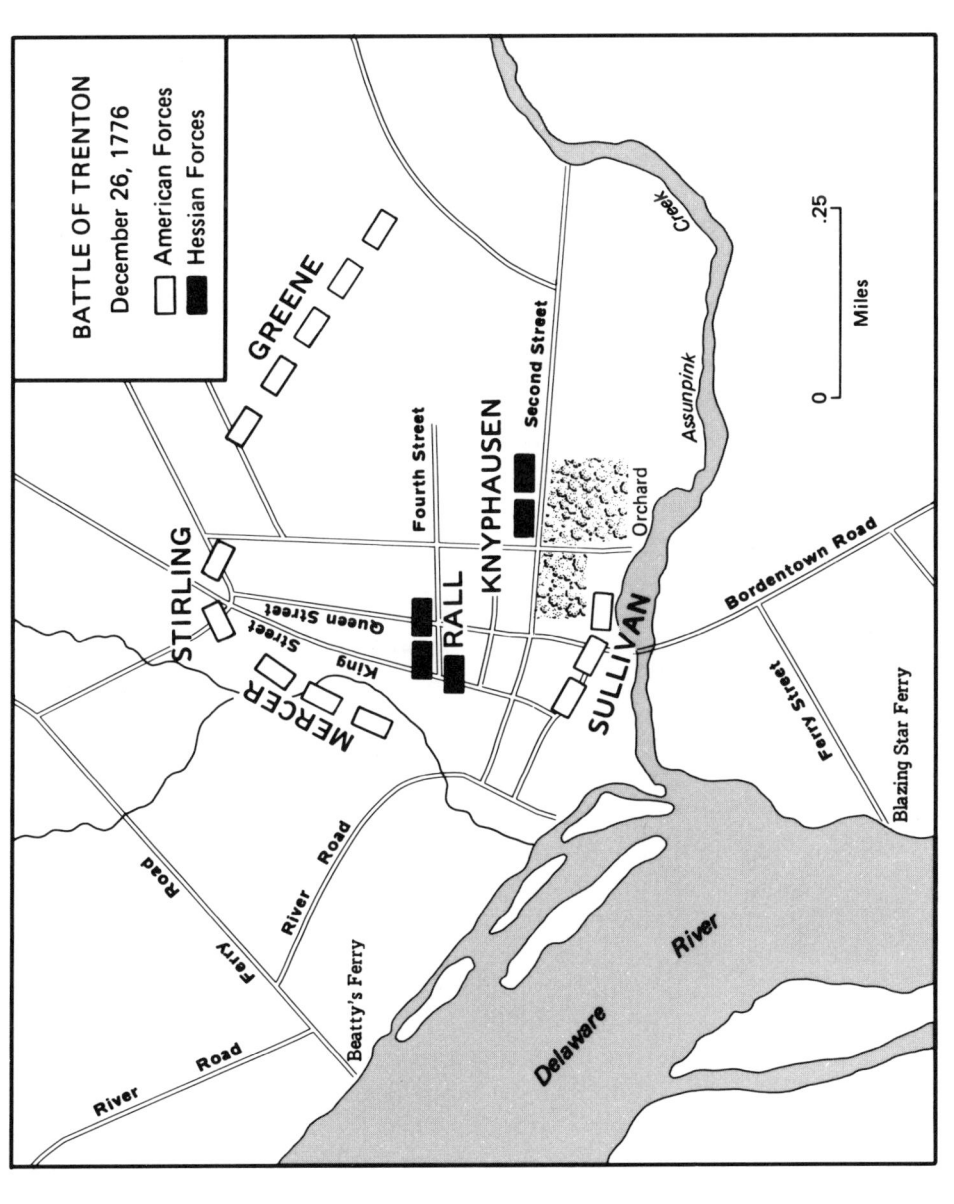

wrote to Governor Livingston that the effects of Washington's victory were "amazing". The morale of New Jersey was aroused and Stirling hoped the governor and legislators would do all in their power to take advantage of the new spirit. The legislature should immediately vote to enroll New Jersey's full quota of Continental troops. The Governor should get out militia raiding parties to fall on the enemy's isolated cantonments on their line of retreat, so that "they would be completely knocked up." Now was the "time to exert every nerve; and if we do, General Howe's Army will be ruined. . . . God bless you, be active, and make the state of New-Jersey what it ought to be."[37]

Stirling's spirit was strong in late December 1776, but his body had failed him. Constant exposure to snow, ice, and freezing winds during the Trenton campaign—"the worst Weather I ever saw," he said—had brought him low with an attack of rheumatism. Hence, he must watch in frustration as Washington recrossed the Delaware River on the night of December 30–31, to conduct another expedition against the British in New Jersey. His only consolation was that General Washington had left him at Newtown in command of all patriot forces along the west bank of the Delaware River, with orders to "secure the ferries and *passes* of the Country against any surprize." In early January 1777, Stirling was carrying out his duty as best he could "with the few I have to Command," while rumors of impending British assaults across the river kept him in a state of constant agitation. He received word from Adam Stephen on the 8th that Howe might attempt to march seven thousand men against Philadelphia while ignoring Washington, who had gone into winter quarters at Morristown after the battle of Princeton. Stirling notified Congress of this report and pointed out that if it were true he had only a few "trifling guards of Militia" with which to fend off such an enemy thrust. The intelligence, of course, was false. In fact, Howe, rather than advancing against the rebels, was withdrawing all his forces from Bordentown, Black Horse, Burlington, and Mount Holly to New Brunswick or other posts eastward of the Raritan River. Belatedly, the campaign of 1776 was at an end. It had concluded, as Stirling realized, on a much more successful note than he had dared hope possible even two weeks before.[38]

Seven

Washington's Loyal Captain: The Campaign of 1777

In mid-January, Stirling proceeded to Philadelphia, where he could more easily conduct military business, now that British activity was ceasing in New Jersey and his presence was no longer required at Newtown. He wrote George Clinton, asking that his baggage, which had been left behind in the march from White Plains the previous November, be forwarded to him so he could live in greater comfort. His primary concern was with recruiting his brigade up to strength for the coming campaign, and he expended much ineffectual effort on this business. He attempted with General Gates, who was also in Philadelphia, to curtail raids by recruiters of one state upon militiamen of another. Apparently, some of his regulations angered the militia, or at least so Washington heard at Morristown, for six hundred citizen soldiers simply marched home, spreading such nasty rumors along the way that others would not serve. Washington hoped the report was untrue. "It has been our great misfortune to have too much to do with Militia," he lectured Stirling, "but while the necessity exists, the most should be made of them; a people unused to restraint must be led, they will not be drove." What Stirling had done, if anything, to arouse his commander's ire is not known.[1]

Stirling received orders from Washington in early February to repair to Basking Ridge and take charge of patriot troops there. He was delighted with these instructions, for at Basking Ridge he could live in the comfort of his family on his estate, be near his friends and colleagues in the army's main encampment at Morristown, and harass the enemy's outposts to his heart's content. He had no sooner arrived there than he received even more pleasant news from Congress: On February 19 he had been promoted major general. Gratefully he wrote the legislators, "I am sincerely devoted to the cause of American Liberty, and . . . I shall not Omitt any occasion of Shewing my self worthy of the Confidence . . . repose[d] in me." Seizing upon this chance to use his present high standing with Congress to gain a favor, he petitioned the legislators to vote him recompense for losses of personal property at the battles of Long Island and Trenton, so that in the future "I may be the better enabled to take the field again with some degree of Credit to them & to my self." He did not have much confidence that his memorial would be heeded, and his pessimism was warranted. Congress on March 18 declared that it dare not pay Stirling for his losses, "lest a dangerous precedent be established." However, a precedent *was* being established, for Congress later used the denial of Stirling's request as excuse to refuse other officers' petitions for financial redress.2

The winter and spring of 1777 were quiet seasons for Lord Stirling, although his post at Basking Ridge was near Howe's troops at New Brunswick. He corresponded with Washington about reorganizing part of his division, which by late March numbered only three hundred soldiers and a sergeant's guard of three cavalrymen. He spied on the British in New York and reported troop movements to the commander in chief. He went on "harassing the enemy with constant scouting parties," allowing "Scarcely a day [to pass] without one or more skirmishes, the success of which are constantly in our favor." He supported General Benjamin Lincoln's detachment at Bound Brook in every way he could and was happy when an enemy assault against that post on April 13 was repulsed. All these duties Stirling carried out in spite of rheumatic attacks that flared up from time to time with symptoms of violent intestinal cramps, intense headaches, and high fevers that lasted for days on end. He also did not allow infirmity to quench his love of the good life, for he and Lady Stirling continued to entertain numerous guests and friends at his Basking Ridge mansion. Nathanael Greene, who stayed a while with his compatriot during April wrote his wife, Caty, that he had had a most enjoyable visit in the springtime lushness of Jersey's Somerset Hills. One sour note was struck during this idyll when Washington on May 6 wrote Stirling a letter of reprimand for treating a Mrs. Livingston "with a degree of roughness and indelicacy, which I am convinced, your cooler reflection must condemn." Washington obviously was embarrassed with this affair and would not have interfered except that such "little quarrels" might be made use of by the enemy. In his reply, Stirling stiffly noted that the lady in question had been leasing a house of his and had not paid her rent. When given six weeks' notice to vacate, she had not, even though she "had no less than four other houses engaged." Apparently, Washington was satisfied with this response, for he let the matter drop.[3]

With the arrival of spring 1777, Washington and his generals expected immediate stirrings from the enemy at New Brunswick, but April turned into May, and Howe continued to remain silent in his camp. The patriots took full advantage of these months to prepare for the coming campaign. By late May, Washington's reorganized and well-equipped Continental army was ready to take the field with nine thousand men in five divisions, commanded by Major Generals Sullivan, Greene, Stirling, Stephen, and Lincoln. In addition to this core of regulars, the commander in chief could augment his forces with thousands of militia when the need arose. To be sure, the commander and his subordinate generals thought this dependence upon militia a dangerous thing, but given Congress' inaction in raising Continental regiments, there was not the remotest chance that the army would ever number the seventy-five thousand men that the law permitted.

The officers' fear of militia dependency stemmed from two sources. First, they expressed the practical military point of view that citizen soldiers were an undependable source of manpower, constantly coming and going, consuming precious stores and rarely performing any useful military function. Second, and perhaps more important, the officers viewed the necessity to fight a militia war as a potentially radicalizing influence on the Revolution itself, with ideological overtones about the establishment of a more democratic society after the war than the generals wished to see. Even while the war continued (as Professor Don Higginbotham has noted), the leaders of the Revolution, who "were conservative in both political and military outlook" (as were most of the officers), feared that dependence upon citizen soldiers might unleash a guerilla struggle that "would pose internal dangers to the cause: such physical destruction, such savagery and blood-letting, that the internal institutions of the country, along with the political and legal processes, might fall sacrifice to the war." General Lord Stirling was among those officers who feared the radicalizing influence of militia armies, and he consistently resisted all attempts to weaken the regular army, as he saw it, by reducing the number of Continentals and increasing the size of militia forces.[4]

With his small army, Washington on May 28 took post on strong and defensible heights at Middlebrook, from which he could move, if necessary, to counter an enemy thrust toward Philadelphia from New Brunswick. On June 14, General Howe went into action, pushing two columns of soldiers toward Middlebush, in hopes of luring the American commander from his secure position into open country and bringing on a general engagement. Washington refused to take the bait, so the Anglo-German forces withdrew. Then, on June 22 Howe evacuated New Brunswick and marched to Perth Amboy with the intention of crossing to Staten Island and embarking for Philadelphia. In his withdrawal, he was harassed by Daniel Morgan's regiment of Anthony Wayne's brigade, but to little effect. Stirling, meanwhile, moved his division upon Washington's order as rapidly as possible to a post between New Brunswick and Perth Amboy to reinforce General William Maxwell's brigade, which had been detached from Stirling's force earlier. The commander in chief intended that Stirling strike Howe's withdrawing army in the left flank, but Stirling's advance was too late. Howe got safely to Perth Amboy.[5]

Slowly following Howe with his main army, Washington on June 24 marched cautiously to Quibbletown and opened his headquarters there. At the same time, he ordered Stirling's detached division to take post roughly between Woodbridge and Metuchen, about five miles northwest of Perth Amboy. Washington was uncomfortable with these positions for two reasons. First, he felt he might have to pull back his troops, which would be "no small misfortune" on account of the effect a retreat might have on American morale. Second, he was worried about the exposed nature of his encampments, especially Stirling's, which was nearest the enemy on "low and disadvantageous ground." The American commander had good cause to worry, for Howe, observing Washington's arrangements, "Judged it advisable to make a movement" that he continued to hope would result in a full-scale battle. Therefore, he rapidly marched two columns toward Washington's army on the 26th. Lord Cornwallis commanded the movement to the right toward Woodbridge, and Howe himself was in charge of the left thrust toward Metuchen. It was Howe's intention that Cornwallis, after taking a swipe at Stirling, would rejoin the main British army at Metuchen. Thereupon, Howe would push against Washington's left flank at Quibbletown, cut the American retreat toward the safe high ground to the northwest, and destroy the Continental army.[6]

Stirling's division was in grave danger on the morning of June 26.

Washington's main army was also threatened, but not as seriously. Immediately, the commander in chief recognized the problem and withdrew his troops into the protective hills at Middlebrook. Stirling also saw the danger and was anxious to get away, but Cornwallis was moving too rapidly for the earl to avoid a brush with the enemy. As the redcoated soldiers of Cornwallis's column came into American view near Woodbridge, Stirling was just pushing seventy wagonloads of ammunition and other precious provisions out of his camp. Hence, he threw his little force of one thousand men into the line of battle and put his three cannons into position for action in order to defend these supplies. Stirling's maneuver was unwise almost to the point of foolhardiness, for although he was "advantagelously posted," as Howe said later, he nonetheless was outnumbered twelve to one. Moreover, by attempting to fight he was running the risk of precipitating a major battle—precisely that Howe wanted—or losing his entire division. Perhaps he felt he had no choice.[7]

As the fight developed, Stirling's line was charged by the elite grenadiers and some light cavalry with "so great impetuousity," as Howe said, that the rebels "dispersed on all sides." In this brief skirmish, a junior British officer was said to have espied Stirling among the Americans and cried, "Come here, you damned rebel; and I will do for you," whereupon Stirling coolly ordered four marksmen to silence, "the hardy fool by killing him on the spot." As Stirling and his troops hastily quitted the field, they were forced to abandon their three pieces of brass ordnance. They also left behind, according to Howe, sixty-three dead soldiers and about three times that number of wounded and captured. The British lost only five killed and thirty wounded. As Stirling hurried his troops toward the passes into the hills at Scotch Plains, he was pursued by British light dragoons. He finally shook off the enemy horsemen at Westfield and on the evening of the 26th reached the safety of New Jersey's mountains.[8]

Lord Stirling and the patriots at this point commenced a period of quiet but anxious waiting to discover what Howe intended to do next. After his skirmish with Stirling, Howe withdrew his army once more to Perth Amboy and on the last day of June retired to Staten Island, which he had quitted a year before to fight Washington. Immediately, he began preparations to embark his army for a voyage southward against Philadelphia. Washington and his generals, ebullient that New Jersey was free of invaders (but not privy to Howe's plans), marched the Continental army back to Morristown. From there it could be ready to strike the enemy's forces in New Jersey, should Howe suddenly attempt to march overland toward Philadelphia, or to push rapidly to the Hudson Valley, if Howe moved northward for a junction with John Burgoyne's forces, which were coming out of Canada. After Stirling put his division on the road under his second in command, Frenchman Thomas Conway, he rode down to Elizabethtown to see if he could find out what the enemy was doing around New York City. He did not have much luck, so he shortly rejoined Washington at Morristown, just in time to share with him the ominous news from Philip Schuyler that Fort Ticonderoga, at the south end of Lake Champlain, had fallen to Burgoyne on July 5. Washington had no choice in face of this disaster but to march northward to the Hudson, for the danger that Howe would proceed up the Hudson to meet Burgoyne seemed vastly greater than that he would make a sudden dash overland toward Philadelphia. Hence, the Continental army from July 11 to 17 wended its way slowly northward until it reached Smith's Clove, where Stirling opened his headquarters at Suffern. He was ordered by Washington two days later to move his division across the Hudson River and take post at Peekskill, which he did with scant enthusiasm. "Peaks Kill," he complained to the commander in chief, "is one of the most melancholy duty holes I ever saw."[9]

Fortunately for Lord Stirling, he did not have to remain there very long. On July 24, Washington and Stirling received definite intelligence that Howe had sailed the day before with most of his army from New York. His destination was almost certainly Philadelphia, although the Americans could not rule out New England entirely. Therefore, the commander put his army in motion southward and ordered Stirling's division to recross the river and march behind him in the general direction of the Delaware fords near Trenton. Stirling complied. At the same time he queried Washington about the possibility of his division marching toward Staten Island, in the likelihood that Howe's withdrawal had left that place weakly defended and open to a surprise assault. Washington seconded this idea, and he wrote Stirling that he was ordering all available boats collected at Perth Amboy in case remaining enemy forces on Staten Island proved to be, as a deserter declared, "Green" regiments numbering only one thousand men. Further analysis of the island's defenses, however, proved to the two generals that Stirling could not carry out a successful attack with the meager forces at his command. Hence, Stirling marched his division quickly to Trenton (bypassing his home at Basking Ridge, although he desperately wished to pause there for even a short visit). In early August he rejoined the main army.[10]

The haste with which Stirling effected his march was due to reports reaching the American officers that Howe's fleet was off the Delaware capes and would soon sail up the Delaware River to Philadelphia. Yet this news had hardly been received before it was quickly superseded by new reports on July 31 that the fleet had sailed eastward over the horizon rather than proceeding into Delaware Bay. It was difficult at this point for Washington and his generals to penetrate Howe's intentions. The commander in chief had already asserted that Howe's "abandoning General Burgoyne" was "unaccountable," but now he was even more mystified. Howe's conduct, he declared in exasperation on August 4, "really is so mysterious that you cannot reason upon it so as to form any certain conclusion." All the Americans could do under these circumstances was wait, while keeping the army alert for action. So, Washington encamped his forces in a convenient spot about twenty miles north of Philadelphia in Bucks County, and for two suspenseful weeks he and his generals sat and fretted about the condition of their men under these trying circumstances. Finally, he broke the tension on August 21, by calling together Greene, Stirling, Stephen, newly arrived Marquis de Lafayette, Maxwell, Knox, and other officers for a council of war to determine a course of action for American forces. The generals agreed without much debate that Howe, after such a long absence at sea, must surely be sailing for Charleston. Since it was obviously impossible for Washington's army to reach that city in time to do anything against Howe, the Continentals ought to march northward against Burgoyne. Thus, Washington, with the approval of Congress (which would be left undefended by this maneuver), began preparations for the advance.[11]

That same evening, Washington's plans were negated by news from Virginia that the British fleet had entered Chesapeake Bay on the 14th of August and was sailing northward toward Head of Elk, Maryland. Howe had appeared at last, and word had reached Washington in time for him to interpose the Continental army between the British and Philadelphia. The Americans might have received much worse news than that. Hence, it was with relief that the patriot generals prepared their men to march southward, and it was in this lighthearted temper that they decided to parade the army through the streets of Philadelphia. In preparation for this show, the commander in chief issued orders for his men to wash their clothes, polish their weapons, and be ready to march smartly.[12]

The soldiers stepped out from their camp near Germantown on Sunday morning, August 24, cavalrymen leading to "scout" the way, pioneers coming next with axes ready as though to hew a road, and the infantry divisions following at an interval of one hundred yards. The Continentals came twelve abreast down Front Street to Chestnut, then west to the Common, fifers and drummers playing a martial air, the generals in front of their commands mounted on their best horses and dressed in their newest uniforms. For two hours, these ragamuffins trudged by the crowds in the streets of Philadelphia, then onto a floating bridge across the Schuylkill River and their destination at Darby. Observers had plenty of time to note their strengths and deficiencies. John Adams, a keen analyst, found the men "extremely well armed, pretty well clothed, and tolerably disciplined," but he also found in them much to criticize. The troopers did not march in time, or hold their heads erect, or turn out their toes correctly, or cock their hats uniformly. But the generals this day, despite the deficiencies in their men's military bearing, were proud of their army.[13]

Stirling and his commander in chief now could do little more than wait for Howe to act. To be sure, all the army's generals did their parts to keep an eye on enemy activities, but there was little activity to keep an eye on. In early September, Howe leisurely disembarked his thirteen thousand men at Head of Elk, and on the 8th of the month he began to march up the road toward Christiana, Delaware. Washington, observing Howe's motions from his post at Wilmington, suspected that Howe intended to turn his flank and get the British army between the Continentals and Philadelphia. Hence, the commander in chief decided to interpose his army to halt the British thrust. On September 9 he marched his troops northward and took post on high ground east of Brandywine Creek at Chadd's Ford. During these movements, Stirling was suffering from a severe bout of rheumatism, and although he did not leave the army he was forced temporarily to yield leadership of his division to General Conway. The earl was back in command by the time Washington completed his maneuver to the Brandywine.[14]

Stirling and the other American generals could plainly see that

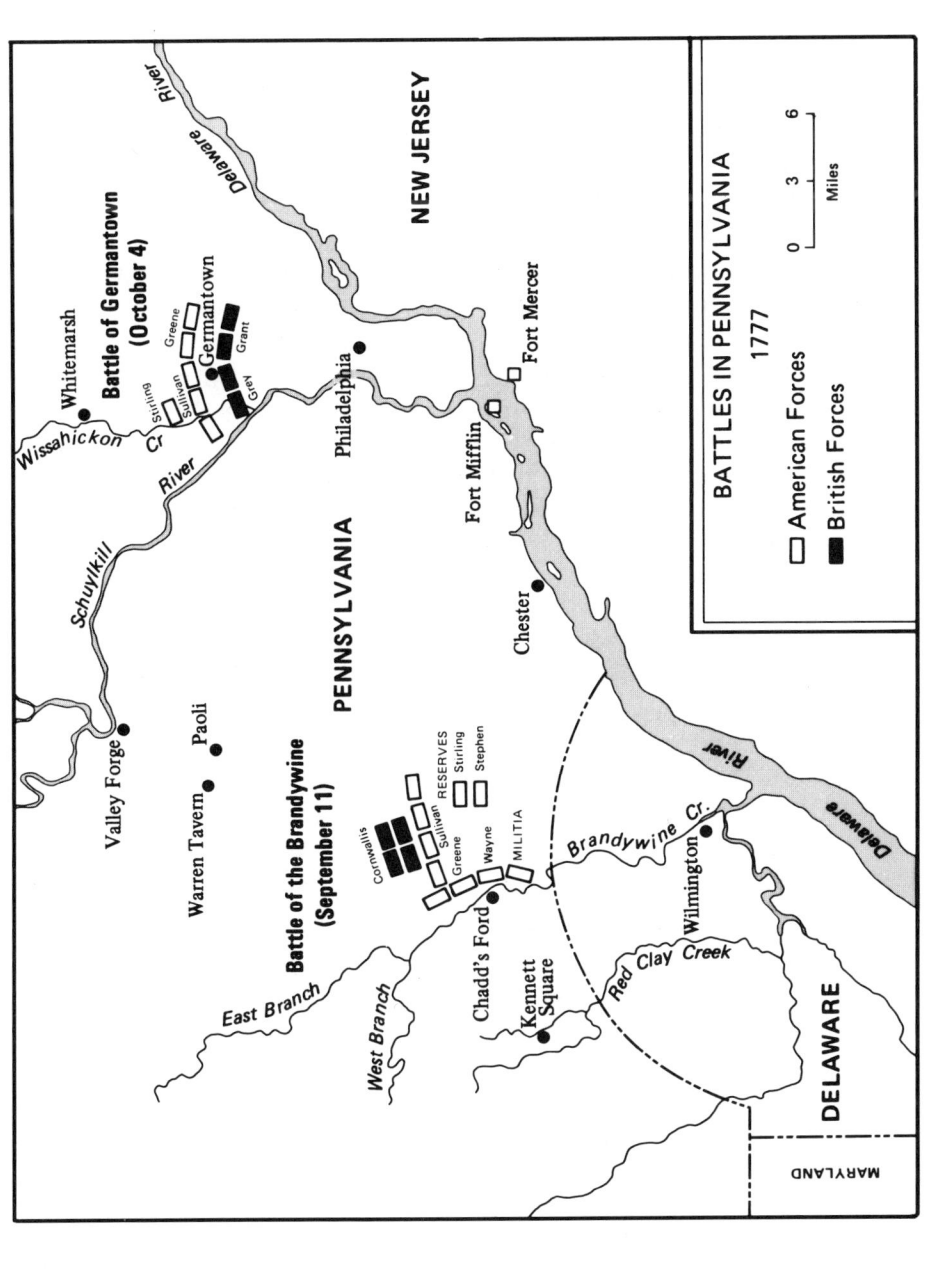

Brandywine Creek was their only line of defense in southeastern Pennsylvania for keeping Howe out of Philadelphia. This stream, running generally from the northeast to southwest, was deep enough to require infantry to use fords—hence Washington's tactic of occupying a defensible position at Chadd's Ford. But even though the patriot commander recognized the vital defensive importance of the creek, he had no intention of holding this line by risking his eight thousand regulars and three thousand militia against Howe's full force of thirteen thousand men. He would harass the Briton's advance to Kennett Square, four miles west of Chadd's Ford, as he did on September 10 by sending out skirmishing parties, and he would cover as many of the seven other Brandywine fords as he could, but beyond that he must leave the initiative to Howe, fighting if he must but yielding should Howe apply superior force in battle. With these ideas in mind, he disposed his army. He stationed John Armstrong's Pennsylvania militia at Byle's Ford, below Chadd's, and posted Lincoln's division, including Maxwell's brigade, on the west side of the creek nearest the enemy. He sent Sullivan to the right of his line on the opposite bank and ordered Greene's division and Wayne's brigade (part of Lincoln's command) to the center, directly behind the ford. In reserve, he placed Stephen behind Greene and Lord Stirling to support either Sullivan on the right or Greene in the center, as circumstances required.[15]

As the foggy morning of September 11 dawned, Stirling and the other American generals learned that Howe intended to give them battle. Riding to Washington's headquarters, Stirling could hear the rattle of musketry and boom of cannon as the enemy pushed up from Kennett Square and engaged Lincoln's men west of the Brandywine. He had just reached his destination when word reached Washington that Maxwell's light troops were taking the brunt of the British assault. After about two hours of fighting, Maxwell withdrew his men at 10:00 A.M. across the creek, and soon the balance of Lincoln's division followed. The American generals now learned that they were opposed by General Baron Wilhelm Von Knyphausen who led an undetermined number of British and German troops, and that Howe's whereabouts could not be accounted for. As noon approached with Knyphausen's force strangely unwilling to advance, Washington and his officers began to suspect that the missing Howe might be attempting a flanking movement to their right. Consequently, Washington immediately increased patrols by his light horse in that direction, and as unconfirmed but nonetheless disturbing reports began reaching him that a British force had been seen far up the Brandywine, he ordered Stirling and Stephen at 11:00 A.M. to march their divisions to the Birmingham Meeting House and take position on strong ground dominating potential enemy routes of advance from the northwest.[16]

Stirling and Stephen began executing their orders without delay. Rallying his little division, Lord Stirling set off on the three-and-a-half-mile march to his objective, but before he had covered half the distance a furiously riding courier overtook him with an order from Washington to halt his column until the commander in chief was absolutely certain that Howe intended to flank the American position. If he did not, then Stirling's and Stephen's men must remain within supporting distance of the American front on the Brandywine, should the enemy be given the option of launching an attack with fifteen thousand troops against fewer than half that number of Continentals. Stirling restlessly waited with his men far from the scene of battle, while Washington wrestled at headquarters with the problem of where Stirling's division ought to be posted. Shortly after 2:00 P.M., Washington's perplexity was ended with the arrival of astonishing news from John Sullivan: "The enemy are in the rear of my right about two miles, coming down," he said. "There are . . . about two brigades of them." Sullivan's troops were shifting to an east-west line to meet the British threat, and Sullivan needed reinforcements desperately. With all dispatch, Washington directed Stirling and Stephen to advance at a trot to the Birmingham Meeting House and take orders from Sullivan, the senior commander on the American right. It was now a race to see whether Stirling and Stephen could reinforce Sullivan before the flanking redcoats smashed the patriot right wing and threatened annihilation of the entire American army.[17]

The Americans won the race, joining Sullivan in a strong position on hills just south of the Birmingham Meeting House and extending the patriot line on its new axis farther to the right. Directly, Lord Stirling set his troops frantically to preparing his new position by throwing up makeshift breastworks and positioning cannon for greatest effectiveness. Before these arrangements were complete, the unequal contest commenced when Stirling descried the British advancing toward him at about 4:30 in the afternoon, under the leadership of the able and valiant Cornwallis. With determination Stirling, Sullivan, and Stephen for a time absorbed the full brunt of British fire and steel, but soon the sheer weight of enemy power began to tell. Just as the American line began to buckle, Washington appeared upon the scene with Greene's division, and the patriots steadied and held their ground. By now, however, William Woodford's brigade of Stirling's division had lost most of its cannon, and all the Continental units had suffered badly. Consequently, Washington ordered his troops to retreat, under the protecting fire of George Weedon's brigade. In the last hour of daylight, the patriot right wing, without harassment from the exhausted British in its front, withdrew in fairly good order from the heights around the Birmingham Meeting House.[18]

During the next day or two, as Stirling and his division recuperated at Chester from the battle of the Brandywine and as Washington reorganized his forces, the earl learned what had happened in the late afternoon of the 11th on the American left wing. Wayne and Maxwell had fought as best they could, but without Greene's division to support them, they had fallen back and lost their cannon. The militia, meanwhile, had withdrawn without engaging the enemy. As for battle casualties, the numbers were uncertain, but it appeared the Americans had lost at least a thousand men while the enemy suffered only half that many deaths, wounds, and captives. Washington, then, had been hurt at Brandywine, but by no means mortally, for his army still had plenty of fight left. His subordinate Stirling, who had proved once again his ability and courage as a battle leader, was itching for another go at the British. General Sullivan, recognizing the quality of Stirling's leadership, praised the earl's division as "a Corps which remarkably distinguished themselves" at Brandywine.[19]

Stirling and the entire patriot army spent the three weeks following the Battle of Brandywine in frustrating march and countermarch, during which time Philadelphia was lost. At first, Washington withdrew his forces northward beyond the Schuylkill River, leaving only enough troops near Howe to harass the enemy's advance and to gather intelligence. The American commander recrossed the Schuylkill on the 15th and the following day disposed his army at Warren Tavern for battle. But a torrential rain drenched his army's cartridges and forced him three days later to pass the Schuylkill again. This time he left Anthony Wayne and William Smallwood with separate troop detachments to vex the enemy's flanks, not dreaming that Wayne's men would be surprised in camp at Paoli on the evening of September 20 and shot up badly. Even worse for the patriots, Howe a day later acted as though he would march toward the valuable Continental depot at Reading, decoyed Washington into following him, then reversed his direction of march, and on the 26th occupied the city of Philadelphia. Humiliated by this setback, Washington called a council of war to ask Stirling and the other officers how the American army should respond. The council decided that since almost twenty-five percent of the Continentals were barefoot, they should remain where they were, at Potts Grove. Washington agreed, but at the same time ordered Stirling to keep close watch on the enemy and go to the assistance of reinforcements under McDougall that were to arrive from the Highlands, should they be attacked. Without incident, these forces marched in on the 27th. Washington, now reinforced, called another council to ask his officers whether the patriot army, numbering eleven thousand men, should assault Howe's main encampment, established at Germantown, to the northwest of Philadelphia. The advice of the council, Stirling concurring, was that the American army should await further reinforcements before attempting anything. The commander in chief acquiesced.[20]

In early October, Lord Stirling and the other officers of Washington's staff changed their minds about attacking the enemy. Word had arrived in the American camp that Howe was sending two detachments of troops from Germantown to help clear rebel forces from the Delaware River below Philadelphia. Since only nine thousand redcoats remained at Germantown, and since Howe had thought it unnecessary to build entrenchments to protect his numerically weaker force from the Americans, Washington hoped he could compel the British soldiers in Germantown to surrender before three thousand grenadiers in Philadelphia could march to their assistance. Such a victory should be disastrous for Howe and was certainly worth the risk to the patriot cause.

It was a welcome change for Washington and his generals on October 3 to begin drafting plans for an offensive. Not since they had put their heads together more than nine months before to plot the attack on Trenton had they done more than react to overwhelming British strength. They planned with care and detail, and they planned intricately, perhaps too intricately for "inexperienced officers and imperfectly disciplined troops," as British historian Sir John Fortescue said. Four columns were to advance on the enemy on the night of October 3–4, over as many separate routes. Although the columns were to be independent of each other except for communication by courier, they were expected to assault the enemy in coordination. John Armstrong on the extreme right and William Smallwood and David Forman on the far left were to lead militia contingents in support of the two main thrusts nearer the center. Sullivan would command his own and Wayne's Continental divisions on the right nearest Armstrong, with Conway's brigade in the van. Greene, on Sullivan's left, was to attack directly down Shippack Road with his and Stephen's regulars, McDougall leading the way. As a corps de reserve, Stirling would command the brigades of William Maxwell and Francis Nash and would follow Greene's command into action as need dictated.21

Before dawn on the morning of October 4, Lord Stirling and his men reached the outskirts of Germantown, where they grounded arms, built fires, and waited tensely, as all reserves since time immemorial have, to be called into battle. Their apprehension was compounded by a terrible fog, with "the weather so Calm," as Stirling wrote later, "that the Smoke of our fires remained Stagnate about us and we Could not see an hundred yards before us." Under these conditions, Stirling listened as Sullivan's advanced parties groped to an engagement with the enemy's light infantry on Chestnut Hill and drove it back through the ghostly murk that enveloped the scene of battle. Soon Stirling, to his relief, was in the fray. Washington, following up on Sullivan's success, ordered Stirling to place his two reserve brigades on either flank of Wayne's division and then for both generals to reinforce Sullivan. As these fresh forces marched forward, with Stirling accompanying Maxwell's brigade, Maxwell came under intense fire from a large stone mansion on his line of advance named Chew House. Washington, after a half hour debate among his officers on how to dispose of this problem, ordered that the house be bypassed and that Maxwell march to Sullivan's support as previously ordered. Therefore, Stirling and Maxwell pushed on after Wayne and Nash, who had long since gone on with their advance.22

At that point in the battle, things began to go wrong for American forces. Wayne's division, which had extended Sullivan's line toward the left, suddenly came under intense fire from out of the fog on its own left flank and broke in panic. Wayne's troops, in fact, were being shot at by their own comrades, men of Stephen's division who had advanced on Greene's orders about forty-five minutes after Sullivan moved forward. Tragically, Stephen's troopers had mistaken Wayne's soldiers for the enemy. Even more disastrously for the Americans, however, the enemy on Sullivan's front had been reinforced by four regiments of infantry, which, under the command of Cornwallis, had double timed out of Philadelphia while the fight progressed. Now, in the confusion of fog and fear, Sullivan's men also gave way to rout, and the American soldiers retreated pell mell, followed closely by British regulars seeking revenge for their earlier humiliation. Stirling, however, had observed that Continentals' withdrawal, and with cool deliberation (despite having a horse shot from under him) posted Maxwell's reserve force to cover the patriot retreat. When the fresh redcoats, therefore, "Attempted to fall on the Rear of our Army the Reserve gave them such a reception as made them retire precipitately, and leave our Army" to withdraw unvexed to Pennypacker's Mill. On this note, the intensely frustrating battle of Germantown, in which the American army had for a short time seemed on the verge of a splendid victory, shuddered to an end. In fact, the Americans were never anywhere near being as victorious as they thought they were. Howe had not the slightest intention of allowing three thousand men to sit quietly in Philadelphia while the Continental army compelled the surrender of his main force in Germantown.[23]

Had Stirling been of a pessimistic cast of mind, he might have been despondent after the battle of Germantown about the course of events over the past four weeks. During that time, the Americans had lost two pitched battles, had been maneuvered by Howe in whatever direction the British general fancied to make them march, and had been forced to abandon Philadelphia. Casualty statistics for the battle of Germantown were also enough to depress an American general, for they showed the Continental forces losing twice as many men as the British, about 1,100 to 534. But Stirling, rather than being melancholic, declared optimistically that the British would now realize "that we can drive them before us for Several miles together, and that we know how to Retreat in good & defy them to follow us. We are now stronger than we were the day before yesterday, large reinforcements are nigh at hand, and the Enemy will find that after every Battle our Army will increase, and theirs diminish, this is fighting at such a disadvantage that they must soon be Convinced that they never can Support the war in America." In these comments, Stirling was not indulging in idle speculation. In fact, he had correctly identified one of America's greatest assets, and Britain's worst liabilities, during the American revolutionary war.[24]

In the weeks following the battle of Germantown, Stirling and the other American general officers were required by British might and strategic advantage to reassume a defensive role. A fortnight after the battle, the enemy evacuated Germantown and withdrew into Philadelphia, but the patriots could do no more than shadow the redcoats as they made their short march, while looking for small openings to skirmish at advantage. Slowly Washington shifted the American camp to Whitemarsh, north of Germantown. Meanwhile, Stirling was kept busy with courts-martial. By October, a number of prominent officers were facing various charges for supposed derelictions in previous actions: Sullivan, for misconduct on an expedition against Staten Island; Wayne, for neglect of duty at Paoli; and Stephen for drunkenness at Germantown. In the cases of Sullivan and Wayne, Stirling had the unwelcome task of presiding over trials conducted before a panel of officers that included Generals McDougall and Knox, and Colonels Oliver, Spencer, and Thomas Clark. The court, which began its business on October 11 and concluded four days later, acquitted both officers of the charges against them and recommended that their records show that they had comported themselves with the highest honor. Adam Stephen's case, however, came out differently; he was convicted of "unofficerlike behavior" and "drunkenness," and the officers hearing his case recommended his dismissal. Washington, in general orders, approved the results of all three courts-martial, and Stirling's comrade Stephen involuntarily retired to his home in northern Virginia.[25]

Shortly afterward, Stirling was forced by rheumatism and injuries sustained in falling from a horse to ask his commander in chief for sick leave. His illness and lameness were so severe that he could not remount his steed, and so he traveled by carriage to Reading, the place where he was sent by Washington for detached duty. Painful as his health problems were, the earl at last had time for reflection on the military situation facing the Americans around Philadelphia, and on October 29, he shared his lengthy thoughts with his commander at Whitemarsh. Stirling believed it was imperative that the patriots not allow the British to open the Delaware River below Philadelphia by eliminating American Forts Mercer and Mifflin. Since Howe would surely try to do so, or be forced to leave the city, it was America's task, said Stirling, to call out militia to harass him. If Howe decided to evacuate Philadelphia, then the army should be shifted to Radnor Meeting House, where it would be close to the Schuylkill fords and between the enemy's army and fleet. Washington for various reasons dissented from these views, and the earl finally agreed that the patriot encampment should remain where it was, since America's Delaware defenses seemed to be driving Howe to desperate measures and since the Continental cause might best be served by allowing this process to continue.[26]

By early November, Stirling's health was "much recovered," and although he still could not ride a horse, he returned to Washington's camp by carriage. Although he did not immediately resume a full work load, he observed affairs that affected the army, especially the final disheartening collapse on November 21 of the American defenses on the Delaware. He also corresponded with Governor Livingston of New Jersey, his brother-in-law, in a vain attempt to get the militia of that state called to full mobilization. He joined Washington in a council of war on the 24th to discuss an issue that the other officers had already debated three times during his absence: whether to attack Howe's redcoats in Philadelphia. Stirling believed such an assault was feasible. Outlining his plan, he advocated that the American army strike the city from two sides, Greene's division in one attack and a body of regulars and militia in a separate diversionary onslaught. The council was not convinced by these plans, and it voted against any attempt to storm the enemy in the immediate future. Washington agreed with the majority of his generals. At the same time, however, he respected Stirling's recommendation, for it clearly showed that the earl had not allowed poor health to weaken his fighting spirit. The commander himself in fact still longed to assault the British, and in early December he reopened the question of attack one last time for the campaign season by asking his officers if a militia army could do the job. Not even Stirling thought his plan would work. Ardor was one thing, utter stupidity another. "Were you Aided by all the Militia the States on this Continent Can furnish," he declared to Washington on December 3, "they would only Serve to make the Carnage, on the Route, the greater." Quickly, the commander in chief dropped the plan.[27]

In fact, Washington's decision to remain on the defensive at Whitemarsh was due as much to Howe's war plans as to any doubts about his own. The British commander, after completing his Delaware River operations, turned his attention on December 4 once more to the American army. That day, Howe pushed his forces to within skirmishing distance of American troops, and for a time it appeared to Washington that his opponent was going to fight him on his own well-chosen ground. But Howe, after maneuvering around the patriot position for a few days, withdrew back to Philadelphia. The campaign of 1777 was finally at an end. Thus, Stirling for the next two weeks spent his time advising Washington about the best place to post the Continentals for the winter. The earl thought they should encamp in the Great Valley, but other generals proposed other places. Washington, after listening at length to his officers' wrangling and mind-changing, finally decided to occupy a place called Valley Forge, about twenty miles northwest of Philadelphia. As he moved his army there the week before Christmas, he ordered Stirling's division to Radnor Meeting House to shield the Continental soldiery from enemy assault, to patrol the roads in that area, and to forage. By December 24, Stirling's men, especially those of Daniel Morgan's corps, were glaring down their musket barrels at an enemy patrol that was in a "post of defiance"; but no fight ensued. Other small skirmishes did occur, and Stirling reported these to Washington on the 26th, only to receive the commander's worried admonition not to bring on any pitched battle such as Stirling had gotten into at Woodbridge the previous June. Washington need not have worried, for by then the Continental army was safe at Valley Forge, and in early January Stirling rejoined the commander in chief at headquarters.[28]

In the quiet winter at Valley Forge, as the army went through crises of short supply, demoralization, and dissolution that always seemed to beset it during that season, Stirling was busy defending his commander, General Washington, from detractors real or imagined during the so-called Conway Cabal. Stirling was one of a number of officers, such as Greene, Sullivan, Knox, and Morgan, who by 1777 had come to view Washington as indispensable to the cause of independence and almost an object of veneration. It was in this frame of mind that Stirling on October 27 had welcomed to his headquarters at Reading young James Wilkinson, aide-de-camp to General Gates. Wilkinson was on his way to inform Congress, at its new seat in York, that John Burgoyne had surrendered to Gates ten days before at Saratoga. The two men had partaken of "a pot luck dinner" and then sat around with Stirling's aides, James Monroe and William McWilliams, while Stirling regaled the company with a long-winded account of the battle of Long Island. Soon the officers became slightly drunk, and Wilkinson, who had taken a liking to McWilliams, carried the latter aside and told him of a letter Gates had received from General Conway, which listed thirteen reasons why Washington had lost the battle of the Brandywine. Next day, a more sober Wilkinson went on his way toward York, and McWilliams told Stirling what had passed between him and Wilkinson the night before.29

Stirling was incensed to learn that Conway had supposedly written Gates, "Heaven has been determined to save your country, or a weak general and bad councillors would have ruined it." Stirling may have been motivated by more than duty in this matter, for he was undoubtedly aware that Conway, while earlier serving in Stirling's division as a subordinate officer, had written Congress accusing the earl of drinking too much liquor. In any case, Stirling wrote Washington what he had learned, concluding that "such wicked duplicity of Conduct, I shall always think it my duty to detect." There the matter rested for some time, as far as Stirling's part was concerned. He did not know that Benjamin Rush, a severe critic of practically the entire officer corps in the Middle Department, was berating Washington and referring to Stirling as being "a proud, vain, lazy ignorant drunkard," Sullivan as "weak, vain, without dignity, fond of scribbling, in the field a mad man," and Edward Stevens as "a sordid, boasting cowardly sot." But Stirling *did* know that Congress on November 6 promoted Conway to major general and made him inspector general of the army; he *did* know that the legislators almost simultaneously reorganized the Board of War, and appointed Gates as its chairman, in a measure seemingly designed to overshadow Washington. To him and the other officers around the commander in chief, these measures smacked of a conspiracy. He would not sit idly by and allow Gates or Conway to erode Washington's power and prerogatives without lifting a finger. Therefore, he wrote his friends in Congress, informing them in no uncertain terms that the army resented these measures, especially the promotion and appointment of Conway. Abraham Clark replied with bewilderment, "Your Lordship mentions the want of *Military* merrit in a Gentleman lately promoted; I always before heard him mentioned as having great Military Abilities . . . was the business now to be done Congress would probably Act otherwise." The legislators, responding to similar cries of protest from many supporters of Washington, quickly placated their commander in chief and officer corps by assuring one and all that Washington's position was secure. As Congressman Eliphalet Dyer declared, there never was "the most distant thought of removing Genll. Washington, nor ever an expression in Congress looking that way."[30]

Meanwhile, Stirling was becoming more and more upset at the possibility that Wilkinson was lying to Conway and others in the officer corps about what he had told McWilliams at Reading. This likelihood arose when Conway told Stirling that he had heard Wilkinson deny the statement that Stirling had attributed to him. If such were true, of course, then Stirling himself must be implicated in a lie, and he knew he had related the exact substance of what McWilliams had told him. He laid these matters before Wilkinson on January 6, 1778, bluntly inquiring as to whether Wilkinson had or had not quoted Conway's letter in the form Stirling had passed on to Washington. If he had not, then *"what are the words of the letter, and I should be very much obliged to you for a copy of that part of it."* Wilkinson replied almost a month later in an equivocal manner that really left Stirling's question unanswered. But there was nothing equivocal about the young man's shock that Stirling would ask for extracts from Conway's letter. "I can scarce credit my senses," the virtuous gentleman expostulated, "when I read the paragraph in which you request an extract from a private letter, which had fallen under my observation. I may have been indiscreet, my Lord, but be assured I am not dishonorable." Stirling could be forgiven if he were unable to grasp Wilkinson's fine distinction.[31]

Stirling's difficulties with Wilkinson were not at an end. The young officer was at Lancaster on February 22, challenging his former mentor, General Gates, to a duel. "The enclosed Letters," he fumed to Gates, "unmask the Villain & evince my Innocence." The "Villain" was Stirling, whom Wilkinson was now openly accusing of lying to Washington and trying to shift blame for his own "devious" behavior. "My Lord shall bleed for his Conduct," he declared, "but it is proper I first see you." There followed, according to Wilkinson's unreliable memoirs, not a duel between himself and Gates but a lachrymose reconciliation in which the latter's joy was exceeded only by the former's forgiveness. Thereupon, Wilkinson betook himself to Valley Forge to seek satisfaction from Lord Stirling for supposed slights to his "integrity." Arriving there in mid-March, he requested a friend "to deliver a peremptory message to Lord Stirling, on the ground of his having misrepresented my conduct to the prejudice of my honor." But his colleagues talked him out of so rash a note, and he finally demanded only that Stirling acknowledge that the discussion at Reading in October had "*passed in a private company,* during a convivial hour." The earl agreed to these terms, although he did point out to Wilkinson that nothing had been said under "injunction of secrecy." So, Wilkinson dropped the idea of a duel with Stirling, but he continued to rail in private that the earl "lacked candor," and to tell Washington that Stirling's comments about him were "cruel misrepresentations." On March 21, Stirling related to Washington his side of these proceedings and declared his relationship with Wilkinson at an end. Washington was pleased with this news, as he also was with the realization that his position as army commander was secure. He and his supporters at Valley Forge could relax their vigil against potential usurpers.[32]

Despite the aggravations of his job during the hard months at Valley Forge, Stirling enjoyed himself as a part of what Pierre Étienne DuPonceau described as Washington's "inner circle." Included in this group, besides Stirling, were Lady Stirling and Lady Kitty, who had joined Stirling for the winter; Mrs. Washington, whom DuPonceau said looked like a "Roman matron"; General and Mrs. Greene; and Miss Nancy Brown, Lady Kitty's friend and a "distinguished belle." This group, with others included from time to time, gathered in the evenings to dine, talk, and sing. Also, Washington and Stirling on occasion indulged in a bit of horse trading.[33] Stirling's own headquarters, as usual, was a lively center of army social life, with the earl and his aides eating and drinking from well-stocked supply rooms. Stirling especially liked one member of his "family," young James Monroe of Virginia, probably because of the man's military record. Monroe, who had served in the 3d Virginia Regiment under Stirling in the retreat across New Jersey in 1776, had been one of the four Americans wounded at Trenton while leading a charge against German cannon and had joined Stirling's staff as aide-de-camp in November 1777. Years later, when Monroe was a prominent politician, making use of his earlier military association with Lord Stirling to advance his campaign for the presidency, Aaron Burr noted with caustic sarcasm that since Lord Stirling "was regularly * * * *" during the war, Monroe's duty as an aide "was to fill his lordship's tankard and hear, with indications of admiration, his lordship's long stories about himself." Burr's comment, although not disinterested, contained a bit of truth.[34]

Eight

•

Monmouth and Its Aftermath, 1778–1779

Even though he had many social diversions during his winter at Valley Forge, Stirling was grateful to see the arrival of spring 1778. With the coming of warm weather, the patriot army stirred to life, shook off the effects of its winter doldrums, and followed the teachings of its new drill instructor, Baron Friedrich Von Steuben. Early in the season, Washington reorganized the army into five divisions, giving Stirling command of the 5th Division, composed of George Weedon's and Peter Muhlenberg's brigades, plus, the 1st, 2d and 3d Maryland brigades. Then the commander in chief called the general officers of the army to a council of war to discuss plans of operation for the upcoming season. The possibilities were an attack on either Philadelphia or New York City or quiet repose in camp while waiting for Howe to make the first move. Generals Wayne and Maxwell wanted to march against Philadelphia; Knox and Muhlenburg recommended an assault on New York; most, including Lafayette and Steuben, wanted to stay on the defensive. Stirling alone was in favor of assailing both New York and Philadelphia at the same time. Washington for the moment decided to remain at Valley Forge while he continued to collect recruits and while he inoculated his soldiers against smallpox.[1]

A few days later, the commander in chief and his officers received the welcome news that France had signed a treaty recognizing the independence of the United States. To celebrate the occasion, Washington had the brigades assembled on May 6 under their officers to hear the treaty read, and afterwards he entertained the officers with food and drink while giving every sodier a gill of rum. Stirling gladly took part in these celebrations. Shortly afterwards he swore an oath of allegiance to the United States, which Congress was requiring of all American officers.²

Meantime, Stirling and the general officers of the Continental army continued to plan for the next campaign. On May 8, at the request of Congress, Washington called a council of war that General Gates was ordered to attend before departing to command the Highlands. Gates was glad to get the business out of the way and leave, because his reception in camp had been frosty, due to his reputation among men like Stirling as a leader of the supposedly infamous Conway Cabal. In the council, Washington, Gates, Greene, Stirling, and the other senior officers agreed that the army's manpower of 11,800 was not enough to challenge the enemy's 10,000 in Philadelphia. Therefore, the Continentals must "remain on the defensive and wait events . . . unless the future circumstances of the enemy, should afford a fairer opportunity, than at present exists." Thus, Stirling continued to wait tensely with everyone else at Valley Forge for the enemy to act. He was flattered when Congressman James Lovell wrote him on June 8 that the possibility always existed that Stirling might one day receive an independent command from Congress. But, "as danger is talked of in your quarter I doubt not your presence there will be most agreeable to the Commander of the Department."³

By the time Stirling received Lovell's message, it was obvious to everyone at Valley Forge that the British in Philadelphia, under the command of a new general, Sir Henry Clinton, were preparing to evacuate the city and return to New York. Washington asked his officers for advice on how to react to this news and received an overwhelming admonition from the majority, which included Stirling, to stay put with the main army while sending out small parties to annoy the enemy from time to time. Stirling later sent a letter to Washington reiterating his strongly held view that at present it would "be imprudent to risque a general battle; if the affairs of the United States can be maintained in their present situation, the enemy loose their point; if we loose a general battle or suffer our army to be much impaired, the United States are ruined." Hardly had the general's opinion been written before news arrived on the 18th that Clinton's army was on the march toward New York. Consequently, Washington immediately ordered his own troops on the road toward the British, with Charles Lee, recently exchanged, in the van and Stirling bringing up the rear. Although their march was delayed by bad weather, the patriots began crossing the Delaware on June 20 and four days later were encamped around Princeton, with Washington's headquarters established at Hopewell. The enemy, meantime, according to intelligence reports, had advanced at least as far as Black Horse and perhaps to Allentown.[4]

These were the circumstances facing the American army when Washington called Stirling and his colleagues to another council of war on June 24. The enemy, reported the commander in chief, numbered about 10,000 men, the Continental army, 10,684 rank and file. Unaccountably, Clinton in seven days of marching had covered only forty miles, and Washington suspected Sir Henry of attempting to lure him into battle. Should the Americans oblige? The officers were divided in opinion. Lee, supported by Stirling and Knox, expressed the strong viewpoint that the patriots should not attack the enemy. In fact, Lee declared, the Americans should build the British a "bridge of gold" to expedite their march, since their withdrawal to New York coincided exactly with patriot interest. Other officers, however, favored at least a partial stroke, and that view finally prevailed. Washington decided that he would send a detachment of fifteen hundred men "to act as occasion may serve, on the enemy's left flank and rear" while the main army stayed clear of a general engagement. Alexander Hamilton, one of Washington's aides, grumbled that the council's decision "would have done honor to the most honorable body of midwives and to them only." Washington, Greene, and Wayne also had serious reservations about the timidity of the plan. The commander in chief wanted to carry out a general assault, but overrode his own scruples for the moment and set the council's program in motion by advancing a detachment under Charles Scott to scout the enemy. He also ordered the main army to march to Kingston, just north of Princeton, for the enemy army was advancing on the road from Allentown to Monmouth Court House, and he wanted to be nearer Clinton's left flank as it passed by.[5]

At this juncture, Stirling became involved in a curious imbroglio about seniority and prerogatives of command. Washington decided on June 25 that he must reinforce Scott's detachment with 1,000 men and replace Scott with a more vigorous, higher ranking officer. The commander believed that under the circumstances Lafayette was the best choice, for the Frenchman was a hearty advocate of military action, while Lee and Stirling, the other officers who might interpose a claim to the position, were on record as favoring no action at all. Washington appealed to Lee for approval of his plan, and Lee immediately acquiesced. Hardly had he made the concession, however, than his friends began to chide him for a bad decision. Moreover, as Hamilton noted later, "Lord Stirling [was also showing] a disposition to interpose his claim." Consequently, Lee changed his mind, asserting that if Lafayette commanded the advanced column, both Lee and Stirling would be "disgraced." In the end, Washington arranged a cumbersome compromise, in which Lafayette would command the advanced troops until Lee came forward to take charge. Stirling's name was no longer mentioned, because he had not pushed the matter.6

By June 27, Stirling and everyone else could see that if the American army intended any action against Clinton, it would have to be soon. The British were at Monmouth Court House, and Clinton, as though anticipating an assault, had reinforced his rear guard with his best troops, the grenadiers and light infantry. Very soon, the redcoats would be beyond the marching range of the Continental army. Washington responded to this situation by ordering Lee to advance with a reinforcement of about twenty-five hundred soldiers to Englishtown, where Lafayette's column was encamped, and to take command. Lee was directed to assault the British rear guard with his five thousand troops as Clinton's army withdrew from Monmouth, while Washington would be marching to his support with the main army by advancing to Penlopen, three miles from Englishtown. Leaving nothing to chance, the commander in chief ordered Stirling and the French engineer Colonel Duportail to reconnoiter around Penlopen to identify a strong defensive position for the Americans to fall back upon, should that operation become necessary. These matters were accomplished by the evening of the 27th. All Washington, Stirling, and the other Americans in the main camp could do after that was await news that the British were breaking camp at Monmouth Court House and that Lee had engaged them in battle.7

Early in the morning of June 28, Washington received the expected message from Lee, and he immediately got his army on the march toward the enemy, with Stirling commanding the left wing and Greene the right. As he rode forward, Washington confidently expected soon to unite his own force with Lee's and overawe the enemy in his front. The reports he was receiving from Lee certainly gave him no cause to doubt that he was at last in a position to bring overwhelming force to bear on a detachment of the British army, for he was being informed that Clinton's rear guard at Monmouth Court House numbered only fifteen hundred to two thousand soldiers. Thus, it was with extreme surprise that Washington and the other general officers with the main army that morning came upon a skulking fifer and were informed that the advanced corps was retreating before the enemy. Washington had received from Lee no report of a withdrawal, and the only firing he had heard from the front had been a single cannon shot at about noon. Nonetheless, the evidence of a retreat soon was abundant, as hundreds, then thousands, of bewildered, exhausted, demoralized men staggered past Washington, Stirling, and the other officers in what was an all too familiar scene of confusion and despair. Meeting General Lee in this chaos, Washington exchanged some hot words with him about his supposed refusal to obey orders, then set about to rectify the situation.[8]

The battle was not beyond salvaging. Although the American generals now learned that the enemies before them numbered not two thousand but three times that many, they had strong ground available upon which to dispose the army. Therefore, while a few regiments of retreating troops halted their flight and turned under Wayne's leadership to hold the pressing redcoats with "well served artillery," (as Washington later reported to Congress), the commander in chief placed Stirling's corps, reinforced by Scott's men, on the left on high, wooded ground with a ravine in front. On the right he disposed the battalions under Greene's command. Behind this main line, he stationed Lafayette with remnants of the advanced corps that had rallied from its retreat. He completed these dispositions with no time to spare, for as Stirling noted later in describing the battle of Monmouth Court House, "by the time [the divisions] were well formed . . . , and the Batteries were all established, the Enemy appeared in the front of us," and the fighting recommenced with the overwhelming weight of attack falling on Stirling's troops. The earl, who loved a fight, now had one on his hands that rivaled in intensity the struggle around Birmingham Meeting House the previous September on the Brandywine.[9]

Through simmering heat (Stirling called June 28 "one of the hottest day's [*sic*] I ever knew"), the earl began cannonading the enemy's lines, while the British reciprocated in kind. "For upwards of two hours," said Stirling, this bombardment continued, "without the least Effect," apparently, to either side, except that the British cavalry and infantry were kept from forming for an assault upon the American line. This

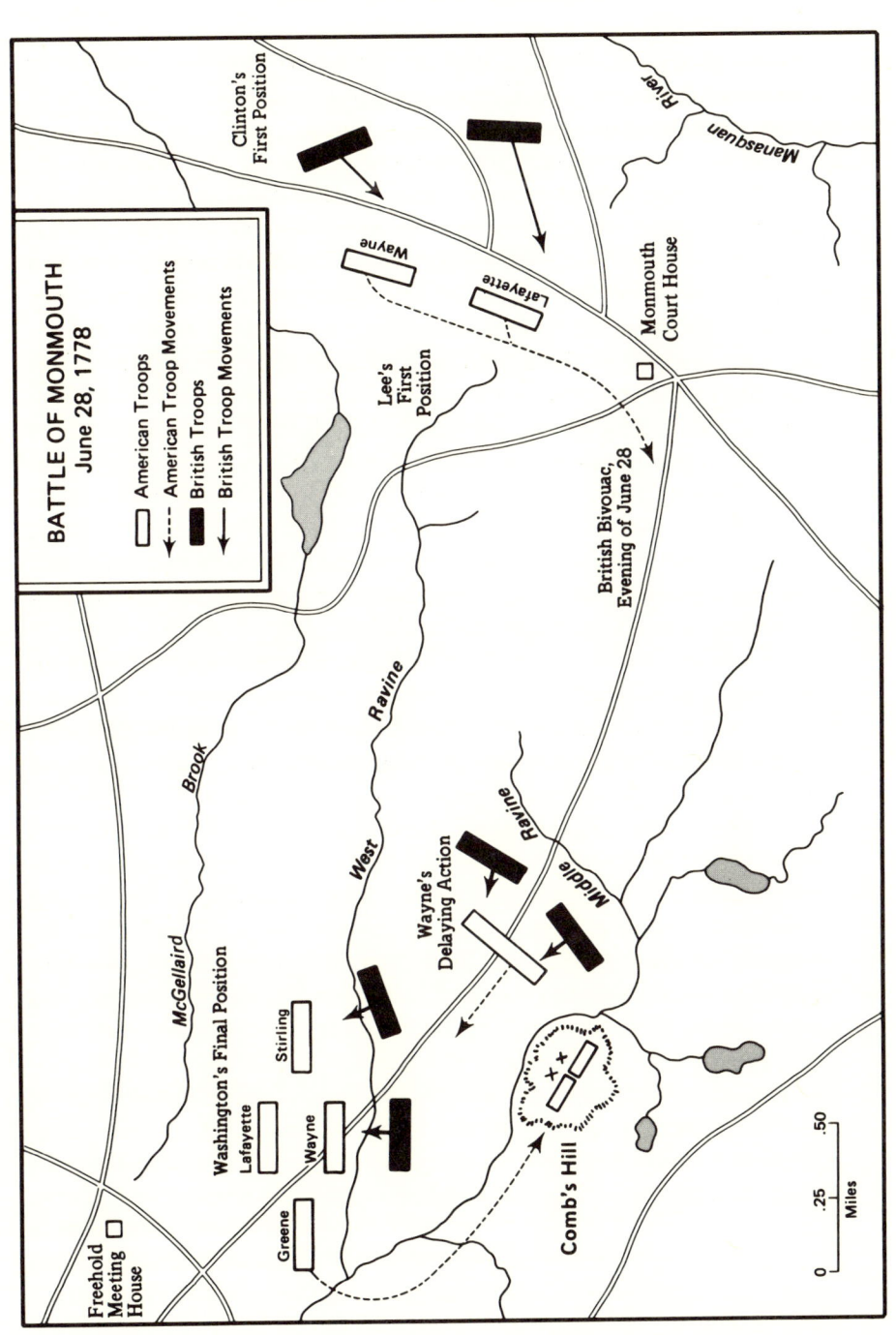

impasse was broken when Stirling sent about six hundred men "along the Ravine on my left in order to gain the Enemy's Right." The earl's measure was so effective that the American troops "were within 100 yards of the Enemy before they were discovered; they immediately directed their fire so well & briskly that the British Granadiers & Royal Highlanders were obliged to shew their backs." While this fighting "was going on so Successfully on the left," said Stirling, "I ordered two Brigades from the Right of my Wing, to Advance from the Woods . . . & gain the Enemy left, which they did with equall Success." The British line thereupon began crumbling, and as "their Canonade Slackened, our musketry pressed hard on them." When Stirling advanced a fresh brigade against them, "the Enemy were immediately reduced to a precipitate flight, which they Continued till they got over a deep Gully . . . behind which their whole force was drawn up." At that point, the American general wisely called off his men, believing that "To press the pursuit further or to go into a New Action on disadvantageous ground, with men who were already fainting" from heat exhaustion "was by no means advisable."[10]

Throughout this fighting, Stirling was in active command of his wing, exposing himself to constant danger from enemy fire. The earl rode back and forth along his lines during the long cannonade that opened his part of the battle, exhorting troops here, complimenting junior officers there, and issuing orders as the need arose. At the height of the conflict, Stirling's adjutant, Lieutenant Colonel Francis Barber, was wounded by a musket ball as Stirling and his aides rode through the whizzing lead that from time to time was directed their way. Taking Barber's place, young James Monroe assisted his commander for the remainder of the engagement. Hamilton later noted that "Lord Stirling rendered very essential service" in the battle, and Washington, in a letter to Congress, remarked upon the great importance of Stirling's well-placed cannon in repulsing the British.[11]

The battle sputtered to an inconclusive end as the torrid day wore on and British assaults against Stirling's stubborn soldiers led to no gains. Although Clinton attempted a few desultory probes against Greene's well-disposed right wing after Stirling's positions refused to collapse, Washington in turn pushed forward two brigades to counter Clinton's thrust. As evening drew near, Sir Henry realized that the American army he now faced was not an untrained rabble, as before, but a disciplined force, ready to meet a European army in a European-style fight.

Also unlike before, it was the British army, not Washington's, that surrendered the ground and retired toward a bastion of security. At midnight, Clinton withdrew in good order toward New York City, leaving behind 217 dead and over 1,000 wounded and missing soldiers, five times the number of American casualties. Washington, his army weakened by continuing heat, by exhaustion, and by the unapproved departure of the militia for home, could not pursue.[12]

Despite American problems after the battle of Monmouth, Stirling saw that the New Jersey campaign of 1778 was symptomatic of even greater difficulties for the British. "This March of General Clintons thro' New Jersey," mused the earl, "has cost him very dear and looks like a rash attempt. But he Conceived it to be the only way of escaping [from Philadelphia] without risqueing the Loss of his whole Army, for he . . . Concluded that the french fleet was already on the Coast." Although Stirling could not be aware of the fact, Clinton's reason for marching overland was lack of British naval transports, not fear of a French fleet. However, Stirling's point about French naval power altering the course of the war in America's favor was certainly true, for no longer could the British presume as a matter of course that they could transport their armies and supplies freely by water. Clinton had reason to be grim and Stirling optimistic in the summer of 1778, and not merely because their personalities inclined them in opposite directions.[13]

On July 1, while the Continental army rested at New Brunswick and observed the enemy in New York City, the officers were shocked by a terse announcement in general orders: "A general court martial whereof Lord Stirling is appointed President will sit . . . tomorrow for the trial of Major General Lee." The charges against Lee, who had demanded the trial, were "disobedience of orders, in not attacking the enemy on the 28th of June, agreeable to repeated instructions; . . . misbehavior before the enemy on the same day, by making an unnecessary, disorderly and shameful retreat;" and "disrespect to the Commander-in Chief in two letters, dated the 1st of July and the 28th of June." Stirling quailed before this duty, which he called "the most disagreeable" he had ever faced; for he had worked in harmony with Lee since early 1776, when Lee had bolstered Stirling's military career with timely praise just as Congress was discussing the earl's promotion to brigadier general. It seemed for a time that Stirling might be relieved of this onerous duty, for he received a letter from Lee on the 2d which, although stating "the highest confidence in your integrity and honesty," noted that Stirling "had the imprudence . . . already to give an opinion" that Lee was guilty as charged. Therefore, Lee believed it would be "more eligible" if the Baron de Kalb should preside over the court-martial. In reply to Lee's note, Stirling frostily assured the general that he had expressed no opinion on Lee's complicity or innocence, for until that moment he had not known "the Charge upon which you are to be tryed." However, "if you have any objection [to my serving] I shall willingly decline [the] office." Perhaps Lee believed that Stirling was too close a friend of Washington to be objective in this matter. Whatever his concern, he let the matter drop, and Stirling was confirmed as president of the court-martial. The trial began on July 4, with Lord Stirling chairing a panel of twelve officers, with Lee speaking in his own defense, and with John Laurance, the judge advocate general, acting as prosecutor.[14]

Throughout the next thirty-nine days, Stirling's primary duty consisted of chairing sessions of Lee's court-martial, and he apparently gave temporary command of his division to another officer. Through three moves of the army—to Paramus on the 9th, Haverstraw on the 14th, and White Plains on the 20th—Stirling transported his court, presiding in the interim over twenty-six lengthy sessions and listening to seemingly interminable evidence. Lee's defense was not terribly impressive, consisting as it did largely of polemics. Yet, the general established doubts as to the veracity of the first two charges against him and proved that he had been a brave man under fire. Against him, however, spoke Maxwell, Morgan, Scott, and Wayne, each insisting in one way or another that Lee had handled his command clumsily on June 28. It was not surprising, therefore, that when Stirling finally announced the court's verdict on August 12, Lee was found guilty of all the charges against him. As Lee's biographer, John R. Alden, has noted, it is doubtful by that time "that even the Gospel according to St. Mark would have sufficed to save Lee," for he had insulted or alienated practically every general officer in the army, and it was clear that he and Washington could no longer work together. While there was not much protest in the patriot officer corps against the court's finding, a few thought the penalty of suspension from the army for one year a curious, even ridiculous, penalty. As Henry Lee later noted in his *Memoirs,* if Lee were truly guilty, he ought to have been shot; if innocent, reinstated to command with full honor. Whatever the merit of this argument, the decision was made, and Lee's military service was at an end. Stirling, whom Lee afterward referred to as "Alexander le Gros," never doubted that justice had been served by the proceedings. Lee, on the other hand, insisted that Stirling had not conducted the trial fairly. "According to my idea," he told Congress in October, the earl "step[ped] . . . egregiously out of the line of his duty."[15]

Stirling's military activities for the remainder of 1778 were bland and routine after the excitement of the battle of Monmouth Court House and Lee's court-martial. These activities consisted primarily of administering the affairs of his encamped division, checking complaints about illegal recruiting, adjudicating disputes among junior officers, and sitting on councils of war that Washington occasionally called to discuss military matters. On July 25, Stirling, Greene, McDougall, Knox, Gates (whose command had been combined with Washington's when the main army moved to the Highlands), Steuben, DuPortail, and other officers advised the commander in chief against trying to assault Clinton in New York or even advancing the army nearer enemy lines. A month later, the officers recommended to Washington that the articles of war be amended to allow convicted soldiers a prison sentence with bread and water as an intermediate punishment between one hundred lashes and death. After the Franco-American expedition against Rhode Island came to grief in early September, the council urged the commander not to shift the army eastward to support Sullivan's forces at that place. Washington reluctantly gave in to the cautious counsels of his senior officers, but he may have been reminded of the popular observation in the Continental army that asking a council of war to take risks was to follow a certain formula for inaction.[16]

Stirling took advantage of his leisurely military duties at White Plains to attend to family matters. In August, he obtained permission from Washington for his wife and younger daughter, Lady Kitty, to cross British lines and visit his elder daughter, Lady Mary, and her infant son in New York City. Mary and her husband, Robert Watts, although loyalist in their political leanings, lived unobtrusively under British occupation of their hometown. After the visit, Lady Stirling wrote her husband ("My Dear Lord") an account of their visit. Sadly, she reported, it had included attendance at the funeral of Stirling's tiny grandson, who died the same day Lady Stirling and Kitty arrived. Somewhat later, Lady Kitty also sent Stirling a sprightly narrative of the trip. According to her, many New York loyalists were becoming sick of British rule, including Mr. Watts, "& as to Mary, her political principles are perfectly *Rebellious*." Old friends of her father, she said, were inquiring after him, especially Colonel Cosmo Gordon, brother of the duchess. Sir Henry Clinton, however, never came around, although he promised that he would. "Upon the whole," she concluded, "I think we may call our Jaunt an agreeable one, tho' it was checker'd with several unlucky circumstances."[17]

Stirling's solicitude for his family's welfare often caused him anxious moments, especially when British armies were on the march in New Jersey. Under normal circumstances, he liked his wife and Kitty to remain under the care of Lady Stirling's brother, Governor William Livingston of New Jersey, at Elizabethtown. Whenever the enemy came too near, however, he would have them move with the governor's entourage to a secluded country estate near Basking Ridge or to Paramus, where a lively hostess, Mrs. Theodosia Prevost, later the wife of Aaron Burr, lived. Hence, it was with gratitude that he received an invitation from Robert Livingston for his family if necessary to spend the winter with the governor, far from the dangers of war. "I thank god," he told Livingston, "I have had my health extremely well ever Since I have been in the Service, except a little Rheumatism and now & then a fall & a Bruise or so." At the time, he was suffering from a "Severe" attack of rheumatism; "however it is in a fair way of doing well."[18]

Stirling's rheumatic attack did abate, just in time for him to lead his division into action against the enemy. On September 24, Sir Henry Clinton landed a force of five thousand men at Paulus Hook on the New Jersey shore, while he simultaneously pushed another three thousand across at Dobbs Ferry. Washington believed these detachments were merely large foraging parties, but just in case the Dobbs Ferry force was intended as a drive upon West Point, he ordered Stirling to march his division from Fredericksburgh, where it was then posted, toward Peekskill. It turned out that the enemy thrust up the Hudson was only a feint to cover what seemed to be the more serious landing in New Jersey. Consequently, Washington four days later ordered Stirling to take command of Maxwell's and Woodford's Continentals in New Jersey and to raise militia as supplemental troops for defense. In a private note to Stirling, he explained his official orders by pointing out that it was "necessary there should be some officer of higher rank, than any there now, to take direction of the whole. Your knowledge of the country will give you a peculiar advantage for this purpose." Moreover, Stirling was particularly suited to the task of closely observing the British in New York City and sending the commander in chief minute reports of their activities. Flattered by Washington's expression of trust, Stirling wrote the general, "I thank your Excellency for the Command and you may be Assured I will use my best endeavours to Carry your Instructions into execution." Next day, he rode with his aides toward his new field of service.[19]

Lord Stirling was a very busy man for the next few days. His immediate worry was the enemy troop that had landed at Paulus Hook. As it foraged between the Hudson and Hackensack Rivers, Stirling shifted Woodford's brigade to Paramus and two regiments of Maxwell's corps to Aquackanoc, on the Passaic River. Stirling feared, groundlessly as it turned out, that an enemy cavalry force under Francis, Lord Rawdon, would make a raid toward patriot storehouses at Morristown. Hence, he was riding daily from one place to another in an attempt to keep control of his department and was engaging in frenetic letter writing, to Washington, to Congress, and to Governor Livingston. He reported to the commander in chief on October 4 that the New Jersey militia was giving him great trouble. The citizen soldiers, he wrote sarcastically, "are all home Sick and are every hour apply[ing] for leave to return to their families. I have used every argument to induce them to Stay at this Critical Juncture," but "the Spirit of going home is universal." He was applying to Livingston for relief from this situation, for if things continued the same, "I shall be obliged to retire to the Hills." The governor attempted to solve the problem but with little success. It was fortunate for the patriots that British forces in New Jersey remained quiescent (except for a minor raid on Little Egg Harbor by Captain Patrick Ferguson, which Stirling ordered General Casimir Pulaski to counter). The number of the enemy facing him, Stirling noted on October 8, was seven thousand, consisting of the best British troops in America. Had these forces attempted anything beyond a forage, Stirling could only fall back before them, a fact that accounted for Washington's constant admonition to him not to get too close to the foe and bring on a general engagement. Despite these handicaps, Stirling boasted to Congress on October 13, after the British finally withdrew their troops from New Jersey, "they have gained not the least advantage of us; on the contrary, they have been confined to a narrow district of country."[20]

With the threat of British soldiery no longer hanging over his head, Stirling established his headquarters on October 12 at Elizabethtown. There he occupied himself for the next two months with various duties, the most important being to observe the British in New York City. It was clear from Clinton's activities that significant numbers of enemy troops were embarking, but Stirling and Washington did not know how many or for what destination. In an attempt to unravel the mystery, Stirling sent detailed and minute reports to Washington on an almost daily basis. Sometimes this intelligence was accurate and sometimes not, but in all respects it showed an exquisite concern for duty. At various times in October and November, Stirling guessed that Clinton intended to seize Charleston or that the British were withdrawing their entire army from North America. In time, he learned that Clinton was merely detaching first his wounded and sick, then (upon orders from London) two large forces to capture the French West Indies island of St. Lucia and to assault Savannah, Georgia.[21] Washington was worried that Clinton might be planning to attack Boston, but upon reflection he doubted the British would try it, for America's adversaries, he said in disgust, "are indecisive and foolish." Henry Knox agreed, declaring that "we cannot draw a conclusion of what will be done . . . for they often act directly against their own interest." All Washington could do was cover the Hudson River approaches to West Point, which he did by ordering Stirling to post Woodford's and Morgan's men so as to defend the Clove, a strategic pass through the Highlands. Then he awaited events that he could not control.[22]

Meanwhile, Stirling went about his routine military duties. Under a flag of truce, he conducted numerous messages from Congress, Washington, and himself to the British. Sometimes he complained and sometimes the British complained about the behavior of emissaries, who were supposed to be bound by strict rules of etiquette but who often breached the regulations. He sent a rude rejection to British commissioners of peace, the so-called Carlisle Commission, when they made overtures for reconciliation between the United States and Great Britain. He also continued to curtail illegal commerce between New Jersey and the enemy, going so far as to question an authorization of Congress allowing a Mrs. Yard to pass with her baggage and some important messages to Congress from New York. As Stirling noted to Henry Laurens, president of Congress it was against New Jersey law to allow goods to cross the lines without condemning them for sale and dividing the profits among the captors. However, he had gotten the seizers, "out of respect to Congress," to sell Mrs. Yard's baggage for only six pence, although it was worth twenty thousand pounds. Stirling's devotion to duty in this case led Washington to write him a mild rebuke. As the commander pointed out, "some instances of commerce between the inhabitants and the enemy may be tolerated for purposes of gaining intelligence." This note had its intended effect. Stirling wrote Washington a month later that although he paid "particular attention to the Law of this State for preempting Trade with the enemy," he did allow spies to carry on a small trade as cover. In a singularly ungallant act, however, he seized cloth intended for a poor patriot girl's bridal dress, and she was "put under the Mortification of being Married in her old Cloths."[23]

As winter approached, Stirling at Washington's behest turned his thoughts to where the army ought to be stationed during the months of military inactivity and whether the Continentals should stay together or disperse. He considered the security of the troops, their subsistence, the protection of the country, the mutual support of American posts, and the patriot's relation to the French fleet. Finally, he recommended to the commander in chief that the army spend the winter in various New Jersey cities, except for small detachments at Danbury, Hartford, and West Point. Washington decided to station most of the army at Middlebrook, although he heeded Stirling's advice at least to the extent of posting small detachments at a number of places. As Washington proceeded to his new encampment in early December, he stopped at Elizabethtown to visit Stirling for a few days. His sojourn was interrupted by an alarm that Clinton was pushing up the Hudson River with fifty transports laden with soldiers. When the report proved false, Washington rode on to Middlebrook.[24]

Not all Stirling's time at his Elizabethtown headquarters was consumed by army business. His wife and daughter joined him there, and they enjoyed the society of Governor Livingston's circle. In late October, everyone had a glorious time at the wedding of Elisha Boudinot, son of Stirling's neighbor and friend, Elias Boudinot. The earl reported to General Washington that the ceremony was "grand," and the bride, a Miss Smith, beautiful. Although Stirling in early November suffered a rheumatic flare-up so intense that for a day or two he could not hold a pen and was forced to dictate his letters to an aide, he renewed his petition to Congress for redress of his battle losses. Writing to Congressman Robert Morris, he noted that although Congress had previously rejected his claims, the legislators had recently passed a law allowing payment of five hundred dollars to an officer for a horse "*killed* in Battle." Stirling noted that even this new legislation was inadequate to his own peculiar situation, for although he had lost six horses in the war, two of them had been stolen by Hessians at the time of his capture at Long Island, three had been worn out by the rigors of campaigning, and only one had actually fallen in battle (at Germantown). In any case, five hundred dollars per horse was wholly inadequate compensation, even if he were paid for all six, for "to replace *one* I had lately been obliged to pay 2200 dollars." In case any narrow-minded legislator should think that sum exhorbitant, Stirling explained that "unless I am well Mounted I can not do my duty as I ought." He concluded, "my Case I think requires a little of the particular attention of Congress." Unfortunately for both Stirling's purse and his dignity, Congress disagreed, and his losses remained unpaid.[25]

By early December, Washington's reasons for having posted Stirling in East Jersey no longer applied. The Britons' foraging raids and the embarkations of troops had ceased. Therefore, the commander in chief ordered Stirling to join the main army at Middlebrook, giving him upon his arrival (in company with his wife and daughter) command of a division consisting of three Virginia brigades. Then, on December 21, Washington turned over to Lord Stirling, the next highest ranking general in camp, command of the entire American army. Washington had been ordered by Congress to Philadelphia to consult with the legislatures on plans for the campaign of 1779. In his instructions to Stirling on how to maintain the army, the commander recommended that particular attention be paid to shelter for the soldiers, to discipline, and to refusing furloughs for officers. Until Washington's return on February 5, 1779, Stirling issued all general orders and subsequently had them approved by the commander in chief. Immediately, he took over the reins of administration, giving orders to expedite the march through New Jersey of the Convention army (captured in 1777 at Saratoga and now being moved from Boston to Charlottesville). He gave every assurance to General Friedrich, Baron Von Riedesel, and Major General William Phillips, both of whom were prisoners with this troop, that he would make their march as comfortable as possible. He did not, however, invite either to dinner on Christmas Day, when he, Lady Stirling, Lady Kitty, and the general officers of the Continental army and their wives feasted together in honor of the season.[26]

Stirling confronted his first real test as acting commander in chief shortly after Christmas, when the American army began to run out of forage. Only a day or two earlier, he had been expounding smugly on the distress of the British in New York, who were low on bread and rice, and bragging about how this situation would be to the patriots' advantage. Now he had before him a letter from Greene, the quartermaster general, declaring that the Americans could not secure grain from nearby farmers and that barges to transport foodstuffs were frozen in the ice of the Raritan River. On December 28, Stirling wrote Washington that the army was in its "last extremity" for want of forage. "Indeed," he declared, "the very existance of it depended on an immediate relief." Therefore he was forced, "however disagreeable the Measure, to grant a Warrant to impress forrage from farmers round us, for a temporary relief, untill some Can be brought in from a greater distance." Unless other measures could be taken to bring in Indian corn from other countries, he declared, the army's distress would soon be even worse, and "we shall have no such recourse to go to." He explained to Greene his "awful" policy of impressment and complained of the bitterly frigid weather. "It never was Colder in Lapland," he swore.[27]

Turning his attention from the problem of forage, Stirling saw a military opportunity arising because of the abnormally low temperatures in the middle states. The enemy, he reported to Washington on December 29, was "in high Rumpus, Confusion & distraction" because of shortages in rice, rum, and bread, while at the same time the water approaches to Staten Island were frozen, "and by the appearance of the weather are like to Continue so for many days." Now, he said, would be a good time to make a "Stroke at the Troops on that Island," who were cut off from either support or retreat because "the Bay is too full of Ice." America, he declared, possessed all the advantages in this situation, "for our Bridge of Ice cannot be broken up by any Storm so Suddenly as to endanger it." Washington was indeed persuaded by Stirling's plan and on New Year's Day, 1779, approved it. But on the 3d, the earl glumly reported that warmer weather had "rotted" the ice and that the scheme must be delayed for the time being. The Staten Islanders, he mused, "may now sleep sound till another Frost alarms their Fears." At least one good consequence of the warmer weather, Stirling noted to Washington, was that the forage crisis was at an end and impressments could cease. "I shall be glad," he said, "to get rid of the Numerous Complaints I have every day from the farmers."28

During the remainder of his tenure as commander of the patriot army, Stirling conducted mostly routine business. With the army in "good order" and "ready for an Exploit," all he needed to do was administer its day-to-day activities and await Washington's return. He built up a supply of cannon balls by having Congress negotiate contracts with three New Jersey blast furnaces—one of them Hibernia—for the production of shot. He sent Nicholas Biddle to the Monmouth region to secure more forage for his army and playfully noted to Greene, "I hope he is well imployed I dont mean in a . . . frolick." He kept up his reconnaisance of New York and at Washington's request sent out a party of 250 men under Lieutenant Colonel Caleb North to interdict illegal commerce between the south Jersey coast and New York City. He published from time to time in general orders such instructions as Washington sent him, and he conducted a survey of the camp to determine how many blankets the commander in chief needed to procure while in Philadelphia.29

By January 26, Stirling's duties, requiring as they did that he remain outdoors on horseback for hours on end, had begun to weigh on his health. He wrote to James McHenry, "I [am now] laid up with my old Companion in Winter and so bad Still in my Right hand that I am now Scarce able to hold my Pen." He sent the same information to General Washington, apologizing for not having written for some time. Stirling's infirmity, however, did not stop him from actively directing military business, and on January 12 he reluctantly allowed James Monroe to resign from his staff, appointing Captain Thomas Marsh Forman in his stead. He admonished Brigadier General Smallwood to remain alert to the possibility of an enemy incursion through Lincoln's Gap near his headquarters, lest the enemy succeed in getting into the American rear by that route. Meantime, he conducted a short negotiation with British General Phillips, who lingered in New Jersey through January, on the possibility of exchanging the Convention troops for American prisoners of war; but Washington objected to these proceedings, and Stirling notified Phillips that "no good can result from any regulation on the subject of exchange." As Washington had reminded him, Stirling told Phillips that Congress forbade discussing the matter of exchanging Convention troops.[30]

Lord Stirling's tenure as commander of the Continental army came to an end with Washington's return to camp on February 5. Upon his resumption of duty, Washington's first act was to publish in general orders thanks for Stirling's "endeavours to preserve order and discipline and the property of the Farmers in the Vicinity of the camp." Stirling, for his part, gladly gave over to Washington the burdens of leading the army and embraced his new assignment of commanding a "division" of three hundred men at Bound Brook. He relaxed with his family for the balance of the winter and did light duty. On February 26, he wrote a lengthy exposition for Washington, comparing two plans for drilling the army. He later worked out an arrangement of signals with New Jersey militia officers who might be called to arms on quick notice if they were needed in the army's next campaign. Finally, on April 10, he took part in a council of general officers, called by the commander in chief, to discuss terms for an exchange of regular prisoners of war with Sir Henry Clinton. He determined with his colleagues, Sullivan, Greene, Arthur St. Clair, DeKalb, Knox, and others, that for purposes of exchange, one American officer was worth a thousand British or German regulars.[31]

Although Stirling had few military duties to keep him busy in the spring of 1779, he was deeply involved in civil-military affairs with the New Jersey legislature. The officers of the New Jersey brigade of Continentals had for many months been petitioning the legislature of their state to readjust their soldiers' pay to keep up with the depreciation of the currency. After bringing the matter up time and time again, to no avail, the New Jersey officers were by 1779 desperate. In April they sent to the legislature what Stirling called a "spirited memorial," pointing out various mischiefs that might result unless "equitable provision" was made for the officers and men of the brigade. Still the legislature refused to act, instead referring the matter to Congress. Finally, twenty-one officers of the 1st Regiment declared on May 6 that unless their grievances were redressed within three days they would resign from the army. This action created a crisis for Washington, who had intended to use the New Jersey troops in Sullivan's expedition against New York Indians during the coming summer. He begged the officers to reconsider, but they had lost all confidence in the legislature and refused to budge. The legislators, for their part, declared that they had no intention of capitulating to military coercion, and some of them swore they would disband the regiment before yielding under duress. This impasse was broken by Lord Stirling, who at this time of crisis was in Trenton on personal business. "As I saw that the Appearance was now the Chief Obstacle in the Way" of a solution, Stirling wrote to Washington, "I proposed to some of the leading Members the expedient of withdrawing the Memorial and the Legislature takeing the Matter up (to all appearance) of their own meer Motion this was Instantly agreed to on all sides, and in a few hours pretty ample resolves were made by both houses, among the rest it was ordered the £200 be paid to each Commissioned officer & $40 to each Soldier." Thus, Stirling helped to avert a major conflict between politicians and military men in New Jersey.[32]

If his proposals of state were astute, Stirling's business acumen was not, and throughout the revolutionary war his finances had continued to remain in a muddle. His creditors, fearing public repercussions because the general served the public as a soldier, did not have the temerity in the first years of the Revolution to pursue repayment of loans. By 1779, however, Stirling knew their patience was wearing thin and that if he could he must act to preserve some part of his estate for his family. Hence, he acquiesced to the advice of his councilor, Hugh Wallace, given four years earlier, to have the New Jersey legislature pass a bill vesting his remaining property in trustees, who were "to Sell the Same or a Sufficient Part thereof for the discharge of his debts; and for Conveying the remainder (if any there by) to him." In May Stirling went to Trenton to lobby for this measure, but his efforts did not go smoothly. He wrote Washington on the 24th, "I have had sufficient experience to teach me that whoever is to be attendant on the Legislature's motions, need to be possessed of a good Stock of patient philosophy." His perseverance finally did pay off. On May 31 his proposal became law, and he could at last hope soon to be free of debts.[33]

Unfortunately for Stirling, his financial problems were not to be so easily solved. Somewhat shadily, he had intended to take advantage of the inflation in Continental currency at the time of his application to the legislature for relief, but the paupered earl shortly found himself caught in a frightful economic trap. Commissioners Richard Stevens and John McHelm, appointed by the legislature to sell Stirling's estate, proceeded to do so, while at the same time Tory creditors in New York

City seized and auctioned off the Alexander family home on Broad Street. These measures, rather than relieving Stirling's economic distress, threw him into even worse financial straits, for in the fall of 1780, before the commissioners could pay the earl's debts, the New Jersey legislature suspended the tender law in force at the time of the sale, and Stirling's creditors refused to accept payment of his obligations in the old currency. Thus Stirling found himself with neither estate nor purchase money. As he noted to William Paterson, his attorney, the suspension of the tender laws had wreaked a "cruel and iniquitous hardship" upon him, and he hoped the legislature would repair the damage to his personal finances.[34]

Such was not to be. The part of Stirling's fortune that had remained intact until the disastrous blow of the New Jersey tender act was now obliterated. Although his creditors for some reason allowed his family to live in the mansion at Basking Ridge until after his death three years later, he went to his grave without ownership of one piece of land, one building, or one stick of furniture from his once-vast holdings. All he had to bequeath his wife were certificates issued by the state of New Jersey for depreciation of his salary as a militia officer. Not even the land promised to soldiers by Congress for service "during the war" would be Lady Stirling's, for the earl died before the peace treaty of 1783 was signed. When the poor woman made a claim to this entitlement, her application was disallowed by the pinchpenny national government. Consequently, Sarah Alexander, who dispensed with the title Lady after her husband's death, had only a few hundred dollars to dispose of in her will, written in 1804. The loyalist historian, Thomas Jones, insisted in his *History* that "his Lordship" Stirling had made money on the depreciation of the currency during the revolutionary war. "He purchased Continental money," said Jones, "and with £1,000 of gold and silver he discharged all his debts, though they amounted to nearly £80,000." This statement is false. Stirling, it is true, had *intended* to take advantage of the inflation, but his financial ploy redounded against him and worked his utter ruin. Proud, vain Lord Stirling's economic agony in his final years was no less pitiable for having been self-inflicted. Neither was his family's distress any less real.[35]

Nine

•

Military and Financial Stalemate, 1779–1780

Believing that his financial affairs were satisfactorily arranged, Stirling in late May 1779, left Trenton for Washington's encampment at Middlebrook. He returned to an army commanded by a general who was perplexed about enemy intentions and about the best way to break the stalemate around New York City. Stirling believed it "practicable" in this situation to assault British lines by conducting a joint operation against the city with the French fleet, commanded by the Comte d'Estaing. First, all Franco-American shipping from New England to the Delaware would rendezvous in the Philadelphia harbor, proceed to New York, and cut communications between Staten Island, Manhattan, and Long Island. Then, troops in New Jersey would land on Staten Island, the "Eastern" army would cross to Manhattan at Kingsbridge, and a body of two or three thousand New England militia would land on Long Island "in order to amuse [the enemy] there." When Staten Island was secured, troops would be ferried across to Manhattan, to join those already besieging New York City until it fell or until British troops in the South were recalled to save it. If the latter event occurred, the Americans would act as circumstances dictated. The plan, noted Stirling, was inexpensive and contained few risks, for American avenues of retreat would always be open, and "at all adventures I think the preparations should immediately take place."[1]

Washington thanked Stirling for his plan and noted that it confirmed much of his own thinking. But, he said, "where circumstances are either not well known, or not duly balanced, a plan may appear very well in theory which would fail in practice." Such was Stirling's scheme. In fact, the commander did not have enough regulars to conduct offensive operations, and the militia was undependable for this type of operation. Moreover the naval force could not be collected, because one would have to apply "to a variety of powers" for cooperation. So, while Washington gave Stirling his "sincere thanks" for the proposal, he must at present set it aside as impractical.[2]

Stirling and Washington forgot all planning for future operations on June 1, when the British marched a powerful force toward White Plains. On the following day, Clinton's troops seized King's Ferry and began to fortify Stony Point on the west bank of the Hudson. The American generals now recognized an imminent threat to West Point, the loss of which they believed would be calamitous to the patriot cause. To counter this enemy thrust, Washington began rushing Continental troops northward from Middlebrook toward Stony Point and on June 2 ordered Stirling and his division to join him there. But by then, trepidation in the patriot camp about Sir Henry Clinton's intentions was waning, for it appeared that if the British general had intended to seize West Point he had moved too slowly. Clinton's "delay has ruined him," noted Horatio Gates; "he will be beat if he attempts [West Point] now." All the same, Washington was taking no chances. On June 13, he drew up a detailed plan for Stirling and the other American general officers to follow in case the British assaulted West Point. He need not have worried, for exactly two weeks later, Clinton withdrew most of his forces from the lower Highlands and left only isolated garrisons at Stony and Verplanck's Points, on either side of the Hudson River.[3]

British inactivity over the next few weeks allowed Stirling the quiet and leisure to conduct mostly routine army business. He sat on July 3 with a committee of officers—himself, Greene, Knox, and Colonels Jeremiah Wadsworth and Nicholas Biddle—to draw up regulations for controlling prices in camp. He heard with pleasure a fortnight later of Anthony Wayne's storming of Stony Point and on the 24th marched his division to Suffern at Washington's order. Although British General William Tryon "and his burning Crew," as Washington noted four days later, were putting Dobbs Ferry to the torch, Stirling was not called upon to react. He only continued to wish that a French fleet would arrive off the mouth of New York harbor, so that he and his Virginians (whom he now commanded) could act in concert with America's Gallic allies and wreak retribution upon the redcoats in Manhattan.[4]

Stirling and his aides took time out from military service in July, with Washington's approval, to ride home to Basking Ridge for the wedding of his younger daughter, Lady Kitty. The service took place on the 27th and was a festive occasion. It was also poignant, for Stirling and his family realized that because of their bankruptcy this might be their last celebration at the mansion. Many prominent guests were in attendance, including civilian, social, and military leaders from New Jersey and New York. According to long family tradition, Kitty and her new husband, William Duer, stepped out on the front lawn after the wedding and received the congratulations of young officers who were clamoring to kiss the bride. The day came to an end with Stirling and his lady presiding over a wedding feast at which many toasts were offered and received.[5]

Upon his return to camp, Stirling played a part in Major Henry Lee's assault on Paulus Hook, the most important military activity that he would see in the campaign of 1779. For some time, Lee had been observing British forces in Paulus Hook, on the west bank of the Hudson, almost directly opposite New York City, and had convinced Washington (who needed little convincing) that an "attempt to surprise the enemy" there was feasible. Since Lee was serving in Stirling's division and would use about 400 of the earl's Virginia Continentals for the attack, Lord Stirling was brought into the planning for the expedition on August 12. Stirling, after consultation with Lee, became as enthusiastic about the proposed assault as Lee and quickly gave it is his full support. Hence, the attack proceeded on the night of August 18–19, with Lee marching toward the enemy and Stirling anxiously posting 500 men under his immediate command as reserve troops at New Bridge on the Hackensack River. The storming of Paulus Hook was a great success, and as Lee withdrew from the British fortifications with 158 prisoners, he notified Stirling that he was on his way back to the patriot lines, marching in good order. Stirling thereupon directed 200 men under Colonel Burgess Ball to intercept Lee's column and give the major whatever assistance he could. Soon the entire American force was safely within patriot lines.[6]

Stirling proudly reported Lee's exploit to Congress on August 20. A day later he noted to Robert Erskine that the only unhappy note in the whole affair was Lee's failure to capture Lieutenant Colonel Buskirk's loyalists, who had been reported to be stationed at Paulus Hook but who on the night of the attack were out "near the Chester Dock in hopes of Catching some of my foragers." Despite Buskirk's escape, Washington was extremely pleased with Lee and Stirling. "The increase of confidence which the army will derive from this affair and that of Stoney Point," he wrote the earl on August 21, "will be the least of the advantages resulting from these events." Congress was also delighted with the news and on the 24th voted a resolution of thanks to Washington for ordering the raid, to Stirling for "the judicious measures taken by him to forward the enterprize and to secure the retreat of the party," and to Lee for executing the assault itself.[7]

Stirling lived a quiet existence for the remainder of the summer in his headquarters at Suffern, near the Ramapo Mountains. He and Washington spent considerable time allaying the anger of Virginia officers who were upset about Lee's being given command of the Paulus Hook expedition. Finally, the matter was laid to rest, but another problem beset Stirling in September: trying to get permission for his daughter Mary to pass through the American lines around New York and visit the family. Washington was willing to allow the visit if Governor Livingston would as well, but the governor declared that only the commander in chief could judge the validity of the case. Hence, Washington was forced into the painful necessity of denying his old friend and colleague this important personal request. He went to great lengths to explain his decision, but if he was worried about a rupture with the earl over this matter, his fears were misplaced. Stirling unhesitatingly supported his commander's position as being consistent and just. Meanwhile, Stirling and Anthony Wayne, whose divisions were encamped near each other, arranged their actions so that foraging parties from their respective camps did not fall afoul of the other's pickets and patrols. When a British sloop, the *Vulture,* took post on the Hudson near Wayne's encampment and began cannonading him, Wayne borrowed two 6-pounders from Stirling to throw "hot shot" in return. In September, Stirling joined with twenty-six of the general officers in sending a memorial to Congress (with Washington's approval) asking for relief from financial distress caused by runaway inflation of the Continental currency.[8]

As fall descended upon the Highlands, Stirling and his officer colleagues began preparations for military cooperation with a French fleet under the command of the Comte d'Estaing, which was then operating off the Georgia coast against Savannah. Washington learned on October 4 that d'Estaing would soon be sailing northward to New York.

He realized that Clinton, in response to this threat, might decide to contract his lines by withdrawing the British garrisons from Stony and Verplanck's Points. Consequently, he ordered Stirling and Wayne to be particularly alert to this possibility and to take advantage of the operation if they could. Lord Stirling, as the senior officer in this situation, alerted Wayne to be ready for action, and the Pennsylvanian immediately began reconnoitering Stony Point to find weaknesses in its defenses. Stirling, who was suffering another lingering bout with rheumatism and gout had to force himself into the saddle to meet Wayne on October 5 to coordinate plans. He wrote to Washington that he was marching his division to Paramus "with a View toward [intercepting enemy troops from Stony Point] and yet maintaining the power of Joining the main Army, should it be Necessary." In his letter, Stirling enclosed a detailed plan for an American assault on Staten Island, which the earl said should be carried out "at all rates."9

It turned out that Lord Stirling had little more to do with these military matters. In the first place, the French fleet never arrived, and the British outpost garrisons were not withdrawn. In the second place, Washington informed Stirling that the patriot army for the moment simply did not have the resources to storm Staten Island. And in the third place, Stirling himself was so ill by October 7 that he was forced to petition the commander in chief for leave to go home. Hence, Stirling departed camp on the 9th in the company of General Knox and the Marquis de Barbé-Marbois, secretary of the French legation at Philadelphia, who were on their way to the city. Stirling left these men at Basking Ridge and rejoined his wife for a period of rest and recuperation. Awaiting him at his home was a letter from Samuel Huntington, president of Congress, notifying him of Congress's vote of thanks for his part in the raid on Paulus Hook. Gratefully he responded, "The very great honor Congress have done me by that Act fills my Bosom with the warmest gratitude, and Swells my Ardor for future opportunities of deserving their approbation."10

Stirling had "greatly recovered" his health by late October and at Washington's request took command of a division of Virginians in central New Jersey for the duration of the campaign. From his headquarters at Morristown on the 26th he raised alarm among his subordinates about a British "invasion" of Jersey. "A party of their Horse were this morning in Quibbletown," he wrote General William Woodford, "and it is said, are Six Thousand in Force, at Amboy." He learned on the next day, however, that the enemy, about seventy Queen's Rangers under Captain John Sanders, had "quited this State," and, he declared, "they must surely be much afraid of our attacking them. Their expedition appears to me almost as ridiculous as the famous Battle of the Kegs." Stirling's allusion here was to an attempt by Americans in early 1778 to destroy British ships in the Delaware by floating kegs of gunpowder downstream against them. British troops had become alarmed by the kegs, believing they were "filled with armed rebels, who were to issue forth in the dead of night, as did the Grecians of old from their wooden horse at . . . Troy," and take Philadelphia. This ludicrous affair had inspired Francis Hopkinson to inscribe a satirical poem about it, called "The Battle of the Kegs," which became popular with Stirling and his American compatriots.[11]

Stirling, with time on his hands, volunteered to Washington to proceed down the southern Jersey coast and act as a welcoming committee should d'Estaing arrive. The commander found this offer "very interesting," but he noted that "it has been anticipated by my sending Gen. du Portail and Lt. Col. Hamilton" to Little Egg Harbor. The French fleet never appeared, so no one got to welcome America's allies. In November, Washington finally realized that his hopes for Franco-American cooperation in 1779 were chimerical. Hence, he began making provisions for posting his army at Morristown for the winter. He delegated to Greene the responsibility for choosing campsites for the individual divisions, and Greene immediately turned to Stirling for assistance. The earl, who knew the countryside well, was glad to oblige his friend and after lengthy reconnaisances provided Greene with detailed descriptions of a number of good camp locations. On November 16, the commander in chief marched his divisions into bitterly cold and snowy cantonments at Morristown, where they would suffer a much worse winter than they had two years before at Valley Forge.[12]

Once the army was settled into camp, Stirling, Greene, and Hamilton decided to take a short furlough in Philadelphia with Washington's approval. Their visit, a wonderful diversion after so many months of army life, was marred by one ugly incident. Major John S. Eustace, aide-de-camp to General Charles Lee, was also in town, and his sojourn "in this infernal hole," as he called Philadelphia, had been ruined by "ill natured whispers" against Lee. In fact, by the time he had occasion one day to meet Hamilton, "in company with the *Favourite Green the Drunkard Stirling,* and their several classes of attendants," he had developed "a rivetted aversion to the whole Tribe of General officers (St. Clair & Gates excepted)." Hence, when Hamilton "advanced toward me . . . with presented hand—I took no notice of his polite intention, but sat down, without bowing to him or any of the clan . . . I cou'd not treat him much more rudely—I've repeated my *suspicions* of his *veracity on the tryall* so often that I expect the son of a bitch will challenge me . . . If he does, he will find me as unconcern'd as he can possibly be anxious."13

The friends of Washington allowed this matter to pass, but even Stirling's equanimity, never easily shaken, was tried when he ran across an anonymous piece from the London *Evening Post* that was circulating in Philadelphia. The author of the essay had Hamilton, "poet and composer to the Lord Protector Mr. Washington," writing a history of the rebellion, "in case Clinton's light bobs should extirpate the whole race of rebels this campaign." Hamilton, a *"tarnation cute obsarver,"* was composing a document enhanced in value "by the presence of a vignette, representing a combat between a Presbyterian deacon, and the flesh and the devil (in which the deacon gets whipped)." The details of two other illustrations were known, "one, of Polly Wayne's brigade 'boldly' retreating from Stony Point, after a 'manly' possession of that fortress for three hours; the other, a rear view (by far the most intelligent and pleasing) of the titular Lord Stirling, on his return from one of his nightly *feu de joies* at Bergen, in Jersey, and supposed to be murmuring his usual boast in a strain something like this:—

> 'Peer's blood I have'—
> Toddied and brave—
> Who-o—'d be a sla-a-ave?"14

Stirling faced two items of business that required immediate attention when he returned to Washington's headquarters in early December. First, he was being criticized by the Reverend Edward Lewis for allowing a church to be taken over by army doctors while Stirling's own buildings were left alone. Stirling wrote Lewis, "to show you and the whole Congregation how satisfactory it would be to me that your place of divine worship be preserved for that purpose only, I do most readily consent that any houses of mine [except the mansion at Basking Ridge] may be made use of as hospitals for the Army." Second, Stirling's division of Virginians was being ordered by Washington to march southward as a reinforcement for General Benjamin Lincoln's army in South Carolina, and Stirling was being given the opportunity of going with them. He declined the offer. "In all arrangements of the army," he wrote Washington on December 9, "I have always been content with the commands that have been alloted to me." He was pleased to be offered leadership of the southern army, but "the very great esteem I have for General Lincoln would prevent my entertaining a wish to take it out of his hands . . . Whatever commands your Excellency may commit to my care, you may be assured will be executed with cheerfulness and faithfulness." Washington accepted Stirling's sincere avowal of duty with gratitude and sent the troops off under William Woodford. Five days later he ordered Stirling to take charge of an army division composed of Maxwell's and Edward Hand's brigades.[15]

As the year 1780 began, Stirling and his comrades at Monmouth were suffering the cruelest weather they had ever seen or heard tell of. Snowdrifts four feet deep piled up as bitter arctic gales blew from the northwest and froze solid the waters around New York City. The Delaware River also froze at Philadelphia, and the Chesapeake Bay, according to Thomas Jefferson, was a sheet of ice from Head of Elk to the mouth of the Potomac. It was in these conditions that Washington proposed to Lord Stirling that he lead an assault against British outposts on Staten Island. Stirling had made the same suggestion on a number of earlier occasions, but for one reason or another the idea had never been implemented. However, Wayne's success at Stony Point, and "Light Horse Harry" Lee's at Paulus Hook in the previous summer, tempted both Washington and Stirling to give the enemy on Staten Island a dose of the same medicine. Consequently, Washington decided on January 12 "to direct the attempt," putting under Stirling's command about 2,700 troops, consisting of the brigades of William Irvine and Moses Hazen, and a smaller detachment under Colonel Walter Stewart. The object of the expedition, noted the commander in chief to Stirling, was to capture enemy troops stationed there, about 1,000 in all, and to bring off public stores, cattle, and sheep. The Americans must secure surprise at all costs, for such would be the key to success for the mission.[16]

General Lord Stirling was in complete agreement with these arrangements, only pointing out to Washington after full consultation with General Irvine and Colonel Stewart that it would be difficult to take the enemy unawares since the British had guards and patrols out "at every accessible place." Moreover, he noted, the difficulties of getting on the island may be greater than Washington believed, for the roads were covered with drifting snow. Thus, while Washington's plans were good, they ought to be delayed for a couple of days. Once surpise *was* secured, it would be no problem to bring the enemy to surrender. American troops would "Suffer greatly from severe weather," but the enemy's would suffer worse. Washington, after receiving Stirling's comments, directed his subordinate on the 13th to use his own judgment about ordering the attack, depending on variables of weather, British alertness, and how fast American officers had been able to bring together patriot soldiers at the places assigned to them for the assault. Stirling responded the following day from Crane's Mills, "it is determined [we will] pass upon the Island by daybreak in the morning."[17]

Stirling spent the frigid and barren night of January 14–15 preparing himself mentally for a morning that might bring success to his arms but would most assuredly cause suffering for his rheumatic body and his half-clad soldiers. Long before daylight, he had his men on sleds, advancing toward DeHart's Point, where he crossed over the ice of Newark Bay and landed near Mercereau's Dockyard. Moving inland, he divided his column at Blazing Star road and sent the two detachments by different routes toward the enemy's main fortified position at the Watering Place. Both groups of Americans gained the heights overlooking the British post at about the same time, and they managed to seize nine vessels anchored near Decker's Fort while the redcoats retreated into their works. The enemy, however, reported Stirling to Washington later, knew of the Americans' coming, and all surprise was completely lost. The fortifications, improved all about by an abatis covered with ice-glazed snow nearly ten feet high, were impregnable. Moreover, as Stirling learned to his consternation, Staten Island's garrison could receive reinforcements from New York by way of unfrozen water communications. Therefore, the British sent for help and several enemy vessels came down before evening of the 15th to harass the patriots. Despite this danger, the Americans fell back only a short distance before taking camp for the night, "upon a bare bleak hill," as Joseph Plumb Martin, a private in Stirling's army, described it, "in full rake of the northwest wind, with no fuel but some old rotten rails which we dug up through the night."[18]

Lord Stirling had no alternative the following morning but to order a withdrawal from his dismal camp, for his men had neither food nor fuel, and they could not mount a siege. In fact, the enemy had been reinforced during the night, and the Americans now found themselves imperiled, more besieged than besieging. After burning Decker's Fort and the nine boats they had seized the day before, the Continentals pulled back in good order. But, said Private Martin, "the British were quickly in pursuit," and a party of dragoons "Attacked our rear guard and made several of them prisoners." After this evening assault was repulsed, "we arrived in camp after a tedious and cold march of many hours, some with frozen toes, some with frozen fingers and ears, and half-starved in the bargain. Thus ended our Staten Island expedition." Stirling's raid, to put it mildly, had not been so successful as he had hoped. Still he reported to Washington that it produced a "considerable quantity of blankets & other stores," these at the expense of three men killed and a few more suffering from wounds or frozen feet. Enemy losses consisted of one killed and a handful taken prisoner.[19]

Both Stirling and Washington were criticized for their conduct of the Staten Island raid, because of the equivocal outcome of the operation. Stirling became the object of sarcastic gibes among his own comrades for his "failure" against the enemy. John Gibson, for instance, described Stirling's expedition in a letter to Horatio Gates as a "slaying frolic." Washington was accused by John Adams of "allowing" civilians to cross over from New Jersey and plunder. In fact, Washington had foreseen this likelihood and had warned Stirling to guard against it "as far as possible," which Stirling had. Washington's and Stirling's real faults in this wretched episode were their willingness to ignore in their planning the obvious dangers and problems from the weather and from incomplete knowledge of enemy activities and dispositions. As late as January 14, Stirling told Washington, "intelligence is not so explicit as we wish." They both became cocksure, let their guards down, and fell into the dangerous military trap of believing a plan will work merely because they willed it.[20]

Following the Staten Island raid, Stirling's health was wrecked for the rest of the winter. His correspondence virtually ceased, and even his location cannot be ascertained with certainty. He probably went to Basking Ridge or to Governor Livingston's place in Elizabethtown; in his condition he would have been of little use to Washington. In any case, for about two months he was lackadaisical in administering his division, and in March he received a severe scolding from Washington for this laxness. Stirling's general orders, said the commander in chief, were not conforming to regulations. He was allowing too much waste of public property, and he was not overseeing the disciplining of his troops, keeping track of how many men he had in his brigades or reporting returns to headquarters, inspecting his men, or keeping his soldiers in camp and away from civilians. "This My Lord is a free and friendly representn. of facts," said Washington, and he pointed out that these problems were by no means confined solely to Stirling's division. "I shall take occasion as soon as the Genl. Officers Assemble to require in explicit terms from them a conduct conformable to these sentiments."[21]

Stirling was "surprised" when he received this letter. As he told the commander in chief, he thought he *had* been policing his division satisfactorily. He agreed with Washington on the general sentiments expressed but pointed out, "I have not, for these two months, been able to be on horseback with so firm a seat as was necessary . . . ; besides, getting my feet wet, which was scarce avoidable, I was sure would have been attended with very serious consequences for me." Moreover, many of the troubles with which his men were afflicted were far beyond *his* control. Even the officers of his regiments were "so naked" they were "ashamed to come out of their huts."[22]

That the Continental army was in frightful condition by spring of 1780 was undeniable. As Nathanael Greene wrote, "there never was a darker hour in American prospects. . . . Our treasury is dry and magazines empty; how we are to support the war is beyond my conception." The men were hungry, snow continued to fall, and even on April 1, eight inches were still on the ground at Morristown. The American army, Washington reported to his officers on March 27, consisted of only seven thousand men, while the enemy in New York had eleven thousand. Sir Henry Clinton, who had gone to Charleston, commanded six thousand against Lincoln's much smaller force. Under these circumstances, Washington and his generals could only stay on the defensive, thwart British movements as best they could, and try to recruit the Continental brigades up to strength. Thus, Stirling, now recovered from his illness, was dispatched into New Jersey to cooperate with Governor Livingston in reorganizing and rebuilding the three Jersey regiments, pursuant to recently enacted state laws. Meantime, Washington was dispatching Harry Lee's Light Horse and the Delaware and Maryland Continentals to South Carolina, to offset an enemy reinforcement of twenty-five hundred troops on the way there from New York. Stirling thought this action extremely dangerous, for by dispersing American strength, Washington was playing into the enemy's hands. "This Army," Stirling argued to Washington on March 30, "I think might Serve the Southern States much more effectually by operating in this part of the Country." But Washington ignored the earl's arguments and sent the forces off as planned. With the coming of spring, conditions did not improve at Morristown, and on May 25 two regiments of Connecticut troops mutinied. When the uprising quickly petered out of its own accord, rather than infecting the entire army as it might have, Stirling and the other American officers breathed a sigh of relief.[23]

Ready or not, the American army and its officers in early June 1780, were forced into action by British operations from Staten Island. Even as Washington was asking a council of war on the 6th what to do with a force of twenty-four thousand men that presumably would be under his command fourteen days later, an enemy troop under the leadership of German General Wilhelm von Knyphausen was landing at DeHart's Point in New Jersey. Washington received news of this invasion on the evening of the 6th from Colonel Elias Dayton at Elizabethtown, who reported that the enemy was advancing his way. Next morning, Washington ordered his army to march toward Knyphausen, even though he did not intend to have it engage in battle. Simultaneously he directed Stirling to move his division immediately toward the enemy's left flank and skirmish if he could. By the afternoon of June 7, Washington reached the Short Hills overlooking Springfield from the northwest and learned that Colonel Dayton, with support from local militia, had stopped the enemy's advance that morning at Springfield Bridge. Knyphausen, it seemed, had fallen back to Connecticut Farms, where he had erected breastworks, and was daring the Americans to assault him. Next morning, the 8th, Washington cautiously approached Connecticut Farms and was surprised to discover that Knyphausen the night before had taken advantage of cover from a ferocious thunderstorm to move back to DeHart's Point.[24]

Washington was puzzled by Knypahusen's withdrawal after such a perfunctory advance, but he was convinced the German had ferried the bulk of his force back to Staten Island, leaving only a rear guard of about five hundred men at DeHart's Point. Hence, he decided to attack this enemy detachment in its small enclave. Choosing Lord Stirling to lead this operation, Washington ordered the earl to put the militiamen "into some form" and to allow them to conform to their own tactics.

Meanwhile, General Edward Hand would lead three battalions, a total of five hundred men, in a "coordinated" attack with the militia. All these forces were to stay in the cover of woods as much as possible, "as this mode will not only be best to harass the enemy, but will be best adapted to security, especially against horse of which the enemy are said to have a considerable body." Under no circumstances was Stirling to bring on a general battle, for Washington's only purpose was to annoy or annihilate Knypahusen's presumably small rear guard. If the enemy proved to be in greater force than expected, Stirling was to exercise extreme care not to be surprised by a counterstroke.[25]

In obedience to his orders, Stirling immediately ordered the militia officers south of Springfield to harass the enemy, while at the same time he cautioned them to conserve ammunition by firing "only when the object is Sure." Then he advanced on the morning of the 8th with Hand's force of five hundred men through Elizabethtown and to within sight of the enemy's works. At that point, according to an observer, Ashbel Green, Stirling turned to Hand and said, "Take your brigade, Hand, and the two brigades of militia and go down and bring up those fellows at the Point." Consequently, General Hand marched his troops into musket range of Knyphausen's lines, hoping to lure the German out of his defenses. All he got for his pains was intense enemy fire that very quickly convinced him and his commander, Stirling, that the number of enemy troops at DeHart's Point was larger than Washington had thought. Hence, Stirling withdrew the American forces to Elizabethtown and reported to Washington that Knyphausen's lodgement was too powerful to budge. "I do not think we are ripe for an attack upon them yet," he observed. "I believe it would be best for the army to halt two or three miles short of this, for the present." The commander in chief agreed.[26]

Washington and his generals were in a quandary for the next few days about enemy intentions. Operating from his headquarters near the Short Hills, Washington reconnoitered with Stirling, heard reports of ships sailing up and down the Hudson with no apparent design, and worried that the British in New York, once more under the command of Sir Henry Clinton, who had recently returned from the South, might make a thrust against West Point. He decided to prepare for such an attack by posting his army within quicker marching distance of West Point. On June 22 he began moving the Continentals to Pompton, sixteen miles north of Springfield. He left Greene's tiny division at Springfield to watch Knyphausen, and he ordered Stirling into central New Jersey to rouse the militia of that state to arms. Washington's soldiers had been on their march for less than a day when the noise of cannon fire from the southward stopped them in their tracks. Soon a courier reported to Washington that Greene was under attack at Springfield. Knyphausen was advancing with six thousand troops, intending to destroy Greene's force so that Clinton could later push with greater ease toward the Highlands forts in the lower Hudson Valley. It was too late for Washington to go to Greene's assistance but, fortunately for the patriots, Greene on June 23 halted Knyphausen without the main army's assistance. The only loss was the enemy's burning of Springfield. Although Stirling notified Greene on the day of battle that he was rushing militia to aid him, Greene replied that these troops were not needed, because Knyphausen was retreating and in fact abandoning New Jersey entirely. Later in the day, Stirling wrote Washington a glowing letter of praise for American arms in the battle of Springfield. "In every part," he declared, "our troops Continentals and Militia have behaved gloriously, and have made the Enemy pay dearly for their Jaunt."[27]

Stirling rejoined Washington's army on the day following Greene's victory at Springfield. The American commander was no longer worried about the safety of American communications and supplies in the Jersies, and so they proceeded to Preakness, New York. There throughout the summer Stirling recuperated his health in warm and comfortable surroundings, generally unvexed by any military business of pressing importance. On July 4, he responded to an earlier query from Washington about possible American operations in 1780. Stirling believed that the Continental army had too few men to attempt anything more that summer than a defense of West Point, for although Washington was supposed to receive a fourteen-thousand-man reinforcement from the states, only thirty troopers had arrived. He noted, however, that a French fleet and army might appear to cooperate with the patriots, in which case he thought New York ought first to be "reduced," then Halifax and Penobscot. After these cities had fallen, the allies might shift their attention southward and carry out a winter campaign in Georgia and South Carolina. Stirling's ambitious program was never implemented, because Franco-American cooperation was inadequate to the task in 1780.[28]

In July Stirling also turned his attention to a second petition of the general officers to Congress seeking financial relief from the effects of runaway inflation. This time the soldiers were petitioning not only for an adjustment of their military pay but also for the establishment of a postwar pension system. Since their first memorial had been ignored, the officers (Stirling, Greene, Von Steuben, Knox, Hand, Wayne, and Lafayette) were instructing an emissary, McDougall, to take their petition directly to Congress and not to "return to the army without a definite answer." They threatened, should they be ignored a second time, to resign their commissions and go home. Stirling's support of his fellow officers in these proceedings was not an academic exercise. To be sure, he did not enjoy defying Congress, but by 1780 he must rely almost entirely upon his public pay, both now and in the future, for support of his family, and he was seriously concerned that congressional mishandling of the compensation issue would aggravate his already straitened financial condition. Thus, he was forced into an activity that he might otherwise have considered to be slightly insubordinate toward his civilian masters.[29]

During his quiet summer at Preakness, Stirling once more became the butt of British satire, brought on this time inadvertently by his friend and colleague Anthony Wayne. In late July General Wayne carried out an attack upon a blockhouse near Bull's Ferry, in territory the Americans called the English Neighborhood. Wayne's raid, intended not only to destroy the blockhouse but also to collect cattle for hungry American soldiers, was by and large a fiasco and became the brunt of enemy derision. The height of British sarcasm was reached when Major John André, aide-de-camp to Sir Henry Clinton, composed a seventy-two stanza ballad entitled "Cow Chace," which was a parody of a fifteenth-century ballad "Chevy Chace." Published by André in three installments in the *Royal Gazette,* the poem described Wayne as a cowardly cowboy, and Lord Stirling, who was supposedly to support his comrade, as not appearing at his station:

> The self-made peer had sure been there
> But that the peer was drunk.

Publicly, Stirling paid no attention to this sarcastic allusion to his excessive drinking, having, by that time, learned to ignore such comments from friend and foe alike. Inwardly, he may have resented them, although he never said so in even his most intimate correspondence.[30]

Stirling was deeply shocked, as were all Americans, when in late

September he learned of an attempt by Benedict Arnold, commander of West Point, to turn that post over to the British. Arnold, a friend of Stirling's, and a long-time colleague in arms, had plotted the scheme for months. This "treason of the blackest dye," as Greene called it, was discovered when John André, who was acting as an emissary between Arnold and Clinton to work out final details of the plot, was captured out of uniform behind patriot lines carrying incriminating documents. Had the conspiracy succeeded, Washington himself might have been seized by Clinton, for the commander in chief arrived at West Point just at the moment the British attack was to occur. General Wayne, upon hearing of the crisis, rushed his division over sixteen miles of road in only four hours, to reach West Point at daybreak on the 27th. Wayne reported that Washington thought this feat "fabulous," and exclaimed, "'all is safe, and I again am happy.'" Arnold, meanwhile, had made his escape to the British warship *Vulture* and had sailed peacefully down the Hudson to New York.[31]

Up to that time Stirling's role in the wretched business of Arnold's treason had been only as a concerned spectator. Now Washington, faced with the sensitive and wrenching question of what to do about André, turned for advice to a board of general officers, composed of Greene, Stirling, Lafayette, Steuben, St. Clair, Robert Howe, James Clinton, Glover, Hand, Stark, Samuel Holden Parsons, Knox, John Paterson, and Jedediah Huntington. The commander in chief instructed the board to examine André and "as speedily as possible to report a precise state of his case, together with your opinion of the light in which he ought to be considered and the punishment that ought to be inflicted." On September 29, Nathanael Greene, the board's chairman, called his fellow members to order in the Dutch Church at Tappan; present in the room besides the generals were the defendant, André, and the judge advocate general, John Laurance. The outcome of the hearing could hardly be in doubt, for Major André, who had been captured while out of uniform, admitted that he had not considered himself under flag of truce. Hence, the board unanimously determined "That Major André, Adjutant General to the British army, ought to be considered a Spy from the enemy, and that agreeable to the law and usage of nations, it is their opinion, he ought to suffer death." Washington approved the sentence, and after various delays the young man was hanged at noon on October 2.[32]

What were Stirling's personal feelings about this matter? Did he see in his approval of André's death a retribution for the major's scurrilous comments about him in "Cow Chace"? Did he feel the same sorrow about André's demise on the scaffold as did other American officers, who admired the genteel fellow, once described as having "the best disposition in the world"? The record does not speak to these points. Considering Lord Stirling's lifetime record of avoiding personal vindictiveness, it is highly likely that he agreed with his colleagues' assessment of André and felt the same "silent gloom" at the scene of execution that affected other observers.[33]

In early November, Stirling participated in his last service of the campaign of 1780 by advising Washington on where to post the meager Continental forces for the winter. He, along with the other American generals, urged the commander in chief to disperse the army from West Point to Morristown. Washington acceded to this proposal, ordering the Pennsylvanians to take post at Morristown and the New Jersey regiments to encamp at Pompton. On the 24th of the month, Stirling attended a breakfast at Washington's headquarters, where he met the Marquis de Chastellux, who was acting as intermediary between American headquarters and the Comte de Rochambeau's French command in Newport. Chastellux was impressed with Lord Stirling's demeanor and liked him instantly, but, as has already been noted, the Frenchman was unimpressed with Stirling's military capabilities. Directly after the breakfast, Stirling left the American camp and proceeded to Trenton, where the New Jersey legislature was debating various laws dealing with military pensions and soldiers' pay. There he took up quarters at merchant Thomas Barclay's home, "Somerset," which was located in a grove of pine trees on a Delaware River bluff. Living in this warm, comfortable house, Stirling was healthier in late 1780 than for many a year, and he enjoyed a busy schedule of lobbying the legislature on behalf of the army and writing routine military letters to his friend Anthony Wayne.[34]

Ten

The Rewards of Duty, 1781–1783

The year 1781 began for Stirling in anything but peace and harmony, as he and his fellow officers were confronted in early January with a full-blown mutiny of the Pennsylvania line at Morristown. This was a perilous situation, for the very existence of the Continental army and perhaps the success of the Revolution seemed to be teetering in the balance. The Pennsylvania troops, as even Wayne, their commander, readily acceded, had serious and genuine grievances. They had been unpaid for months; their clothes were in tatters; their food was "dry bread and beef"; their blankets had long ago worn out, leaving them prey to the bitter cold of the second abnormally frigid winter in a row; and, worst of all, they were being told that their enlistments for "three years or the duration of the war" were being interpreted by Congress and Washington to mean the latter.[1]

The Pennsylvanians mutinied on January 1 and marched toward Philadelphia to present their grievances to Congress. Although General Wayne could not suppress the uprising, he did get the mutineers to encamp two days later at Princeton while awaiting word of Congress's intentions. Meantime, they promptly put under arrest two spies sent by Sir Henry Clinton to seduce them from their allegiance to the American cause. Joseph Reed, president of the Executive Council of Pennsylvania, allowed the mutineers to dawdle for a week, then came to them with proposals from Congress, which they readily accepted. The agreement called for the Pennsylvania soldiers to receive an immediate discharge upon their personal appeal, to be given pay warrants for redemption as soon as the state could get the money, and to be provided a full set of clothes as replacement for their worn-out or rotten uniforms. Their grievances settled, the Pennsylvania soldiers dutifully placed themselves once more under the command of General

Wayne (who successfully persuaded about a third of his men to reenlist), and turned over Clinton's spies to him. These poor wretches, tried on the 11th before a court-martial consisting of Wayne and other Pennsylvania officers, were condemned to death and executed before the end of day. Thus, said Stirling, the entire "affair" had concluded "in a manner more pleasing than Could have been expected."[2]

With an uneasy peace restored to military life in New Jersey, Stirling returned to the duties that had brought him to Trenton in the first place. He advised the state legislature for the next three months on how to recruit the Jersey regiments to full strength. He also managed to lobby in his own behalf for relief from the state's legal tender law, which had wrecked his personal finances. In both projects he had little success. The New Jersey Continentals remained few in number and his own financial plight in unhappy chaos. His spirits were not roused by military news from the South, for on January 9, he received an account of enemy depredations in Virginia, inflicted by that patriot nemesis Benedict Arnold, and as winter continued he also heard that Greene had been defeated at Guilford Court House in North Carolina. Undeterred by bad news, Stirling surveyed and constructed a military road in central New Jersey to increase troop mobility when the campaigning season returned. As this work proceeded, another anecdote about Stirling was making the rounds of the Continental army. Two soldiers, it was said, had deserted Stirling's division that winter to return home to their father. The father, a patriotic and virtuous man, returned his sons to Stirling in chains, despite his fear of what the stern earl might do to them. When Stirling pardoned them, "as any officer would do," the father was astonished and filled with gratitude. "My Lord," he declared to the general as tears filled his eyes, "'Tis more than I hoped."[3]

Stirling rejoined Washington's army at New Windsor in June 1781, and with the other general officers gave the commander in chief advice on how military operations ought to be conducted during the coming summer. For the first time in years, optimism pervaded American councils, for the French were sending a fleet under Admiral Comte de Grasse to cooperate with a Franco-American army in common effort against the British. Washington and French army commander, Comte de Rochambeau, had already met in May at Wethersfield, Connecticut, and agreed to assault New York City when the fleet arrived. Consequently, Rochambeau's army of five thousand men had marched from Newport to join the patriots in camps around the city. Taking advantage of his opportunity to advise Washington, Stirling on June 16 strongly urged the commander to assault New York from the west. Not only would the artillery and shot at Monmouth have to be hauled a shorter distance, but also possession of Paulus Hook and Staten Island would give great advantages to the Continentals even if Manhattan itself did not fall. This was a well-matured plan and deserving of Washington's attention, but already events had outrun Stirling's thoughts. By August, Rochambeau was justifiably pessimistic about the possibility of succeeding in an attack against Clinton's well-established lines at New York and urged Washington instead to march against the army of Lord Cornwallis in Virginia. Washington agreed to these plans and notified Lafayette, commanding a small Continental force in Virginia, to do all within his power to hold Cornwallis at Yorktown.[4]

Stirling spent the next two months in first assisting Washington to coordinate American and French army activities and then in preparing for the big move southward. On June 17, the earl accompanied the French engineer Louis Duportail on a survey expedition to Peekskill, and on the first day of July he dined with Washington and other officers at an entertainment for Claude Blanchard, commissary of the French army. Five days later, Stirling was "mortified" at having to miss the ceremonies celebrating the junction of the American and French forces at Philipsburg, New York, but his feet were so swollen that he could not leave his tent. Finally, the American and French commanders received the news they had long awaited. Admiral de Grasse was on his way to Chesapeake Bay from the West Indies with twenty-nine warships and three thousand troops. As Washington began preparations to march toward Yorktown with two thousand Continental army veterans, he was faced with the delicate problem of whom to appoint as divisional officer over them. Heath, the senior general, obviously should remain on the Hudson as commander of that region, and Stirling, whose "Age and Infirmities" made him "unequal to the Toils and Fatigues of the March and Consequent hard Duties of the Expedition," could not accept the honor. Consequently, the commander settled on Stirling's good friend Benjamin Lincoln to lead these troops to possible glory. On August 19, Heath and Stirling observed with melancholy jealousy the departure for the South of their more fortunate colleagues in arms. Their own scene of command, the Hudson River Valley, had suddenly become a military backwater.[5]

At least Stirling's military quietude had one good effect, for it allowed him plenty of time to attend to matters both public and private that otherwise might have taxed his fragile health. His financial situation, already clouded by forced property sales and adverse legal tender laws, was being compounded by languor on the part of New Jersey and Congress in sending him his allowances for depreciation in pay. He wrote his lawyer, William Paterson, to complain about New Jersey's neglect, only to be informed that the state, recognizing no rank of major general, could pay no major general's salary. Hence, Stirling noted to his friend Robert Morris, on September 7, that only the national government could provide relief. Despite his appeal to Morris, he never received any depreciation allowance. He did, however, get some good news: He had a granddaughter, born to Kitty and William Duer on September 16. "The little Babe," wrote the proud father to Stirling, "is as fat as a Mole." To celebrate this occassion, the earl promptly ordered five gallons of Madeira for himself and his staff.[6]

A month later, Lord Stirling for the first time in his military career was given an independent field of command when he was ordered by General Heath to proceed immediately to Albany and take charge of the Northern Department. Heath informed him that his assignment, to counter an eruption by General Barry St. Leger and about two thousand troops out of Canada toward Fort Ticonderoga, might prove a severe test of his military abilities. In reality, Stirling had no reason to fear St. Leger's expedition, for unknown to the Americans its sole aim was to lure Vermont from its allegiance to the United States. Stirling, however, not being aware of St. Leger's purpose, was sure the British general intended to seize and burn Albany. John Stark at Saratoga, convinced of the same thing, welcomed Stirling to the Northern Department, noting to the earl that his "influence and military experience" would be a great asset in "this critical and important command." Stirling thanked General Stark on October 24, but suggested sardonically that Stark's "observations on my abilities rather paint me as the person I wish to be, than the one I sincerely think I am." He hoped that Stark would think as well of him after the campaign as before.[7]

Shortly after his arrival at Albany, Stirling assessed intelligence reports on St. Leger's intentions and became convinced that the enemy thrust was not as dangerous as he had been led to believe. St. Leger was at Bull's Bay, on Lake Champlain and might possibly pose a threat to the Mohawk Valley settlements of Johnstown and Schenectady. Moreover, another enemy troop of about six hundred men under Major John Ross were reportedly proceeding from Montreal by way of the St. Lawrence River toward Lake Ontario. But Stirling quickly neutralized these dangers by ordering Colonel Benjamin Tupper, commander of a New Hampshire Continental regiment at Albany, to march up the Mohawk immediately. Then he sent all militia forces home. He learned on October 23 that St. Leger had moved farther southward on Lake Champlain, occupied Fort Ticonderoga, and was threatening to move on to Lake George. Stirling still doubted that St. Leger intended to come on toward Albany, but he did take the precaution of ordering Tupper's Continentals to redirect their march toward Ticonderoga, and he also wrote militia generals Robert Van Rensselaer and Peter Gansevoort to recall their men and be ready to take the road at a moment's notice. He informed Governor George Clinton of all these measures, in order that he and the governor might coordinate their military activities on the frontiers of New York.[8]

At around noon on October 25, Stirling received from Schenectady the seemingly horrendous news "that a large body of the Enemy," Major Ross's men, were within eight miles of that city. He quickly dispatched Gansevoort's militiamen and sixty mounted volunteers toward that town, at the same time directing poor Colonel Tupper once again to bend his line of march that way. Before Stirling could even respond to this crisis, however, Governor Clinton had already ordered a body of troops under Colonel Marinus Willet to thwart Ross's career in the Mohawk Valley, so none of the earl's forces were anywhere near Schenectady when Willet on October 25 attacked Ross and his redcoats near Johnson Hall. The first word that Stirling received of this battle was that Willet had been defeated, so he made plans on the 26th to ride up the Mohawk and take personal command of the fight for Schenectady. All that kept him in Albany that day were reports from Stark at Saratoga "that the enemy were certainly advancing by Lake George, and that he expected to be attacked in twenty-four hours." With Stirling's approval, Stark now ordered Tupper's footsore regiment to return to Saratoga, for even though the situation to the westward seemed dangerous, the threat of St. Leger's Ticonderoga force appeared more so. Stirling also ordered every militiaman not employed at Schenectady "to move towards Saratoga as briskly as possible." In these circumstances, it was a relief for Stirling to learn from Willet on the 27th that rather than being defeated by Ross he had actually whipped Ross soundly, put him to retreat, and was at that very moment pursuing him relentlessly.[9]

Stirling was now free to concentrate on the enemy force at Ticonderoga, and on October 30 he rode with General Philip Schuyler to Saratoga to take personal command of Stark's troops at that place. He was infomed on the same day by a number of Stark's patrol leaders that St. Leger was advancing up Lake George with his troops. Therefore, Stirling surveyed the ground at Saratoga, began construction of defensive works, and ordered Gansevoort to march from Schenectady with his militiamen to this main camp. Stirling weighed his options and decided that if he must meet the British he would do so upon the west bank of the Hudson directly across from Fort Miller. That decision made, he began fortifying his position and disposed his army in such a way as to have Tupper's New Hampshire regulars bear the brunt of battle. He also bolstered the spirits of his men on November 1, by announcing "the glorious news" from General Heath "of the surrender of the army under the command of Earl Cornwallis" at Yorktown. Stirling noised these tidings "at noon with Thirteen cannon, adding one in compliment to our friends in Vermont, who were cooperating with us against the common enemy."[10]

By early November, Stirling was convinced that St. Leger had no intention that winter of pushing any farther south than Fort Ticonderoga, that in fact the Briton would soon abandon the inhospitable shores of Lake Champlain and return to Canada. Before St. Leger could depart, Stirling sent a message to him under a flag of truce suggesting that the two armies exchange prisoners. In passing, the earl also announced Cornwallis's surrender. St. Leger, furious at the news of Yorktown, not only refused to conduct exchange talks with his American counterpart but also ranted to Stirling about the American general's debased character and referred to his letter as a "prostitution of Honour." However, St. Leger was so shaken by news of Cornwallis's fate that he immediately began withdrawing his army down the lake. Stirling, in consequence, decided that no more was to be feared for the moment from St. Leger and dismissed the militia from service. The earl also wrote Washington, Heath, and Governor Clinton letters of congratulations on the surrender of Cornwallis, and then returned to Albany. Shortly after his arrival there, he received a letter from Colonel Willet (whom he later highly recommended to Washington's attention), reporting the further retreat of Major Ross's men and their loss of all their supplies during the withdrawal. Stirling considered it entirely appropriate that Willet had left these wretched men eight days from Fort Oswego without food or shelter, for he described them as a plundering pack of murderers, who deserved to die from hunger and exposure.[11]

Although Stirling had succeeded in forcing St. Leger to retire from upstate New York in late 1781, he was not satisfied that he had done all that he might before terminating the campaign. Therefore, he proposed to General Heath on November 10 that the patriots conduct winer operations in Canada, "at least so far as to reduce St. Johns, Chambly, and Montreal, and be ready to proceed to Quebec, early in the spring." Preparations for such an expedition, he noted, would be few and inexpensive. He could not doubt "the propriety" of the incursion, for only when the British were thrown out of Canada could the United States rest easy that the British would not have access to "the rear of any of the States" through the Great Lakes after the war was over. The American republic, he declared, "shall always be at their mercy" as long as this possibility existed. "Treaties of peace will never secure us. . . . It will be a constant check to the growth of the States." If a peace treaty were concluded during the winter, he summed up, "it will be on terms of possession at the date of the treaty. This is a sufficient inducement to push as far as we can this winter." Stirling's comments were full of strategic good sense and proved over the next thirty years to be prescient, but he knew that Heath had neither the resources nor the authority to conduct such a winter campaign and was not surprised when his proposal was ignored.[12]

In late November, Stirling terminated his campaign by writing General Washington a long, detailed report outlining all his doings since his arrival at Albany. He then set out to rejoin General Heath at Heath's headquarters in the Highlands above New York City, stopping on his way for an extended visit with his beloved daugher Kitty and her husband, William Duer, in their home at Rhinebeck. Like a dutiful grandfather, Stirling spoiled his infant granddaughter and in general thoroughly enjoyed the conviviality of his family reunion. The pleasure of his stay, however, was marred by an incident on the evening before he was to depart for Heath's headquarters. Loyalists in Wittemberg, a German town nearby, had learned of Lord Stirling's visit to the Duer home and had collaborated on a scheme to capture the earl. A servant of the Duers, however, learned of the plan and informed Kitty, whereupon measures were taken to thwart it. On the night the attack was to take place, Stirling posted his dragoon bodyguard inside the house, barricaded the windows and doors, and issued muskets to all the men.

Consequently, when the Tories made their supposedly surprise assault, they were met by a volley of gunfire that caused them to disperse in all directions.[13]

Lord Stirling rejoined General Heath on December 23 and found awaiting him a letter from Washington, who was in Philadelphia, congratulating him upon the "happy Success" of "military Operations in the Northern District." The consequences, said the commander in chief, "cannot fail to be very important." Stirling, pleased with this praise, declared that he was "honored" by Washington's words; noting to the commander in chief that he intended to visit Princeton soon, the earl hinted that "a line from your Excellency will bring me to your quarters." Washington sent the line, and in late December Stirling left for Philadelphia, where he welcomed the new year of 1782 at his temporary headquarters in that city.[14]

During January, Stirling was busy with a number of military duties. Governor Livingston of New Jersey wrote him on the 11th that "a motley of British and refugees," numbering about three hundred, had carried out an "irruption into the city of Brunswick" and done some damage. After that insipid foray, however, the British in New York settled down for the duration of Stirling's stay in Philadelphia. Thus, Stirling spent his energies in trying to convince Washington that some sort of military operation ought to be attempted that winter. He sent Washington a "memo. for Imeed. consideration" on January 14, suggesting that the Americans send an expedition against St. Leger's ships, which were frozen in the ice of Lake Champlain. The enterprise would require only eight hundred to a thousand men, all of whom could easily be transported on three hundred sleds, and might result in the ships' destruction. If that idea was impractical, then Washington should consider assaulting New York City if the harbor froze over. American troops could be on Manhattan within twenty-four hours by moving in sleighs from the Highlands. Perhaps, mused Stirling, Washington would wish to carry out both these operations, or if the commander in chief really wanted to do good for the American cause that winter he might implement Stirling's earlier suggestion to Heath and send an expedition north to reduce St. Johns and Montreal, thereby cutting off British "access to the Rear of every State on the Continent." General Washington received all these ideas from the earl with polite courtesy, but he, like Heath, had to ignore them because of constraints upon American manpower and supplies.[15]

Stirling's visit to Philadelphia ended in late January when General Washington appointed him president of a court-martial to hear a case against Alexander McDougall at Fishkill. Earlier that month, General Heath had charged McDougall with "conduct unmilitary and unbecoming an officer," because the latter supposedly had called Heath a "fool, a knave, and an obstinate man." Stirling, as his new duty required, proceeded to Fishkill where on February 18 he assembled a court at the house of a Mr. Cooper. It was only then that he learned that McDougall strenuously objected to his presiding at the hearing. In fact, McDougall had already protested to Washington that Stirling had proved himself incompetent for his task by committing many "capital defects" during Charles Lee's trial.[16]

McDougall, not sparing of Stirling's feelings on the first day of the court-martial, asserted in a speech that he considered the earl to be given to prejudgments and ill-will against anyone even suspected of a breach of military duty. Although Stirling noted later to Heath that McDougall also "declar'd he has the highest opinion of my honor and the goodness of my heart," the earl nevertheless felt constrained to defend himself against McDougall's charges, and he insisted both to the court and to Heath that McDougall had no grounds for protest. At this point, General Heath appealed to Washington for advice on the technical question of whether a defendant could refuse to be tried by someone to whom he objected. The commander in chief, to avoid getting mired in technicalities, recommended to Stirling that he simply resign. Stirling aceded to this request, declaring that since McDougall had impugned his competency he could not in any case serve on the court. Finally, Washington appointed Robert Howe to replace Stirling as president of McDougall's court-martial, and the matter seemed closed.[17]

Lord Stirling, however, had not forgotten McDougall's comments about him, and he emerged from the incident determined to get satisfaction from his former friend at the first opportunity. He had no chance to carry out his plan during the next few months while McDougall was involved in an embarrassing and tedious trial, because Stirling did not think it proper to complicate the man's life by insisting on personal retribution. However, McDougall was partially cleared of the charges against him on August 30, and Stirling now told him that the time had come for a reckoning. Putting the matter bluntly, Stirling declared, "you must be sensible that you have injured me, you have greatly injured me indeed, you have attacked my professional character, you have endeavoured to wound my character in the most cruel manner, you have endeavoured to make the world believe me unable to Support the Character of an officer or a good man." It was up to McDougall to decide what he intended to do in response to Stirling's charges; meantime, the earl "anxiously" awaited his answer. Since Stirling was required at that point to leave the Highlands and return to his command in the Northern Department, McDougall did not answer his letter until November 12. Even then, McDougall refused to give Stirling the satisfaction of an apology, and the quarrel between these two strong-willed men was unresolved when Stirling died in January 1783.[18]

Stirling's duty assignment after his resignation from the presidency of the McDougall court-martial was administering the army at Newburgh under conditions that were close to peacetime. Working directly under Washington, who had returned to the Highlands after Cornwallis's surrender at Yorktown, he assisted Heath in examining the honesty of businessmen who dealt with the army. A Mr. Sands, said Stirling to Heath, was gouging the public unmercifully under the "extasy of grasping the golden fruit his avaritious imagination had just erected." He wrote a letter of recommendation for William Stephens Smith and Matthew Clarkson to the Marquis de Bouille, worried about the shortness of provisions for the troops, and composed a three-page paper to no one in particular airing his disgust with the Rockingham ministry's miserly peace proposals. Meantime, Stirling watched the British army in New York, imagining (in his desire for the genuine event) evacuations that did not occur. Washington, alert to any possible military gain, polled his officers on April 15 about the feasibility of attacking New York City. Only Stirling of all the respondents was in favor of storming British positions around the city. His ideas, too grandiose for Washington's meager army of eight thousand men, were almost identical to his earlier proposals for assaults on New York City.[19]

Stirling was hampered in carrying out his duty in the early summer of 1782 by recurring bouts of rheumatism and gout. He had been compelled as early as March 16 to petition Heath for a medical leave of absence, and in May his hands were so crippled that he could not write for days on end. He was confined to his bed in July with a "dangerous illness," and Washington, in a pathetic gesture of friendship, sent him six lemons "to contribute to restoration of Yr. Lordship's health." This attack was so acute that Stirling almost died, and he signed into his wife's care two certificates of depreciation for his military salary, worth $6,904 with accrued interest. He recovered his health sufficiently by mid-August to pay attention to hiring a servant "who is capable of providing for a Table that would admit a few Friends." But by the end of the month he "had a slight return of the fever" and was confined to quarters. His enforced idleness had one good effect. He now had time to do some reading, and he recommended to Washington an "admirably well written" biography of John Sobieski, a seventeenth-century Polish king, whom Stirling described as "one of the first characters that have appeared."[20]

By late summer, Stirling's health had improved enough for Washington to order him back to Albany as commander of the Northern Department for the coming winter. It was clear that Washington wanted to give his subordinate an easy duty post for the next few months, for as Stirling wrote Washington later from Albany, "The attention your Excellency has manifested to my convenience and accomodation during the winter, gives me the highest satisfaction, more particularly so, as I find my health very far from being established. The superior advantages this place will afford me in effecting my recovery, renders your Excellency's assignment particularly agreeable, and will have its influence in reconciling me to my absence from Head Quarters." To make his situation even more pleasant, Stirling prevailed upon his wife to join him during the winter.[21]

Turning to business, Stirling petitioned a return from all his officers in order to determine how many men he had in his theater. He then wrote a long letter to Washington reiterating his long held wish to cut off British access to the Great Lakes before a treaty of peace ended the war. Although he did not even hint that he might try to interdict enemy communications on the St. Lawrence River, he did muse that a good American post at Oswegotie or La Gallete would certainly fulfill the requirement. Stirling's statement agitated Washington, for the commander in chief believed his subordinate was planning a shoestring operation into Canada that would almost surely fail. Hence, he quickly sent off to Stirling a list of the manifold "insuperable obstacles" in the way of such an undertaking and in no uncertain terms ordered the earl to forbear. Stirling was surprised at the excitement he had roused at Washington's headquarters, and he hastened to inform the commander in chief that he "had not the most distant idea of an attempt to that kind under our present Circumstances." He was merely giving his "Ideas of some consequential points that should hereafter be attended to in Settling the boundaries" between Canada and the United States.[22]

In early October, Lord Stirling received intelligence from his scouts and from John Sullivan, who was in retirement in New Hampshire, that British forces were moving into the Lake Champlain region. According to Sullivan, Baron Von Riedesel, commanding a force of four thousand Germans, was at Île aux Noix, planning to drive on Albany. Another enemy contingent under John Johnson was said to be moving down the Mohawk Valley, intending to fall on Schenectady. "There seems some reason," said Sullivan, "to be apprehensive." Stirling reported this intelligence to Washington, even though he doubted its veracity, as did the commander in chief when he received it. Washington did not want to underrate British capabilities, he told Stirling, but he believed the advanced season alone was enough to thwart an assault on Albany. He was sure Riedesel's activities at Île aux Noix were intended solely to improve Canadian security. His observations were confirmed when Stirling shortly afterward received reports from Governor Clinton and others that Riedesel was building a fort upon the island. Lord Stirling was bemused by the activities of his enemies, for even from a defensive point of view, the Germans' construction there made no sense. "What can be their object at this Season," he asked Washington. "However, I shall follow that good old Rule never to despise any intelligence."[23]

As the excitement over enemy activities at Île aux Noix abated, Stirling set out on an inspection tour of American army posts in the Mohawk Valley. He discovered on October 20 that Johnstown was a commodious town that could house a regiment for the winter, should Washington wish to post one there. The soldiers at all stations, he noted to the commander in chief, "appear'd to be better than I expected to have found them." Even the state troops had at least a slightly martial appearance and would cut an even better figure were they adequately armed and clothed. At Rennselaer, he found a blockhouse that was strong and well built, capable of holding off any force the enemy could send against it that winter. Stirling had intended to ride farther upstream, but a heavy snowstorm impeded his progress and detained him for two days. Hence, he returned to Albany on October 22, reported to Washington the condition and needs of his troops, and sent the commander a summary of his numbers. He also noted that all was peaceful on the frontiers, and although "Some tracks and some parties have been seen near Ticonderoga and the Lake Oneida, . . . I am inclined to think they are our own Indians Hunting." The enemy was so busy "in rendering their fortifications tenable" at Île aux Noix that they could spare neither time nor men to alarm the Americans with patrols or raids.[24]

When General Washington received this report, he registered his pleasure that all was well in upstate New York and informed Stirling that the New Hampshire regiment had been relieved of duty there. It would be replaced with a Rhode Island regiment, once Stirling sent the New Hampshiremen southward to Newburgh. Stirling found this arrangement satisfactory, indicating to Washington on November 2 that since the frontier was peaceful he would post the Rhode Island Continentals at Saratoga rather than sending them to Rennselaer. Ten days later, all these troop exchanges had been completed, and Washington had ordered to Albany supplies that the state troops needed. Stirling was delighted at the smoothness of these operations, especially since he was all too familiar with the frustrating way that army administration usually proceeded.[25]

It is well that Lord Stirling was not vexed with petty annoyances in the last months of 1782, for his long public service to America was drawing swiftly to an end. He actively led his troops until December 23, maintained a happy and buoyant family life, and gave no hint in any of his correspondence that he expected to die any time soon. But he realized that he was seriously ill and that his gout and rheumatism were becoming progressively worse. He knew that the previous July he had come very near to dying when gout settled in his stomach and caused his temperature to soar to dangerously high levels. Nevertheless, he bravely told Washington on November 2 that he still hoped for a full recovery. Even as he composed these lines he was losing the use of his hands, and within twenty-four hours he was reduced once more to dictating his letters. He showed some signs of a rally on November 23, or so he convinced himself. That day, in an ink-blotted letter that he inscribed with a feeble hand to Washington, he said, "I thank God I am recovering, 'tho it is but Slowly." A month later, his condition had deteriorated once more. On December 19, he wrote Charles Stewart "I have pretty well recovered my health, so far as relates to the Vile

Bilious fever I was Seized with about five months ago; But my bowels are weak, and I still want strength; the proper medicine is not to be had at this place; good, old, Genuine Madeira is the only Cordial I stand in need of," and he asked Stewart to send him some.[26]

If good wits, high courage, hearty optimism, and the desire to enjoy earth's bounty were enough to keep a man from death, Lord Stirling would not have succumbed at this time. But his hard service in the field and his hard drinking at headquarters finally caught up with him at Albany in late December 1782. Forced to his bed with a violent attack of gout, his temperature soared to lethal heights, and his body was seared with pain. Unable to keep anything in his stomach, he began to die of dehydration before the helpless gaze of family members and friends, who stood in mute sorrow by his bedside. Days merged into weeks as the brave, suffering general fought a desperate but losing battle for life. On January 15, 1783, William Alexander, claiming to be the sixth Earl of Stirling, died in the 57th year of his life. The following day, he was given a military funeral befitting his rank and interred with Protestant Episcopal rites in a vault set aside for his wife's ancestors within the Dutch Church at Albany. These ceremonies, awesome in their severe dignity, were long recollected by the inhabitants of the city as an outstanding incident of the revolutionary war in that region.

When word of Stirling's death spread through the ranks of the United States Army, many officers paused in their busy rounds to declare their grief for, and admiration of, the personable general. Washington, who felt "sharp distress" over Stirling's demise, comforted Lady Sarah on January 20 by expressing "how deeply I share the common affliction, on being deprived of the public and professional assistance, as well as the private friendship of an Officer of so high Rank with whom I had lived in the strict habits of amity; and how much those Military Merits of his Lordship which rendered him respected in his life time, are now regretted by the whole Army." Washington also wrote Congress, "The remarkable bravery, intelligence, and promptitude of his Lordship to perform his duty as an Officer, has endeared him to the whole Army; and now make his loss the more sincerely regretted." Two days later, the commander in chief announced to the army in general orders that anyone who so desired might mourn the death of the popular officer for a month, "by wearing a Crape, or weed during that time."[27]

Congress also took note of Lord Stirling's untimely death. In a solemn and unanimous resolution, the legislators "*Resolved*, that the President signify to the commander in chief, in a manner the most respectful to the memory of the late Major General the Earl of Stirling, the sense Congress entertain of the early and meritorious exertions of that general in the common cause, and of the bravery, perseverance and military talents he possessed." Elias Boudinot, a congressman from New Jersey and a neighbor of the late earl, conveyed a copy of this resolution to Washington and called Stirling's death "unexpected and melancholy." The "special services rendered to his country by that Nobleman," noted Boudinot, "from the very earliest period of the present war, to the day of his death, rendered his memory in the highest degree, respectable to Congress."[28]

Thus, Lord Stirling, merchant, family man, landed aristocrat, monarchist, republican, and soldier, concluded his varied and often exciting life. Although he made significant contributions to politics, commerce, and especially warfare, his overriding personality characteristic was an all-engrossing enthusiasm for whatever he set his mind to do. As a consequence, he often carried things to extremes. His pursuit of a lapsed Scots earldom, his attempts to live as an American country gentleman, his profligacy with money, his sudden embrace of the rebel cause in 1775, his overindulgence in food and drink, all were signs of a tendency to excess or unpredictability. Nevertheless, his contemporaries admired and respected him, his fellow citizens elevated him to important public positions, his enemies were few, and his adoring wife, left penniless by his wasteful ways, addressed him as "my dear Lord."

The reasons for Stirling's fame are many. His natural abilities, while not of the highest rank, were sufficient to allow him a good working relationship with men whom he recognized to possess greater aptitude. During his service in the Continental army, he combined the aggressiveness of Anthony Wayne and Benedict Arnold with the wit and good humor of Henry Knox, and his devotion to Washington was equal to that of Nathanael Greene or Lafayette. He had extraordinary courage, which manifested itself in his battlefield ardor and his constant search for ways to take the war to the British. Additionally, he was imaginative in his military analyses and responsible and dependable in his role as a divisional officer under General Washington.

While Stirling's personal extravagances worked hardships upon his family, they did not affect his role as an army officer. His addiction to the bottle quite likely aggravated his gout and shortened his life, but his alcoholism (if that is what it can be called) did not interfere with his other duties throughout his career. Although he never received just compensation for his military services—and in this regard he was like many of his officer colleagues—he was not embittered by his lack of financial reward, even though his need for money was much greater than that of his comrades. His pretensions to a title certainly showed him to be more than a little conceited, but he never allowed the fact that he claimed an earldom to become an excuse for hurt feelings or sulking when Washington rejected his military ideas.

In sum, Lord Stirling, through natural inclination and by conscious intention, went out of his way as few of his colleagues did to be agreeable to and supportive of superiors. So, while the Marquis de Chastellux was correct in noting that Stirling's "birth, his title, and rather extensive estates" had entitled him to "more importance . . . than his talents could ever have acquired for him,"[29] the Frenchman overlooked in this otherwise shrewd assessment of Stirling an important reason why the earl's fellows were anxious to elevate him to positions of leadership and power. Stirling simply was a genuinely likable, decent, trustworthy man, whose laughter and enthusiasm infected those around him with his joy and good humor. His buoyant optimism and his ability to make people more self-confident during crises helped to endear him to Lady Stirling and their daughters, to General Washington, to Boudinot, and to a host of others. These qualities contributed to his value to America as a social, political, and military leader. The loss of these endearing traits was among the very important reasons why his compatriots mourned his passing.

Notes

Chapter 1

1. James Thacher, *A Military Journal During the American Revolutionary War* (Boston, 1827), 245–46; George W. Corner, ed., *The Autobiography of Benjamin Rush* (Princeton, 1948), 157; Albigence Waldo, "Diary, Valley Forge, 1777–1778," *Pennsylvania Magazine of History and Biography* 21 (1897): 320, hereafter *PMHB*; Charles Lee to George Washington, February 19, 1776, in *Lee Papers,* New-York Historical Society Collections, 4–7 (New York, 1872–76), 1: 309, hereafter *Lee Papers;* Thomas Warren Field, *The Battle of Long Island, With Connected Preceding Events and the Subsequent American Retreat* (Brooklyn, 1869), 525; Leonard Lundin, *Cockpit of the Revolution: The War for Independence in New Jersey* (Princeton, 1940), 90. Most historians agree that bravery was one of Stirling's strongest points as a soldier. See Earl Schenck Miers, *Crossroads of Freedom: The American Revolution and the Rise of a New Nation* (New Brunswick, 1971), 164; George F. Scheer and Hugh F. Rankin, *Rebels and Redcoats* (Cleveland, 1957), 145; John R. Alden, *General Charles Lee: Traitor or Patriot?* (Baton Rouge, 1951), 110; George Bancroft, *History of the United States* (10 vols., Boston, 1834–74), 4: 251; William S. Stryker, *The Battle of Monmouth* (Princeton, 1927), 207n; James Thomas Flexner, *George Washington in the American Revolution* (Boston, 1968), 108n; Christopher Ward, *The War of the Revolution,* ed. John R. Alden (2 vols., New York, 1952), 1: 207; Douglas Southall Freeman, *George Washington: A Biography* (7 vols., New York, 1947–57), 3: 321–22, 4: 241A.

2. Waldo, "Diary," *PMHB* 21: 320; Thacher, *Journal,* 245–46; G. O. Trevelyan, *The American Revolution* (4 vols., New York, 1915), 2: 179; Marquis de Chastellux, *Travels in North America in the Years 1780, 1781 and 1782,* tr. Howard C. Rice, Jr. (2 vols., Chapel Hill, 1963), 1: 106–7; Corner, ed., *Autobiography of Rush,* 157.

3. Corner, ed., *Autobiography of Rush,* 157; Chastellux, *Travels,* 1: 106–7, 142; Thacher, *Journal,* 246; Lundin, *Cockpit,* 21–24.

4. Lyman H. Butterfield, ed., *Letters of Benjamin Rush* (2 vols., Princeton, 1951), 1: 163–65; Corner, ed., *Autobiography of Rush,* 157; Chastellux, *Travels,* 1: 106–7; "Historical Notes of Dr. Benjamin Rush," *PMHB* 27 (1903): 147; Charles Lee to Miss Rebecca Franks, December 20, 1778, cited in Alden, *Lee,* 271; Don Higginbotham, *The War of American Independence: Military Attitudes, Policies,*

and Practice, 1763–1789 (New York, 1971), 208; W. J. Rorabaugh, *The Alcoholic Republic: An American Tradition* (New York, 1979), 40.

5. Moses Colt Tyler, *The Literary History of the American Revolution, 1763–1783* (2 vols., New York, 1897), 2: 120; Ward, *Revolution*, 1: 207; Trevelyan, *Revolution*, 1: 179; John C. Miller, *Triumph of Freedom, 1775–1783* (Boston, 1948), 248.

6. Marquis de Lafayette, *Mémoires, Correspondance et Manuscrits* (6 vols., Paris, 1837–38), 1: 19–20; Louis Gottschalk, *Lafayette Comes to America* (Chicago, 1935), 32; Chastellux, *Travels*, 1: 106–7; Freeman, *Washington*, 4: 480.

7. William Smith, *History of the Late Province of New York,* ed. Michael Kammen (2 vols., Cambridge, Mass., 1972), 1: 271; George Rose III, "James Alexander," *Dictionary of American Biography,* ed. Allen Johnson and Dumas Malone (22 vols., New York, 1928–44), 1: 167–68, hereafter *DAB;* Henry Noble MacCracken, *Prologue to Independence: The Trials of James Alexander, American, 1715–1756* (New York, 1964), passim; Herbert L. Osgood, *The American Colonies in the Eighteenth Century* (4 vols., New York, 1924), 2: 417, 431–32.

8. Patricia U. Bonomi, *A Factious People: Politics and Society in Colonial New York* (New York, 1971), 56–75.

9. Michael Kammen, *Colonial New York: A History* (New York, 1975), 202–5. Other useful modern studies of eighteenth-century New York politics are Stanley Nider Katz, *Newcastle's New York: Anglo-American Politics, 1732–1753* (Cambridge, Mass., 1968), and Milton M. Klein, *Politics of Diversity: Essays in the History of Colonial New York* (Port Washington, N.Y., 1974).

10. MacCracken, *James Alexander,* 40, 43–44, 51–72; Osgood, *Colonies,* 2: 442–45; Rose, "James Alexander," *DAB,* 1: 168; William Alexander Duer, *The Life of William Alexander, Earl of Stirling* (New York, 1847), 5; Benjamin W. Labaree, *America's Nation-Time, 1607–1789* (New York, 1972), 80; James Alexander, *A Brief Narrative of the Case and Trial of John Peter Zenger, Printer of the New York Weekly Journal,* ed. Stanley Katz (Cambridge, Mass., 1963).

11. Rose, "James Alexander," *DAB,* 1: 168; Adolph B. Benson, ed., *The America of 1750: Peter Kalm's Travels in North America: The English Version of 1770* (2 vols., New York, 1937), 1: 140; MacCracken, *James Alexander,* 84–85, 87, 131–32; Duer, *Stirling,* 5; Theodore Sedgwick, Jr., *A Memoir of the Life of William Livingston* (New York, 1833), 57–58; Herbert and Carol Schneider, eds., *Samuel Johnson, President of King's College: His Career and Writings* (4 vols., New York, 1929), 4: 206; Martha J. Lamb, *History of the City of New York* (2 vols., New York, 1877–80), 1: 647, 2: 539; Smith, *History of New York,* 2: 150; Austin B. Keep, *History of the New York Society Library* (New York, 1908).

12. Carl Van Doren, *Benjamin Franklin* (New York, 1938), 220; Labaree, *Nation-Time,* 5, 335–37, 335n; Osgood, *Colonies,* 2: 316.

13. MacCracken, *James Alexander,* 17–18; Livingston Rutherfurd, *Family Records and Events: Compiled Principally from the Original Manuscripts in the Rutherfurd Collection* (New York, 1894), 37; Wills of James and Mary Alexander, March

13, 1745, and July 27, 1756, New Jersey Colonial Documents, Liber F, 345–54, Liber G, 199–210, New Jersey State Library, Trenton; John Shy, *Toward Lexington: The Role of the British Army in the Coming of the American Revolution* (Princeton, 1965), 355; Miers, *Crossroads,* 81; Lamb, *New York,* 1: 503–4.

14. I. N. Phelps Stokes, *The Iconography of Manhattan Island, 1898–1909* (6 vols., New York, 1915–28), 2: 296; Will of Mary Alexander, New Jersey Colonial Documents, Liber G, 199–210, New Jersey State Library; Samuel Eliot Morison, *Builders of the Bay Colony* (Cambridge, Mass., 1930), 156.

15. Stokes, *Iconography,* 6: 517; George H. Danforth, "The Rebel Earl" (Ph.D. diss., Columbia University, 1955), 6.

16. MacCracken, *James Alexander,* 85.

17. William Alexander to James Alexander, August 7, 1747, James and Mary Alexander to William Alexander, July 27, 1748, James Alexander to William Alexander, February 14, 1748, September 12, 1751, William Alexander, Lord Stirling, Papers, Box 1, New-York Historical Society, hereafter Stirling Papers, NYHS; William Alexander to James Alexander, February 14, 1750, Rutherfurd Collection, vol. 3, New-York Historical Society, hereafter Rutherfurd Collection, NYHS.

18. Elizabeth Clarkson Jay, "The Descendants of James Alexander," *New York Genealogical and Biographical Record,* 12 (1881), 13; Lamb, *New York,* 1: 599; Sarah Alexander to William Alexander, July 8, 1752, Stirling Papers, 1, NYHS.

19. Moses Gambeau to William Alexander, August 3, October 3, 1748, William Alexander to John Stevens, March 13, 15, 17, 20, 1749, January 2, 15, 1750, John Stevens to William Alexander, August 29, 1748, June 8, 30, July 4, 13, 29, 1749, William Alexander to T. Pemberton, Jr., October, 1752, James Alexander Papers, Boxes 1 and 9, New-York Historical Society, hereafter James Alexander Papers, NYHS.

20. William Alexander to W. Alexander, December 8, 1743, December 22, 1746, September 28, 1749, October 3, 1750, W. Alexander to William Alexander, August 12, September 12, 1746, Catherine Alexander to William Alexander, January 10, 1749, March 26, 1750, June _____, 1750, July 25, 1750, Stirling Papers, 1, NYHS.

21. Henry Livingston to William Alexander, July 9, 15, 1748, May 28, 1749, William Alexander to John Winthrop, May 21, 1753, Stirling Papers, 1, NYHS.

22. Daniel Horsmanden, *The New York Conspiracy,* ed. Thomas J. Davis (Boston, 1971); John Hope Franklin, *From Slavery to Freedom: A History of Negro Americans* (4th ed., New York, 1974), 64; G. W. Williams, *History of the Negro Race* (New York, 1883), 151; Herbert Aptheker, *American Negro Slave Revolts* (New York, 1943), 192–95; William Alexander to John Stevens, November 19, 1748, July 30, August 1, 4, 1749, John Stevens to William Alexander, August 11, 18, 31, 1749, January 19, 31, 1750, James Alexander Papers, 9, 12, NYHS.

23. William Alexander to John Stevens, June 20, 21, 25, 26, July 17, 1750, James

Alexander Papers, 9, NYHS. See also Receipts, 1765–75, James Alexander Papers, 14, NYHS, Dutch and German Emigrants' Correspondence with John Steadman, July 30, 1753, James Alexander Papers, 1, NYHS, and Danforth, "Rebel Earl," 51.

24. Charles M. Andrews, *The Colonial Period of American History* (4 vols., New Haven, 1934–38), 4: 180; George J. Miller, ed., *Minutes of the Board of Proprietors of the Eastern Division of New Jersey* (3 vols., Perth Amboy, 1949–60), esp. vols. 2 and 3; Elisha Parker to William Alexander, August 19, 1747, James and Mary Alexander to William Alexander, July 27, 1748, James Livingston to Captain William Alexander, n.d. [1748], William Alexander to John Provoost, November 15, 1750, Stirling Papers, 1, NYHS.

25. Milton M. Klein, ed., *The Independent Reflector, or Weekly Essays on Sundry Important Subjects More Particularly Adapted to the Province of New-York* (Cambridge, Mass., 1963), 16, 446–47; C. H. Levermore, "Whigs of Colonial New York," *AHR* 1: 242–43; John A. Krout, "William Livingston," *DAB*, 11: 326; Richard B. Morris, "John Morin Scott," *DAB*, 16: 495. In 1755, as part of their general attacks on established religion, Alexander helped Livingston publish the *Narrative of a New and Unusual American Imprisonment*, the story of high-handed treatment given Francis Makemie, a Presbyterian minister, a half century before in New York by the governor, Lord Edward Cornbury (Lawrence C. Wroth, *An American Bookshelf, 1755* [Philadelphia, 1934], 72–73, and Sedgwick, *Livingston*, 110n). A by-product of the "Whig Club" may have been the founding of the New York Society Library. In March 1754, William Livingston, Robert R. Livingston, Philip Livingston, William Alexander, William Smith, and John Morin Scott collected six hundred pounds to start the library (Smith, *History of New York*, 2: 150). Later, older men, such as Lieutenant Governor James DeLancey and James Alexander, were added to the roll of sponsors (Lamb, *New York*, 1: 647).

Chapter 2

1. For Washington's account of these proceedings, see Donald Jackson and Dorothy Twohig, eds., *The Diaries of George Washington* (6 vols., Charlottesville, 1976–80), 1: 162–210.

2. William Alexander to Richard Peters, March 7, 1754, Peters to Alexander, March 22, 23, 28, April 17, May 23, 1754, Stirling Papers, 1, NYHS; Julian P. Boyd and Robert J. Taylor, eds., *The Susquehannah Company Papers* (11 vols., Wilkes-Barre and Ithaca, 1930–71), 1: 59, 75–78, 85–86, 91–92; Leonard W. Labaree and William B. Willcox, eds., *The Papers of Benjamin Franklin* (20 vols. to date, New Haven, 1959–), 5: 335–37, 335n.

3. A copy of James Alexander's views, which he gave his son orally, are in *The*

Colden Papers, New-York Historical Society Collections, 9–10 (New York, 1876–77), 4: 460, hereafter *Colden Papers;* Labaree and Willcox, eds., *Franklin Papers,* 5: 335–37, 337n, 351. Franklin's plan is published in E. B. O'Callaghan and Berthold Fernow, eds., *Documents Relative to the Colonial History of the State of New York* (15 vols., Albany, 1856–57), 6: 889–91; William Johnson to Robert Monckton, November 12, 1762, and to William Smith, Jr., May 11, 1763, James Sullivan, et al., eds., *Papers of Sir William Johnson* (13 vols., Albany, 1921–25), 3: 934, 4: 116.

4. William Alexander to Richard Peters, March 7, 1754, Peters to Alexander, March 22, 1754, Stirling Papers, 1, NYHS; Boyd and Taylor, ed., *Susquehannah Papers,* 1: 13; Deposition of William Alexander, Lord Stirling for the Supreme Court of New York, December 19, 1782, Boyd and Taylor, eds., *Susquehannah Papers,* 7: 242–45.

5. William Alexander to Robert Hunter Morris, December 1, 1754, Boyd and Taylor, eds., *Susquehannah Papers,* 1: 181–83; other relevant quotes in Boyd and Taylor, eds., *Susquehannah Papers,* 7: 172–240, 242–45; William Alexander to Thomas Penn, December 18, 1760, Penn Papers, 6: 243, Historical Society of Pennsylvania, hereafter Penn Papers, HSP.

6. George Washington to William Fairfax, April 23, 1755, John C. Fitzpatrick, ed., *The Writings of George Washington from the Original Manuscripts, 1745–1799* (39 vols., Washington, D.C., 1931–44), 1: 116; Sullivan, et al., eds., *Johnson Papers,* 1: 454–55.

7. O'Callaghan and Fernow, eds., *Documents,* 6: 920–22; Stanley M. Pargellis, *Lord Loudoun in North America* (New Haven, 1933), 36; Douglas Edward Leach, *Arms for Empire: A Military History of the British Colonies in North America, 1607–1763* (New York, 1973), 355–56.

8. William Shirley to John Erving, Jr., William Alexander, and Lewis Morris, Jr., April 24, 1755, Rutherfurd Collection, 3, NYHS. This paragraph and subsequent ones dealing with Alexander's role in army contracts during 1755–56 is based upon Theodore Thayer's extremely useful article, "The Army Contractors for the Niagara Campaign, 1755–1756," *William and Mary Quarterly,* 3d ser., 14 (January 1957): 31–45.

9. William Alexander to John Shirley, May 24, 1755, Stirling Papers, 1, NYHS; Thayer, "Army Contractors," *WMQ* 14: 33; Oliver DeLancey's Remarques Made on the Accounts of the Agents Employed by General Shirley, [1758], Loudoun Collection, Henry E. Huntington Library, hereafter Loudoun Collection, Huntington Library.

10. Pargellis, *Loudoun,* 155; Lawrence H. Gipson, *The British Empire Before the American Revolution* (15 vols., New York, 1936–70), 6: 181; Smith, *History of New York,* 2: 186; DeLancey's Remarques, Loudoun Collection, Huntington Library; Thayer "Army Contractors," *WMQ* 14: 33.

11. William Shirley to John Erving, N., William Alexander, and Lewis Morris,

Jr., April 24, 1755 (2 letters), Shirley to Alexander, April 28, 1755, Rutherfurd Collection, 3, NYHS; Alexander to Erving, May 2, 1755, Stirling Papers, 1, NYHS.

12. William Alexander to John Bradstreet, May 5, 1755, to William Shirley, May 17, 27, 1755, Stirling Papers, 1, NYHS; Alexander to Shirley, May 10, 1755, Penn Papers, 7: 33, HSP.

13. William Alexander to Robert Dinwiddie, May 10, 1755, to Robert Livingston, June 11, 1755, and Peter Van Brugh Livingston to Alexander, July 10, 1755, Stirling Papers, 1, NYHS; Dinwiddie to Alexander, May 19, 1755, Rutherfurd Collection, 3, NYHS; Alexander to William Shirley, May 10, June, 27, 1755, Penn Papers, 7, 33, 37, HSP; Alexander to Robert Livingston, June 6, 1755, Etting Collection, 3, 14, HSP.

14. William Alexander to James Stevenson, May 8, 1755, to Van Eppes and Fisher, May 21, 26, 27, 1755, to William Shirley, May 27, 1755, to William Williams, June 11, 1755, Stirling Papers, 1, NYHS; Alexander to Shirley, May 18, June 6, 1755, Penn Papers, 7: 33–35, 37, HSP; Thayer, "Army Contractors," *WMQ* 14: 36.

15. William Alexander to John Bradstreet, May 5, 1755, to William Shirley, May 27, June 6, 1755, to William Johnson, June 11, 1755, and to William Williams, June 11, 1755, Stirling Papers, 1, NYHS; Thayer, "Army Contractors," *WMQ* 14: 38.

16. William Alexander to William Shirley, May 10, 1755, Penn Papers, 7: 33, HSP; Alexander to Robert Livingston, June 6, 1755, Etting Collection, 3: 14, HSP; Alexander to Reese Meredith, May 10, June 22, 1755, to Shirley, May 17, June 7, 1755, to John Bradstreet, May 26, 1755, to Robert Hunter Morris, June 9, 1755, to Moses Emerson, June 23, 1755, Stirling Papers, 1, NYHS; Alexander to Peter Van Brugh Livingston, August 4, 1755, Rutherfurd Collection, 3, NYHS; Thayer, "Army Contractors, *WMQ* 14: 34–35; Labaree and Willcox, eds., *Franklin Papers,* 6: 58n.

17. William Alexander to William Shirley, May 18, 1755, Stirling Papers, 1, NYHS; Alexander to Shirley, May 10, 18, 27, June 6, 1755, Penn Papers, 7: 33–35, 37, HSP.

18. William Alexander to John Shirley, June 9, 1755, and to Robert Hunter Morris, July 6, 1755, Stirling Papers, 1, NYHS.

19. Peter Van Brugh Livingston to William Alexander, July 9, 10, 25, 29, 1755, Stirling Papers, 1, NYHS; Robert Orne to Shirley, July 18, 1755, Charles Henry Lincoln, ed., *Correspondence of William Shirley* (2 vols., New York, 1912), 2: 207–8; John A. Schutz, *William Shirley: King's Governor of Massachusetts* (Chapel Hill, 1961), 198–207.

20. William Johnson to Thomas Pownall, July 31, 1755, and to James DeLancey, August 8, 1755, Sullivan, et al., eds., *Johnson Papers,* 1: 803–6, 841–42, 2: 400–1; Arthur Pound and Richard E. Day, *Johnson of the Mohawks: A Biography of Sir William Johnson* (New York, 1930), 186–87.

21. William Alexander to Peter Van Brugh Livingston, August 4, 1755, Ruther-

furd Collection, 3: NYHS; Alexander to James Stevenson, August 4, 1755, Stirling Papers, 1, NYHS; Statement of John H. Lydus, September 21, 1756, Loudoun Collection, Huntington Library, cited in Thayer, "Army Contractors," *WMQ* 14: 39.

22. Peter Van Brugh Livingston to William Alexander, August 5, 6, 15, 26, 29, 1755, and Alexander to Livingston, September 7, 17, 1755, Stirling Papers, 1, NYHS; William Williams to Lord Loudoun, September 10, 1755; Loudoun Collection, Huntington Library; Thayer, "Army Contractors," *WMQ* 14: 39.

23. William Alexander to Peter Van Brugh Livingston, October 4, 1755, Stirling Papers, 1, NYHS; Pierre Rigaud de Vaudreuil to Baron de Dieskau, August 15, 1755, O'Callaghan and Fernow, eds., *Documents,* 10: 327–30; Gipson, *British Empire,* 6: 157; Leach, *Arms for Empire,* 373.

24. William Alexander to Peter Van Brugh Livingston, July 22, August 31, September 17, November 10, 1755, Livingston to Alexander, September 8, 13, 14, 22, November 4, 17, 19, 1755, Abraham Martier to Livingston, October 9, 1755, Stirling Papers, 1, NYHS; Alexander to Livingston, March 28, 1756, Rutherfurd Collection, 3, NYHS; Thayer, "Army Contractors," *WMQ* 14: 41.

25. William Alexander to Peter Van Brugh Livingston, August 31, September 7, October 4, 1755, to James Stevenson, September 2, 1755, Stevenson to Alexander, September 5, 1755, Peter Van Brugh Livingston to Alexander, October 16, 1755, Stirling Papers, 1, NYHS; Alexander to William Williams, September 6, 11, 1755, Loudoun Collection, Huntington Library; Alexander to Messrs. Corn. and John Cuyler, January 2, 1756, to James Stevenson, January 3, 1756, to Abram Dow, January 4, 1756, to James Stevenson, January 3, 1756, to John Petrie, January 5, 1756, William Alexander (Lord Stirling) Papers, New York Public Library, hereafter Stirling Papers, NYPL; Pargellis, *Loudoun,* 149.

26. George Demler's Report on Oswego, May 28, 1756, Loudoun Collection, Huntington Library, cited in Thayer, "Army Contractors," *WMQ* 14: 40.

27. Lord Loudoun to Duke of Cumberland, October 3, November 12, 1756, William Williams to Loudoun, September 10, 1756, Loudoun Collection, Huntington Library; Stanley Pargellis, ed., *Military Affairs in North America, 1748–1765: Selected Documents from the Cumberland Papers in Windsor Castle* (New York, 1936), 268; Account of William Alexander & Company with Francis Lewis, Oswego, May 1, 1756, Colonial Office, 5/46, f. 487, cited in Pargellis, *Loudoun,* 54, quote, 155; "Calendar of the Emmet Collection," New York Public Library, *Bulletin* (New York, 1900), 165.

28. Notes by William Alexander in Defense of Himself and General Shirley, September 15, 1756, Stirling Papers, 2, NYHS. These notes were written by Alexander in response to a "voluminus pamphlet" attacking Shirley and his aides, published by Lewis Evans in early 1756. See Alexander to William Smith, Jr., March 23, 1756 (ibid.).

29. Alexander's Notes of Defense, September 15, 1756, Peter Van Brugh Livingston and Lewis Morris, Memorial to Lord Loudoun, December 5, 1756, Petition of William Alexander, John Erving, Jr., Lewis Morris, Jr., and Peter Van Brugh Livingston to the Right Honourable the Lords Commissioners of His Majesty's Treasury, [July 1757], Stirling Papers, 2, NYHS; Schutz, *Shirley,* 236–43; John A. Schutz, *Thomas Pownall, British Defender of American Liberty: A Study of Anglo-American Relations in the Eighteenth Century* (Glendale, Calif., 1951), 59–70.

30. William Alexander to Colonel Otis, March 2, 1756, to William Smith, Jr., March 23, 1756, to Philip Schuyler, March 27, 1756, Stirling Papers, 2, NYHS; Alexander to Philip Van Brugh Livingston, March 22, May 9, 1756, Rutherfurd Collection, 3, NYHS; Alexander to Robert Hunter Morris, June 8, 1756, Robert Hunter Morris Papers, 2, 74, New Jersey Historical Society, hereafter Morris Papers, NJHS; Robert Rogers, *Journals* (London, 1765), entry of March 15, 1756, 13–14.

31. William Alexander, undated note fragment, and to William Smith, Jr., March 23, 1756, Stirling Papers, 2, NYHS; Alexander to Peter Van Brugh Livingston, March 28, 1756, Rutherfurd Collection, 3, NYHS.

32. William Alexander to Peter Van Brugh Livingston, March 15, April 5, May 6, 8, 1756, Rutherfurd Collection, 3, NYHS.

33. W. A. Whitehead, et al., eds., *Archives of the State of New Jersey, 1631–1800* (30 vols., Newark, etc., 1880–1949), 1st ser., 9: 274, 17: 60–61, hereafter *New Jersey Archives;* Edgar Jacob Fisher, *New Jersey as a Royal Province, 1738 to 1776* (New York, 1911), 57–66. Alexander's appointment to the Council of New Jersey was approved by the Privy Council on April 1, 1758. W. L. Grant and James Munro, eds., *Acts of the Privy Council of England: Colonial Series* (6 vols., London, 1908), 4: 371.

34. William Alexander to Lord Loudoun, August 5, 15, 1756, Loudoun Collection, Huntington Library; William Shirley to Loudoun, September 13, 1756, Lincoln, ed., *Shirley Correspondence,* 2: 556; Francis Parkman, *Montcalm and Wolfe* (2 vols., Boston, 1884), 1: 422ff; Pargellis, *Loudoun,* 148ff; Gipson, *British Empire,* 6: 196ff.

35. William Shirley to Robert Hunter Morris, July 5, 1756, Lincoln, ed., *Shirley Correspondence,* 2: 481n; William Alexander's Inventory, 1756, Stirling Papers, 2, NYHS.

Chapter 3

1. Miller, ed., *Minutes, Board of Proprietors,* 3: 338; *Journal of the Commissioners for Trade and Plantations* (14 vols., London, 1920–38), 10: 261; William Cobbett and John Wright, eds., *The Parliamentary History of England* (36 vols., London, 1806–20), 27: 683, 686, 706, 724, 752, 754, 760, 761, 762–68, 778; Pargellis, *Loud-*

oun, 295; Schutz, *Shirley,* 82. Acting as agent for the Board of Proprietors of New Jersey, Alexander was present in 1760 at the signing of an agreement between the Penns and Baltimores that settled the boundary between Pennsylvania and Maryland (Alexander to Lewis Morris, July 7, 1760, Papers on Science, American Philosophical Society Library, hereafter Papers on Science, APSL).

2. Alexander Colden to Cadwallader Colden, July 12, 1757, *Cadwallader Colden Papers,* New-York Historical Society Collections, 49–56 (New York, 1917–23), 5: 158–60, hereafter *Cadwallader Colden Papers;* Wroth, *American Bookshelf,* 54–55; Smith, *History of New York,* 2: 223. The complete title of the pro-Shirley pamphlet is *Review of the Military Operations in North-America, from the Commencement of the French Hostilities in the Frontiers of Virginia in 1753, to the Surrender of Oswego, on the 14th of August, 1756; in a Letter to a Nobleman* (1757), reprinted in Massachusetts Historical Society Collections, 7 (Boston, 1801), 67–163.

3. William Alexander to Andrew Stuart, April 24, 1758, Stirling Papers, 2, NYHS.

4. Petition of William Alexander, July 1757, Stirling Papers, 2, NYHS, Memorial by William Shirley, n.d., Report of the Paymaster General and Secretary of War, November 1, 1757, and J. West, Treasury Chambers, to Auditor of Imprests, January 27, 1758, Stirling Papers, 2, NYHS.

5. Thomas Farraine to William Alexander, December 12, 1759, Alexander to Samuel Martin, August 3, 1760, Martin to Alexander, January 28, 1761, Stirling Papers, 2, NYHS; Alexander's "Answers" in a suit against his partner, Peter Van Brugh Livingston, July 1, 1768, Stirling Papers, 3, NYHS, and Records, Court of Chancery, Albany, New York, cited in Edward Floyd Delancey's notes to Thomas Jones, *History of New York During the Revolutionary War,* ed. Edward Floyd DeLancey (2 vols., New York, 1879), 2: 50–81.

6. William Alexander to Major Walter Rutherfurd, December 7, 1759, Rutherfurd Collection, 3, NYHS; Alexander to Gouverneur Morris, November 10, 1759, Stirling Papers, NYPL.

7. William Alexander to William Turnbull, February 23, 1760, Stirling Papers, 3, NYHS. Much of Alexander's correspondence with these men has been lost. Someone collected it as well as his letters to George Washington to be laid aside for greater security, and the entire bundle disappeared (Duer, *Stirling,* xiii–xiv). A few letters survive, but most of the information we now have on Alexander's relationships with persons in Britain is gleaned from hints, snippets, and suggestions from a variety of sources. The newspaper account is quoted in Trevelyan, *American Revolution,* 2: 176n.

8. Patrick Graeme to William Alexander, February 3, 1758, Alexander to Graeme, April 24, 1758, John Penn to Alexander, October 9, 1761, Staats Morris to Alexander, January 18, 1758, Stirling Papers, 2, 3, NYHS; Benson J. Lossing, *The Life and Times of Philip Schuyler* (2 vols., New York, 1860–72), 1: 183.

9. Duchess of Gordon to William Alexander, February 3, 1758, Alexander to Andrew Stuart, April 24, June 3, 1758, Duke of Argyle to Alexander, July 20, 1758, Charles Townshend to Alexander, October 1, 1758, Alexander to Stuart, [October or November] 1758, Stirling Papers, 2, NYHS.

10. William Alexander to Robert Hunter Morris, November 10, 1759, Stirling Papers, NYPL; William Shirley to Duke of Newcastle, June 8, 1759, Lincoln, ed., *Shirley Correspondence,* 2: 604–5.

11. William Alexander to William Trumbull, November 9, 1759, Stirling Papers, 3, NYHS; Petition of William Alexander, Lord Stirling . . . before the Privy Council, June 12, 1760, Colonial Society of Massachusetts Publications (50 vols. to date, Boston, 1895–), 24: 207–9; Grant and Munro, eds., *Acts of Privy Council,* 4: 457–58; John Lord Hayes, *Vindication of the Rights and Titles, Political and Territorial, of Alexander, Earl of Stirling and Dovan and Lord Proprietor of Canada and Nova Scotia* (Washington, 1853), 38.

12. Alexander Colden to Cadwallader Colden, July 12, 1757, *Cadwallader Colden Papers,* 5: 158–60.

13. William Alexander to Mr. Dagge, August 16, 1757, to Andrew Stuart, February 24, April 24, June 3, 1758, to Patrick Graeme, April 24, 1758, Stuart to Alexander, September 15, October 14, 25, 27, 29, December 3, 1757, April 5, 8, 12, 1758, Stirling Papers, 2, NYHS.

14. William Alexander to Andrew Stuart, June 3, August 29, 1758, Stuart to Alexander, June 6, 27, July 6, August 19, 22, 29, October 5, December 5, 12, 1758, March 24, 28, 1759, Stuart to Alexander Wedderburne, March 10, 1759, William Trumbull to Alexander, April 11, 1759, James Porteus to Alexander, April 21, 1759, Stirling Papers, 2, NYHS; Charles Rogers, *Memorials of the Earl of Stirling and the House of Alexander* (2 vols., Edinburgh, 1877), 1: 282–83.

15. Andrew Stuart to William Alexander, March 28, 1759, Stirling Papers, 2, NYHS.

16. Andrew Stuart to William Alexander, September 11, October 10, 1759, Alexander to Stuart, October 27, 1759, Stirling Papers, 2, 3, NYHS.

17. Andrew Stuart to William Alexander, May 16, 1760, Alexander to Stuart, June 22, 1760, Henry Digge to Henry Drummond, April 10, 1762, Drummond to Alexander, April 10, May 21, 1762, Stirling Papers, 3, NYHS; *Journals of the House of Lords* (46 vols., London, n.d.), 29: 667, 30: 92–93, 110, 131–32, 186. As late as 1763, Alexander was trying to get the House of Lords to recognize his title by signing "Stirling" to some business papers of the New Jersey Council that must go from the Board of Trade to Parliament. The Lords refused "to act on a bill so stiled" and would not even accept "William Alexander claiming to be Earl of Stirling" (Henry Wilmot to Alexander, November 25, 1763, Stirling Papers, 3, NYHS).

18. Andrew Stuart to William Alexander, December 5, 12, 1758, Alexander to William Trumbull, November 9, 1759, February 7, 1760, Trumbull to Alexander,

December 13, 1759, February 21, 1706, William Philipps Lee to Alexander, January 12, 1760, Alexander to Lee, February 7, 1760, Stirling Papers, 3, NYHS.

19. William Bollan to Andrew Oliver, February 12, 1762, *Jasper Mauduit, Agent in London for the Province of Massachusetts-Bay, 1762–1765,* Massachusetts Historical Society Collections, 84 (Boston, 1918), 27, hereafter *Mauduit;* Alexander to Lewis Morris, July 7, 1760, Papers on Science, APSL; Grant and Munro, eds., *Acts of Privy Council,* 4: 457–58; Colonial Society of Massachusetts Publications, 24: 239–40.

20. James Porteous to William Alexander, April 21, 1759, Stirling Papers, 2, NYHS.

21. William Philipps Lee to William Alexander, July 16, 1760, John Penn to Alexander, October 9, 1761, Thomas Hasley to Alexander, October 15, 1761, Stirling Papers, 3, NYHS; Alexander to Lewis Morris, July 7, 1760, Papers on Science, APSL.

Chapter 4

1. Freeman, *Washington,* 6: 212–13.

2. Will of Mary Alexander, July 27, 1756, Liber G, 199–210, New Jersey Colonial Documents, New Jersey State Library; Duer, *Stirling,* 262; Stirling to Lord Bute, April 1, 1762, Thomas Hawley to Stirling, October 15, 1763, Stirling Papers, 3, NYHS. In 1765, Stirling realized a profit of £1,333 on the sale of New Jersey lands in Hunterdon County that he had invested in thirteen years before (Charles W. Parker, "Shipley: The County Seat of a Jersey Loyalist," New Jersey Historical Proceedings, new series, 16 (1931), 117–18).

3. Eliza Susan Morton Quincy, *Memoir of the Life of Eliza S. M. Quincy* (Boston, 1861), 23–24; *New Jersey Archives,* 2d ser., 1: 66; New Jersey Historical Society Proceedings, new series, 4: 133–34, 5: 125–26; Henry Mulman to Stirling, October 27, 1761, Thomas Hartley to Stirling, June 12, 1762, Stirling Papers, 3, NYHS; Stirling to Richard Peters, February 14, 1763, The Dreer Collection: Revolutionary Generals, Historical Society of Pennsylvania, hereafter Dreer Collection, HSP; Andrew D. Mellick, Jr., *The Story of an Old Farm, or Life in New Jersey in the Eighteenth Century* (Somerville, N.J., 1889), 402; Thomas Balch, ed., *The Journal of Claude Blanchard, Commisary of the French Auxiliary Army Sent to the United States during the American Revolution, 1780–1783,* tr. William Duane (Albany, 1876), 133; Ludwig Schumacher, *The Somerset Hills* (New York, 1900), 75; James P. Snell, *History of Hunterdon and Somerset Counties* (Philadelphia, 1881), 421. According to Thomas Jones, a scathing critic of Stirling, the earl brought with him from England "a valet de chambre, a butler, a steward, a friseur, a cook, a coachman, and a mistress." I am unable to verify his claims, despite diligent—and hopeful—search. In any case, said Jones,

when Stirling later fell into debt, "he was obliged to retrench. The valet went first, then the friseur, next the butler, then the coachman, at last the cook, and madam finding cash low, prudently returned to England" (Jones, *History,* 2: 322). It *is* verified that when Stirling returned from England, he brought with him "fifteen cases of household goods" (Thomas Hasley to Stirling, October 15, 1761, Stirling Papers, 3, NYHS).

4. On Stirling's library: List of Goods Sold at Baskenridge in Vendue Sale, November 23, 28–29, 1775, April 22–24, 1776, Park Collection, Morristown National Historical Park, hereafter Park Collection, Morristown. On his wardrobe: Ned O. Howlett, "Lord Stirling in Basking Ridge," New Jersey Historical Society Proceedings, new series, 15 (1930): 266. On viniculture: Stirling to Lord Shelburne, August 6, 1763, Stirling Papers, 3, NYHS; Sworn Statement of Thomas Burgie, Principal Gardener of Right Hon. The Earl of Stirling, October 6, 1766, before Fre. Smyth, Chief Justice, Province of New Jersey, in Selected Materials Relating to America, 1754–1806, Royal Society of Arts, London, copy, American Philosophical Society Library, cited by permission of the RSA, hereafter Selected Materials, RSA; Derek Hudson and Kenneth W. Lockhurst, *The Royal Society of Arts, 1754–1954* (London, 1954), 163; Richard P. McCormick, "The Society, the Grape, and New Jersey (i–ii)," *Journal of the Royal Society of Arts* 110 (January 1962, March 1962): 119–120; Carl Raymond Woodward, *Ploughs and Politicks: Charles Read of New Jersey and His Notes on Agriculture, 1751–1774* (New Brunswick, 1941), 264.

5. Stirling to Lord Bute, April 1, 1762, Stirling Papers, 3, NYHS.

6. Stirling to Lord Shelburne, August 6, 1763, Stirling Papers, 3, NYHS; Oliver M. Dickerson, *The Navigation Acts and the American Revolution* (Philadelphia, 1951), 118.

7. Cadwallader Colden to Majors of New York, February 17, 1762, *Colden Papers,* 1: 165; Smith, *History,* 2: 271; Jeffery Amherst to Stirling, June 19, 1763, Stirling Papers, 3, NYHS.

8. Stirling to Thomas Harley, April 1, 1762, to Governor William Franklin, January 30, 1764, Harley to Stirling, June 12, 1762, Henry Wilmot to Stirling, September 27, 1766, Stirling Papers, 3, NYHS; Joseph Sherwood to Samuel Smith, June 16, 1761, Joseph Sherwood Letters, New Jersey Historical Society, hereafter Sherwood Letters, NJHS; William Franklin to Benjamin Franklin, November 13, [1766], Benjamin Franklin Papers, 42: 3, American Philosophical Society Library, hereafter Franklin Papers, APSL; Woodward, *Read,* 20; Jack M. Sosin, *Agents and Merchants: British Colonial Policy and the Origins of the American Revolution, 1763–1775* (Lincoln, Neb., 1965), 68n; Larry R. Gerlach, *Prologue to Independence: New Jersey in the Coming of the American Revolution* (New Brunswick, 1976), 138; Fisher, *New Jersey,* 99; Edward P. Alexander, *A Revolutionary Conservative: James Duane of New York* (New York, 1938), 70.

9. John Penn to Stirling, September 3, 1762, Stirling Papers, 3, NYHS;

Stirling to Benjamin Franklin, November 12, 1755, Emmet Collection, New York Public Library, hereafter Emmet Collection, NYPL; Peter Collison to Benjamin Franklin, October 21, 1762, Labaree and Willcox, eds., *Franklin Papers,* 10: 151; *New Jersey Archives,* 1st ser., 18: 135; Lamb, *New York,* 1: 705.

10. Minutes of Councils of New York, September 4, October 23, November 6, 1765, *Cadwallader Colden Papers,* 7: 59–71; Council Meeting, November 13, Lamb, *New York,* 1: 730–31.

11. Assembly Meeting of New Jersey in Burlington, May 21, 1765, discussed in Donald L. Klemmerer, *Path to Freedom: The Struggle for Self-Government in Colonial New Jersey, 1703–1776* (Princeton, 1940), 281; Stirling to William Franklin, November 6, 1765, *New Jersey Archives,* ser. 1, 17: 437–38; Gerlach, *Prologue,* 121. Lundin, *Cockpit,* 88, aruges that Stirling was being crassly expedient in the stamp affair. Perhaps so, but to me the evidence shows him being simply neutral.

12. Lundin, *Cockpit,* 88; John Wolfe Lydekker, *The Life and Letters of Charles Inglis* (London, 1936), 127, 151n; William Franklin to Stirling, April 2, 1767, Walter Rutherfurd to Stirling, May 29, 1767, Stirling to Archibald Kennedy, December 16, 1767, Stirling Papers, 3, NYHS; Council Meeting, March 15, 1765, William Johnson to Stirling, March 23, 1773, Sullivan, et al., eds., *Johnson Papers,* 4: 683–84, 8: 742–43; Gerald Bancker to Stirling, January 9, 26, 28, 1769, John Stevens to Stirling, January 28, 1769, Peter Hansklever to Stirling, September 1, 1769, Stirling Papers, NYPL; Council Meetings, Lord Stirling's House, January 26, April 7, 1774, Sabine, ed., *Smith,* 1: 169; Speech by Lord Stirling to New Jersey Council, March 20, 1770, *New Jersey Archives,* ser. 1, 27: 106–8, 114–16.

13. Philip Livingston to Stirling, October 25, 1762, Henry Clinton to Stirling, November 22, 1762, Thomas Gage to Stirling, July 26, 1767, Daniel Coxe to Stirling, October 27, 1767, Stirling Papers, 3, NYHS; Walter Barland to Stirling, December 14, 17, 1767, Stirling Papers, NYPL; Henry Clinton to Stirling, [1764], Sir Henry Clinton Papers, William L. Clements Library, hereafter Clinton Papers, Clements Library.

14. William Amherst to Stirling, October 11, 1763, Stirling to _____, January 7, 1768, Stirling Papers, 3, NYHS; Benjamin Franklin to Deborah Franklin, June 16, 1763, Labaree and Willcox, eds., *Franklin Papers,* 10: 290; Gerlach, *Prologue,* 28; Van Doren, *Franklin,* 305.

15. James Rivington to Stirling, January 7, 1767, Stirling Papers, 3, NYHS; Jackson, ed., *Washington Diaries,* 3: 180–81; Joseph Jackson, "Washington in Philadelphia," *PMHB* 56 (1932), 116–17; Harry Emerson Wildes, *Anthony Wayne: Trouble Shooter of the American Revolution* (New York, 1941), 30; Joseph Chew to George Washington, March 10, 1774, Stanislaus Murray Hamilton, ed., *Letters to Washington and Accompanying Papers* (5 vols., Boston, 1892–1902), 4: 351–53.

16. Columbia University, *Minutes of the Governors of the College of the Province of New York in the City of New York in America, 1755–1768* (New York, 1932), entry of April 15, 1762, no page number; *Catalogue of Officers and Graduates of Columbia*

University, from the Foundation of King's College in 1754 (New York, 1916), 12; Stirling to Lord Romney, President, Society for Preservation of Arts, May 22, 1762, to Lord Bute, May 24, 1762, to Henry Drummond, May 24, 1762, Stirling Papers, 3, NYHS. James Jay's efforts were so strenuous for King's College that he even engaged the support of George III in his canvass for funds, and he collected ten thousand pounds. The college received the money, but only after it had prematurely instigated a lawsuit against Jay and turned him against the Board of Governors. Stirling's role in this affair is unknown, although Jay thought Stirling supportive enough to solicit the earl's assistance when the board was deciding his case (see Jay to Stirling, June 2, 1773, Stirling Papers, 3, NYHS, and Milton Halsey Thomas, "Sir James Jay," *DAB*, 10: 4–5).

17. Richard Peters to Stirling, November 1, 1761, Stirling Papers, 3, NYHS; Stirling to Peters, November 9, December 29, 1761, Richard Peters Papers, 5: 105, 109, Historical Society of Pennsylvania, hereafter Peters Papers, HSP; Stirling to Peter Templeton, Chief Secretary, Royal Society of Arts, July 21, 1765, enclosed in Benjamin Franklin to Same, October 19, 1766, Selected Materials, RSA; Woodward, *Read*, 49. The Paper on Venus is in NYHS; the one on the compass in Papers on Science, APSL.

18. John E. O'Connor, *William Paterson: Lawyer and Statesman, 1745–1806* (New Brunswick, 1979), 32, 108; Richard Haskett, "William Paterson, Attorney General of New Jersey: Public Office and Private Profit in the American Revolution," *William and Mary Quarterly*, 3d ser., 7 (1950): 29; John Emley to Stirling, June 27, 1769, Stirling Papers, NYPL. On Stirling's flax and timber ventures, see Agreement with Justice Edw. Lewis, November 9, 1767, Stirling Papers, 3, NYHS.

19. Records of Stirling's land deals are in the collections of Princeton University Library; the Park and Lloyd W. Smith (hereafter Smith) Collections of Morristown; the Emmet Collection, NYPL; and the New Jersey Manuscripts of New Jersey Historical Society. Bills to Stirling are in the Stirling Papers, 3, NYHS, and NYPL. For money owed Stirling, see a bill of February 11, 1772, Burton Historical Collection, Detroit Public Library, and William Johnson to Goldsbrow Banyan, February 10, 1769, Sullivan, et al., eds., *Johnson Papers*, 12: 697. For Henry Drummond's comments, see his letter to Stirling, April 10, 1762, Stirling Papers, 3, NYHS. Job Stockton to Stirling, July 11, 1769, Stirling Papers, 3, NYHS.

20. Lewis Morris to Stirling, August 14, 21, 1768, Whitehead Hicks to Stirling, March 10, 1770, William Livingston to Stirling, May 7, 1770, Stirling to William Smith, Jr., August 18, 1770, and to James Duane, August 18, 1770, Stirling's Statement in a Suit with his Partner, P. V. B. Livingston, July 1, 1768, Stirling Papers, 3, NYHS; Records, Court of Chancery, Albany, cited in DeLancey's notes to Jones, *History*, 2: 581–82.

21. Stirling to Francis Bernard, August 10, 1768, enclosing Stirling's Adver-

tisement, July 20, 1768, Colonial Society of Massachusetts, *Publications* 24: 239–40; Andrew Oliver to Jasper Mauduit, April 24, 1762, *Mauduit,* 35; Stirling to Jared Ingersoll, July 25, 1768, Jared Ingersoll Papers, New Haven Colony Historical Society; Lawrence Henry Gipson, *Jared Ingersoll: A Study of American Loyalism in Relation to British Colonial Government* (New Haven, 1920), 232n.

22. Massachusetts Council Meeting, September 7, 1768, Colonial Society of Massachusetts, *Publications* 24: 240–42; Grant and Munro, eds., *Acts of Privy Council,* 5: 220. See also William Willis and James Phinney Baxter, eds., *Documentary History of the State of Maine* (24 vols., Portland, 1869–1916), 3: 111 n, 4: 195–96, 253, 342–43, 7: 305, 311.

23. Stirling to Robert Hunter Morris, December 1, 1754, Penn Papers, 6: 243, HSP; Stirling to Lord Shelburne, August 6, 1763, Garret Rapage to Stirling, March 30, 1767, Stirling Papers, 2, NYHS; Charles S. Boyer, *Early Forges and Furnaces in New Jersey* (Philadelphia, 1931), 93; John B. Pearse, *Concise History of the Iron Manufacture of the American Colonies Up to the Revolution* (Philadelphia, 1876), 53; George H. Danforth, "Lord Stirling's Hibernia Furnace," New Jersey Historical Society Proceedings, 71 (1953), 177.

24. William Neilson to Stirling, January 15, 1770, Stirling's Accounts with William Neilson, 1771–72, James Alexander Papers, 1, 11, NYHS; Samuel Allinson, ed., *Acts of the General Assembly of the Province of New Jersey, 1702–1776* (Burlington, 1776), 319, 338; Victor S. Clark, *History of Manufactures in the United States* (3 vols., New York, 1929), 1: 45.

25. Joseph Hoff to Stirling, November 8, 27, December 10, 1773, Park Collection, Morristown; Agreement Between Lord Stirling and William Neilson, November 3, 1773, to Stirling, December 23, 1773, January 13, 1774, Stirling Papers, 3, 4, NYHS; Stirling to Elias Deaton, December 15, 1773, Edwin A. Ely Autograph Collection, New Jersey Historical Society, hereafter Ely Collection, NJHS.

26. Stirling to Daniel Cooper, January 1, 1774, Agreement, January 19, 1774, Samuel Ogden to Stirling, December 3 (2 letters), 4, 1773, Stirling to Ogden, December 11, 1773, Stirling Papers, 3, 4, NYHS; Stirling's Notice of Sole Ownership, dated January 26, 1774, *Rivington's New York Gazeteer,* February 3, 1774, cited in *New Jersey Archives,* 1st ser., 29: 255; Danforth, "Stirling's Hibernia Furnace," New Jersey Historical Society Proceedings, 71: 182.

27. Joseph Hoff to Stirling, June 2, 1774, William Franklin to Stirling, May 3, 1774, Stirling Papers, 4, NYHS; Account of Stirling-Ogden confrontation, n.d., James Alexander Papers, 16, NYHS; Hoff to Stirling, May 2, 21, 1775, Park Collection, Morristown; Samuel Ogden to Jonathan D. Sergeant, February 19, 1775, General Manuscripts, Princeton University Library; *New Jersey Archives,* 1st ser., 18: 366–69, 511–18, 522, 23.

28. Stirling Memorandum, October 4, 1774, Stirling Papers, 4, NYHS; Stirling's List of Movables, December 10, 1774, James Alexander Papers, 11,

NYHS; Joseph Hoff to Stirling, June 19, November 14, 1776, October 23, 1777, March 20, July 10, 1778, Park Collection, Morristown; Lease between Stirling and John Jacob Faesch, November 8, 1779, Charles Hoff to Stirling, July 5, 1780, Daughters of the American Revolution, Nova Caesarea Collection, New Jersey Historical Society; Thomas M. Doerflinger, "Hibernia Furnace During the Revolution," *New Jersey History* 90 (1972): 100.

29. Hugh Wallace to Stirling, January 6, 1772, James Alexander Papers, 1, NYHS; E. M. Morris, *The Story of Princeton* (Boston, 1917), 41–43. For lottery statistics, see *New York Gazette,* April 12, 1773, April 3, 1775, and *New Jersey Archives,* 1st ser., 28: 485–86, 31: 101–2.

30. Stirling to Samuel Allinson, March 9, 1772, Samuel Allinson Papers, Rutgers University Library, hereafter Allinson Papers, Rutgers; Stirling to James Hamilton, November 22, 1772, Etting Collection, 3: 14, HSP; Stirling to W. & T. Bradford, June 11, 1773, Dreer Collection, HSP; Stirling to John Penn, May 5, 1772, Huntington Library; U. Scott to Stirling, May 20, 1772, William Kelly to Stirling, December 8, 1772, Henry Cruger to Stirling, January 22, 1773, Stirling Papers, 3, NYHS.

31. *New York Journal,* September 9, 16, 23, 30, October 28, November 4, 11, 1773; *New York Gazette,* April 12, September 27, 1773; *Rivington's New York Gazeteer,* March 14, 1774; Stirling to James Hamilton, November 22, 1772, Etting Collection, 3: 14, HSP; Washington's diary, entries, January 2, 4, 1772, Jackson, ed., *Washington Diaries,* 3: 153–54.

32. *New York Gazette,* November 1, 1773; *Rivington's New York Gazeteer,* March 17, 1774; *New Jersey Archives,* 29: 79; Memorandum, March 14, 1774, James Alexander Papers, Box 12, NYHS.

33. Stirling to William Smith, Hugh Wallace, John Harris, etc., August 14, 1774, *New York Gazette,* August 22, 1774, *Pennsylvania Journal,* August 31, September 28, 1774; *Rivington's New York Gazeteer,* September 15, 1774; *Pennsylvania Gazeteer,* October 12, 1774, Stirling to George Washington, October 31, 1774, George Washington Papers, Library of Congress, hereafter Washington Papers, LC; Washington to Stirling, January 20, 1775, Fitzpatrick, ed., *Washington Papers,* 3: 264–65; *New Jersey Archives,* 1st ser., 29: 101–2, 465, 481, 488, 492–95; *New York Gazette,* April 3, 1775; DeLancey's notes in Jones, *History,* 2: 586.

34. DeLancey's notes in Jones, *History,* 2: 324; Stirling to Hugh Wallace, October 26, 1775, Wallace to Stirling, November 13, 1775, Stirling Papers, 4: NYHS.

35. Stirling to Philip Livingston, October 27, 1775, Cortlandt Skinner to Stirling, November 15, 22, 1775, Cornelius Blanchard to Stirling, March 11, 1775, Stirling Papers, 4: NYHS; *Minutes of the Provincial Congress and the Council of Safety of the State of New Jersey* (Trenton, 1879), December 22, 1775, January 12, 1776, 314, 336; List of Goods Sold at Baskenridge in Vendue Sale, November 23,

Notes to Chapter 5   193

28–29, 1775, April 22–24, 1776, Park Collection, Morristown; Lundin, *Cockpit*, 22n.

Chapter 5

1. *Minutes of New Jersey Council of Safety*, January 13, 18, 25, 26, February 13, 1775, 56–60.

2. Jones, *History*, 2: 323; Ambrose Serle to Earl of Dartmouth, September 5, 1776, Benjamin F. Stevens, ed., *Facsimiles of Manuscripts in European Archives Relating to America, 1773–1783* (25 vols., London, 1889–95), 24: 2042; Allinson, ed., *Acts of the General Assembly*, May 31, 1779; Duer, *Stirling*, 263.

3. Gerlach, *Prologue*, 286.

4. Stirling to William Franklin, September 25, 1775, Stirling Papers, 4, NYHS.

5. Eliphalet Dyer's quote in George E. Groce, Jr., "Eliphalet Dyer," Richard B. Morris, ed., *Era of the American Revolution: Studies Inscribed to Everts B. Greene* (New York, 1939), 300; Gerlach, *Prologue*, 286.

6. Charles Pettit to Stirling, September 7, 1775, Stirling Papers, 4, NYHS; Stirling to William Franklin, September 19, 1775, Park Collection, Morristown; *Minutes of New Jersey Council of Safety*, 212; Fisher, *New Jersey*, 465.

7. William Franklin to Stirling, September 15, 1775, Stirling to Franklin, September 25, 1775, Stirling Papers, 4, NYHS; Stirling to New Jersey Provincial Congress, October 4, 1775, with enclosures, and Franklin to Earl of Dartmouth, January 5, 1776, Peter Force, ed., *American Archives: A Documentary History of the Origin and Progress of the North American Colonies* (9 vols., Washington, D.C., 1837–53), 4th ser., 3: 1218, 1872.

8. Battalion Organization Charts, October 28 and n.d., 1775, William Livingston to Stirling, November 8, 1775, Stirling Papers, 4, NYHS; *Minutes of New Jersey Council of Safety*, October 28, 1775, 245; Worthington C. Ford, ed., *Journals of the Continental Congress, 1774–1789* (34 vols., Washington, D.C., 1904–37), 3: 335; Edmund C. Burnett, ed., *Letters of Members of the Continental Congress* (8 vols., Washington, D.C., 1921–38), 1: 250.

9. Stirling to William Maxwell and to William Winds, November 21, 1775, Stirling to Hendrick Fisher, November 28, 1775, Stirling Papers, 4, NYHS; Stirling to Congress, December 3, 1775, William Alexander, Lord Stirling Papers, Papers of the Continental Congress, no. 162, vol. 2, 329, hereafter PCC, 162; Ford, ed., *Journals of Congress*, 3: 335.

10. Stirling to Congress, December 3, 1775, enclosing Return of the Eastern or First Regiment of Foot of New-Jersey, in the Continental Service, December 2, 1775, Stirling Papers, PCC, 162, 2: 329–34.

11. John McKesson to Stirling, November 30, 1775, Nathaniel Woodhull to

Stirling, December 5, 1775, Joseph Hallet to Stirling, December 5, 1775, Stirling to Congress, December 5, 1775, Stirling Papers, PCC, 162, 2: 336–37, 340–41, 344–45, 402; Stirling to William Maxwell, December 2, 1775, Maxwell to Stirling, December 17, 1775, Stirling Papers, 4, NYHS; Stirling to New York Provincial Congress, December 4, 1775, Stirling to New York Committee of Safety, January 20, 1776, Committee of Safety to Stirling, January 25, 1776, Force, ed., *American Archives,* 4th ser., 4: 173, 1065, 1079.

12. Stirling to Captain John Polhemus, December 14, 1775, to Captain John Conway, December 14, 16, 1775, to Captain Elias Longstreet, December 16, 1775, William Winds to Stirling, December 7, 1775, William DeHart to Stirling, December 7, 1775, Samuel Tucker to Stirling, December 10, 16, 1775, Thomas Lowrey to Stirling, December 10, 1775, John Conway to Stirling, December 11, 1775, Joseph Morris to Stirling, December 11, 1775, John Polhemus to Stirling, December 15, 1775, William Livingston to Stirling, December 19, 1775, William Maxwell to Stirling, December 6, 17, 1775, PCC, 162, 2: 349, 352–54; Ford, ed., *Journals of Congress,* 413; Stirling to New Jersey Committee of Safety, December 12, 1775, President of Congress to Stirling, January 3, 1776, Force, ed., *American Archives,* 4th ser., 4: 246–47, 561.

13. Stirling to Congress, December 19, 1775, PCC, 162, 2: 356–57; Charles Lee to George Washington, January 5, 1776, Washington to Stirling, January 10, 1776, Washington Papers, LC; *Lee Papers,* 1: 235; Ford, ed., *Journals of Congress,* 4: 18; Allen French, *The First Year of the American Revolution* (Boston, 1934), 583–84. The regiment of New Jersey troops commanded by Colonel William Maxwell was sent to Albany in early 1776 (President of Congress to Stirling, January 10, 1776, Miscellaneous Manuscripts, Box 2, Library of Congress, hereafter Misc. MSS, LC; Stirling to Maxwell, January 18, 1776, PCC, 162, 2: 405.)

14. Stirling to Congress, January 6, 8, 1776, PCC, 162, 2: 359, 364.

15. Stirling to Congress, January 6, 8, 1776, PCC, 162, 2: 359, 364; William Franklin to Lord Dartmouth, January 7, 1776, Historical Manuscripts Commission, *The Manuscripts of the Earl of Dartmouth* (3 vols., London, 1887–99), 2: 411; Franklin to William Temple Franklin, January 22, 1776, Franklin Papers, 101: 10, APSL; Gerlach, *Prologue,* 309.

16. J. J. Boudinot, ed., *The Life, Public Services, Addresses, and Letters of Elias Boudinot* (2 vols., Boston, 1896), 1: 12; George Adams Boyd, *Elias Boudinot, Patriot and Statesman* (New York, 1952), 27–28; Stirling to Congress, January 8, 10, 11, 1776, PCC, 162, 2: 360, 364, 372; Ford, ed., *Journals of Congress,* 4: 42; Gerlach, *Prologue,* 310.

17. Stirling to New York Committee of Safety, January 12, 1776, New York Committee of Safety to Stirling, January 17, 1776, New Jersey Provincial Congress to Stirling, February 5, 1776, Force, ed., *American Archives,* 4th ser., 4: 655, 965–66, 1053–1054; Charles Lee to George Washington, January 16, 1776, *Lee*

Papers, 1: 240; Stirling to Samuel Tucker, February 2, 1776, to Congress, February 5, 1776, PCC, 162, 2: 398–99, 404–5; *Minutes of New Jersey Council of Safety,* February 5, 1776, 347–48; Danforth, "Rebel Earl," 202.

18. New York Committee of Safety to Stirling, January 21, 22, 1776, Stirling to Robert Ogden, February 9, 1776, Stirling to John Blanchard, February 9, 1776, Blanchard to Stirling, February 15, 1776, Samuel Tucker to Stirling, March 4, 1776, Force, ed., *American Archives,* 4th ser., 4: 795–96, 1065, 1199–1200, 5: 55; Stirling to Congress, January 24, 27, February 19, 1776, PCC, 162, 2: 384–85, 388, 442–43; Copy, Bill of Lading, *Blue Mountain Valley,* Made 30 Sept. 1776, Burton Historical Collection, Detroit Public Library; Ford, ed., *Journals of Congress,* 4: 100; President of Congress to Stirling, February 2, 1776, Benson J. Lossing Papers, Historical Society of Pennsylvania, hereafter Lossing Papers, HSP; Stirling to Cornelius Blanchard, March 8, 1776, Stirling Papers, 4, NYHS.

19. Stirling to Charles Lee, February 4, 1776, Lee to George Washington, February 14, 19, 1776, *Lee Papers,* 1: 271, 295, 309; Stirling to Congress, February 5, 9, 19, 1776, PCC, 162, 2: 408, 416, 442–43.

20. Henry Knox to Lucy Knox, January 5, 1776, Henry Knox Papers, Massachusetts Historical Society, hereafter Knox Papers, MHS; North Callahan, *Henry Knox: General Washington's General* (New York, 1958), 38–39; Charles Lee to Congress, February 22, 1776, Lee to George Washington, February 14, 29, 1776, *Lee Papers,* 1: 295, 322, 335–38; Rhinelander cited in Thomas J. Wertenbaker, *Father Knickerbocker Rebels: New York During the Revolution* (New York, 1948), 71.

21. Stirling to New York Committee of Safety, February 5, 20, 1776, New York Provincial Congress to Stirling, February 20, 1776, New York Committee of Safety to Stirling, February 20, 1776, Stirling to Colonel Thomas Lowrey, February 19, 1776, Force, ed., *American Archives,* 4th ser., 4: 1109, 1200–1201, 5: 233, 239; Stirling to Congress, February 3, 19, 1776, PCC, 162, 2: 428, 442–43. For information on civil-military tensions in New York at this time, and for the quote "skittish members of Congress," see Roger J. Champagne's fine biography, *Alexander McDougall and the American Revolution in New York* (Schenectady, 1975), 104.

22. John Adams to James Warren, February 18, 1776, *Warren-Adams Letters,* Massachusetts Historical Society Collections, 72–73 (Boston, 1917–25), 1: 208, hereafter *Warren-Adams Letters;* Charles Lee to George Washington, March 3, 1776, Jared Sparks, ed., *Correspondence of the American Revolution* (4 vols. Boston, 1853), 1: 161; Ford, ed., *Journals of Congress,* 4: 181; James Duane to Stirling, March 1, 1776, Stirling Papers, 4, NYHS; President of Congress to Stirling, March 1, 1776, Burnett, ed., *Letters,* 1, 370; Stirling to Congress, March 3, 1776, PCC, 162, 2: 428. When Stirling received his promotion and de facto command of New York, he offered, through Elisha Boudinot, the position of

brigade major in his "family" (or staff) to a young New Yorker named Alexander Hamilton. Boudinot, thinking Hamilton would be delighted with the news, hastened to inform the young man of his good fortune. But Hamilton turned him down coldly, on the grounds that he wanted to fight and expected soon to receive a colonelcy in the militia. Not wanting to offend Stirling, Elisha Boudinot wrote him on March 10 that "M. Hamilton had already accepted the command of Artillery, and was therefore deprived of the pleasure of attending your Lordship's person" (Stirling Papers, 4, NYHS; Nathan Schachner, *Alexander Hamilton* [New York, 1946], 46).

23. Stirling to New Jersey Provincial Congress, March 3, 1776, to Elias Dayton, March 10, 1776, to Philip Schuyler, March 10, 1776, Stirling Papers, 4, NYHS; Stirling to George Washington, March 11, 1776, Washington Papers, LC.

24. Stirling to Philip Schuyler, March 10, 1776, to New Jersey Provincial Congress, March 2, 3, 5, 1776, to Colonel _____ Ward, March 8, 1776, New Jersey Provincial Congress to Stirling, March 4, 7, 9, 1776, Stirling Papers, 4, NYHS; Stirling to New Jersey Provincial Congress, February 20, 1776, Force, ed., *American Archives,* 4th ser., 4: 1597; *Minutes of New Jersey Council of Safety,* February 21, 1776, 380–81; Stirling to Congress, March 10, 1776, PCC, 162, 2: 447–48; Stirling to George Washington, March 11, 1776, Washington Papers, LC.

25. Minutes, New York Provincial Congress, March 13, 1776, Regulations Agreed to Between . . . Stirling and a Committee of the Provincial Congress of New York to Defend New York City, [March 13, 1776], Stephen Moylan to Stirling, March 8, 1776, Force, ed., *American Archives,* 4th ser., 5: 374–75, 459–60; Stirling to Congress, March 13, 14, 16, 1776, PCC, 162, 2: 455–56, 457, 567–68; Moylan to Stirling, March 9, 1776, Stirling to George Washington, March 15, 1776, Washington Papers, LC.

26. Stirling to Congress, March 13, 14, 1776, to Lieutenant Colonel Allen, Commander, 2d Pennsylvania Regiment, March 13, 1776, PCC, 162, 2: 455–56, 457, 462; Stirling to Committees of Safety of Morris, Essex, Middlesex, Somerset, Sussex, Hunterdon, Bergen, and Monmouth Counties, March 13, 1776, to Elias Dayton, March 16, 1776, Dayton to Stirling, March 13, 1776, Stirling Papers, 4, NYHS; President of Congress to Stirling, March 15, 1776, Burnett, ed., *Letters,* 1: 392–93; President of Congress to Stirling, March 15, 1776, Force, ed., *American Archives,* 4th ser., 5: 233.

27. George Washington to Stirling, March 14, 1776, Stirling to Washington, March 15–17, 1776, Washington Papers, LC.

28. Stirling to Congress, March 16–17, 18, 19, 1776, to Trumbull, March 17, 1776, PCC, 162, 2: 466–68, 471, 481–82; Alexander McDougall to Stirling, March 16, 1776, Stirling to Schuyler, March 27, 1776, Force, ed., *American Archives,* 4th ser., 5: 248, 519; George Washington to Stirling, March 17, 1776,

Stirling to Washington, March 20, 27, 1776, Washington Papers, LC; Stirling to New York Committee of Safety, March 18, 1776, Philip Schuyler to Stirling, March 16, 20, 28, 1776, Jonathan Trumbull to Stirling, March 21, 1776, Stirling Papers, 4, NYHS; *Proceedings of the Provincial Congress, Committee of Safety and Convention of New York Relating to Military Matters,* O'Callaghan and Fernow, eds., *Documents,* 15: 88.

29. Lewis Ogden to Stirling, March 14, 1776, Stephen Crane to Stirling, March 14, 1776, Morris County Committee of Safety to Stirling, March 16, 1776, William Burnet to Stirling, March 18, 1776, Stirling to Alexander Carmichael, March 17, 1776, Stirling to Committees of Safety of Morris, Essex, Middlesex, Somerset, Sussex, Hunterdon, Bergen, and Monmouth Counties, March 17, 1776, Stirling to New Jersey Committee of Safety, March 17, 1776, Stirling Papers, 4, NYHS; Essex County Committee of Safety to Stirling, March 15, 1776, Elias Boudinot to Stirling, March 17, 1776, John Witherspoon to Stirling, March 19, 1776, Force, ed., *American Archives,* 4th ser., 5: 237, 397, 414; Jacob Foord, Jr., and Ellis Cooke to Stirling, March 21, 1776, Park Collection, Morristown.

30. Stirling to Congress, March 16, 1776, PCC, 162, 2: 467–68; Stirling to Bergen County Committee of Safety, March 18, 1776, to Essex County Committee of Safety, March 18, 1776, to New Jersey Committee of Safety, March 23, 1776, to William Livingston, March 24, 1776, Stirling Papers, 4, NYHS; William Thompson to Stirling, March 23, 1776, New Jersey Letters, Rutgers University Library; Thomas Williams Baldwin, ed., *The Revolutionary Journal of Col. Jeduthan Baldwin, 1775–1778* (Bangor, Maine, 1906), 31–34.

31. Stirling to Elias Dayton, March 23, 1776, Stirling Papers, 4, NYHS; Stirling to George Washington, March 27, April 1, 1776, Washington Papers, LC; Stirling to Dayton, April 9, 1776, Ely Collection, NJHS; Stirling to New York Committee of Safety, April 12, 1776, Force, ed., *American Archives,* 4th ser., 5: 1439.

Chapter 6

1. General Orders, April 24, 29, August 12, 1776, Fitzpatrick, ed., *Washington Papers,* 4: 512–13, 535–36, 5: 422; Freeman, *Washington,* 3: 89.

2. George Washington to New York Commitee of Safety, April 27, 1776, General Orders, May 13, 1776, Washington to Israel Putnam, May 21, 1776, Washington to Secret Committee of New York Legislature, July 21, 1776, Fitzpatrick, ed., *Washington Papers,* 4: 524, 524n, 5: 39, 69, 318; Putnam to Washington, May 27, 1776, Washington to Commanders in the Highlands, June 10, 1776, Extract, Minutes of the New York Provincial Congress, June 3, 1776, Force, ed., *American Archives,* 4th ser., 6: 584, 592, 1359; Stirling to Washington, June 1, 1776, Washington Papers, LC.

3. Fitzpatrick, ed., *Washington Papers,* 5: 182n; Freeman, *Washington,* 4: 115–17.

4. Jones, *History,* 1: 109.

5. Jones, *History,* 1: 104, 2: 297; Henry Brockholst Livingston to Stirling, June 11, 1776, Washington Papers, LC; Livingston to Stirling, June 14, 1776, Force, ed., *American Archives,* 4th ser., 6: 901.

6. Council of War, July 12, 1776, and Stirling's Plan to Attack Staten Island, July, 1776, Washington Papers, LC.

7. Rudolphus Ritzema to Stirling, June 11, 1776, Stirling to George Washington, July 1, 1776, Washington Papers, LC; General Orders, July 17, 1776, Fitzpatrick, ed., *Washington Papers,* 5: 287; Freeman, *Washington,* 4: 141n.

8. William L. Calderhead, "British Naval Failure at Long Island: A Lost Opportunity in the American Revolution," *New York History,* 57 (1976), 333–38; Freeman, *Washington,* 4: 153–54; John R. Alden, *The American Revolution, 1775–1783* (New York, 1954), 96–97.

9. Description of terrain in Samuel Holden Parsons to John Adams, October 8, 1776, Long Island Historical Society, *Memoirs,* 2–3 (Brooklyn, 1865–69), 35 hereafter LIHS, *Memoirs.*

10. George Washington to John Sullivan, August 20, 1776, and General Orders, August 20, 1776, Fitzpatrick, ed., *Washington Papers,* 5: 469; Sullivan's Orders, August 25, 1776, Field, *Long Island,* 30. For Israel Putnam's appointment, see William Bradford Reed, ed., *Life and Correspondence of Joseph Reed* (2 vols., Philadelphia, 1847), 1: 220. General Sullivan's biographer, Charles P. Whittemore (*A General of the Revolution: John Sullivan of New Hampshire* [New York, 1961], 34), says Sullivan "probably" commanded outside the lines at Long Island. Douglas S. Freeman, in his biography of Washington (4: 159n), declares there is "no doubt whatsoever" that this was the case.

11. LIHS, *Memoirs,* 2: 370–71, 3: 64; Freeman, *Washington,* 4: 159. Wertenbaker (*Father Knickerbocker Rebels,* 92) blames Putnam for the patriot debacle at Long Island, claiming that general had no "well defined purpose" in his orders. Francis Vinton Greene (*The Revolutionary War and the Military Policy of the United States* [New York, 1911], 40) says Washington was responsible. John C. Miller, in *Triumph of Freedom,* 122n, charges Putnam and Stirling jointly, although he does not clarify how Stirling could be derelict, especially since the earl had had nothing whatsoever to do with disposing any troops except those under his immediate command on the right.

12. Stirling to George Washington, August, 29, 1776, Washington Papers, LC; Freeman, *Washington,* 4: 162–63; William Smallwood's and Samuel Holden Parson's accounts of the battle, LIHS, *Memoirs,* 2: 387ff, 3: 33ff; Samuel J. Atlee's account, Force, ed., *American Archives,* 5th ser., 1: 1251.

13. William Howe to Lord George Germain, September 3, 1776, Force, ed., *American Archives,* 5th ser., 1: 1255–1256; Stephen R. Lushington, *Life and Ser-*

vices of General Lord Harris (2d ed. rev. London, 1845), 76; LIHS, *Memoirs,* 2: 406.

14. Stirling to George Washington, August 29, 1776, Washington Papers, LC; Robert G. Albion and Leonidas Dodson, eds., *Philip Vickers Fithian: Journal, 1775–1776, Written on the Virginia-Pennsylvania Frontier and in the Army Around New York* (Princeton, 1934), 219; Frederick Mackenzie, *Diary of Frederick Mackenzie, Giving a Daily Narrative of His Military Service . . . During the Years 1775–1781* (2 vols., Cambridge, Mass., 1930), 1: 53; Washington to Massachusetts Legislature, September 19, 1776, Fitzpatrick, ed., *Washington Papers,* 6: 75–78; Christopher Ward, *The Delaware Continentals, 1776–1783* (Wilmington, 1941), 28–42.

15. Stirling to George Washington, August 29, 1776, Washington Papers, LC; Stirling to Congress, March 3, 1776, PCC, 162, 2: 523–24; Edward J. Lowell, *The Hessians and the Other German Auxiliaries of Great Britain in the Revolutionary War* (New York, 1884), 67. Grant's comment is quoted in William S. Stryker, *The Battles of Trenton and Princeton* (Boston and New York, 1898), 48n; Stryker says, obviously incorrectly, that Stirling heard Grant make this remark in Parliament in 1775.

16. Sir Henry Clinton, *The American Rebellion: Sir Henry Clinton's Narrative of his Campaigns, 1775–1782,* ed. William B. Willcox (New Haven, 1954), 43; William Howe to Lord Germain, September 3, 1776, Force, ed., *American Archives,* 5th ser., 1: 1755–1756; George Washington to Congress, August 31, 1776, Fitzpatrick, ed., *Washington Papers,* 5: 506–8; Howard H. Peckham, ed., *The Toll of Independence: Engagements and Battle Casualties of the American Revolution* (Chicago, 1974), 22, puts the total American casualties at 1,097, the British at 932.

17. Frank Moore, ed., *The Diary of the Revolution* (2 vols., Hartford, 1876), 1: 915; Edward H. Tatum, ed., *The American Journal of Ambrose Serle, Secretary to Lord Howe, 1776–1778* (San Marino, 1940), entry of August 29, 1776, 80–82; Ira D. Gruber, *The Howe Brothers and the American Revolution* (New York, 1972), 116–17.

18. Stirling to George Washington, August 29, 1776, Washington Papers, LC; Washington to Congress, August 29, 21, 1776, Fitzpatrick, ed., *Washington Papers,* 5: 496, 506–8; Joseph Reed to William Livingston, August 30, 1776, Force, ed., *American Archives,* 5th ser., 1: 1231; John Morin Scott to New York Convention, September 6, 1776, Richard B. Morris, ed., *John Jay: The Making of a Revolutionary: Unpublished Papers, 1745–1780* (New York, 1975), 312; Reed cited in Trevelyan, *Revolution,* 2: 280.

19. Tatum, ed., *Serle Journal;* Edward Serle to Lord Dartmouth, September 5, 1776, Stevens, ed., *Facsimiles,* 24: 2042; George Weedon to _____, October 10, 1776, George Weedon Papers, Chicago Historical Society; Moore, ed., *Diary,* 320.

20. General Orders, August 21, September 5, 11, 1776, Fitzpatrick, ed., *Washington Papers,* 5: 501, 6: 1842.

21. George Washington to William Howe, September 6, 19, 23, October 6, 1776, to Congress, September 6, October 8, 1776, to Governor Trumbull, September 23, 1776, General Orders, October 8, 1776, Fitzpatrick, ed., *Washington Papers,* 6: 22, 24, 74, 97, 100, 172–73, 179, 183–84; Howe to Washington, September 21, 1776, Sparks, ed., *Correspondence,* 1: 289; Ford, ed., *Journals of Congress,* 5: 735; John Haslet to Caesar Rodney, October 10, 1776, George H. Ryden, ed., *Letters to and from Caesar Rodney, 1756–1785* (Philadelphia, 1933), 137.

22. Council of War, October 16, 1776, Force, ed., *American Archives,* 5th ser., 2: 1118; General Orders, October 17, 1776, George Washington to Robert R. Livingston, October 20, 1776, Fitzpatrick, ed., *Washington Papers,* 6: 216, 37: 534.

23. Rufus R. Wilson, ed., *Heath's Memoirs of the American War* (New York, 1904), 84–87; John Haslet to Caesar Rodney, October 28, 1776, Sparks, ed., *Correspondence,* 4: 526; William Howe to Lord Germain, November 20, 1776, Force, ed., *American Archives,* 5th ser., 3: 922; Robert Rogers, *Journals,* cited by John R. Cuneo, *Robert Rogers of the Rangers* (New York, 1959), 262, 271–73; George A. Billias, *General John Glover and His Marblehead Mariners* (New York, 1960), 114. Said Glover later, "I would have given a thousand worlds to have had General Lee or some other experienced officer present" (Force, ed., *American Archives,* 5th ser., 2: 1188).

24. Robert H. Harrison to Congress, October 29, 1776, Washington Papers, LC; Wilson, ed., *Heath's Memoirs,* 86–87. Tench Tilghman, on October 31, 1776, described Stirling's march to White Plains as "Keeping Pace with the enemy's left flank" (Force, ed., *American Archives,* 5th ser., 2: 1311–1312). This appears to be an inaccurate statement, since Stirling had marched to his destination in only one day, rapidly *passing* Howe's left on the 18th. For a description of the heights at White Plains, see *The [Stephen] Kemble Papers,* New-York Historical Society Collections, 16–17 (New York, 1884–85), 1: 95, hereafter *Kemble Papers.*

25. Wilson, ed., *Heath's Memoirs,* 87–89.

26. Robert H. Harrison to Congress, November 1, 1776, and Return of Stirling's brigade, November 3, 1776, Force, ed., *American Archives,* 5th ser., 3: 464–65, 499; Freeman, *Washington,* 4: 233.

27. Return of Washington's Army, November 3, 1776, Minutes, Council of War, November 6, 1776, Force, ed., *American Archives,* 5th ser., 3: 499–502, 543–44; Charles H. Lesser, ed., *The Sinews of Independence: Monthly Strength Reports of the Continental Army* (Chicago, 1976), 36–39.

28. Thomas Mifflin to Congress, November 10, 1776, PCC, 161, 1: 1; Stirling to George Washington, November 10, 1776, Fitzpatrick, ed., *Washington Papers,* 6: 272; Wilson, ed., *Heath's Memoirs,* 95; Clement Biddle to New Jersey Congress, November 17, 1776, Force, ed., *American Archives,* 3d ser., 740; Stirling to

Congress, November 18, 1776, PCC, 162, 2: 495; Stirling to William Livingston, November 18, 1776, William Livingston Papers, Massachusetts Historical Society, hereafter Livingston Papers, MHS.

29. George Washington to John Augustine Washington, November 19, 1776, Fitzpatrick, ed., *Washington Papers*, 6: 245–56; Stirling to Congress, November 21, 1776, PCC, 162, 2: 499; Stirling to William Livingston, November 21, 1776, Livingston Papers, MHS; Moore, ed., *Diary*, 358.

30. George Washington to Charles Lee, November 21, 1776, to Congress, December 3, 5, 9, 1776, Fitzpatrick, ed., *Washington Papers*, 6: 299, 331–33, 339.

31. George Washington to Congress, December 9, 1776, to General Officers, December 14, 1776, Fitzpatrick, ed., *Washington Papers*, 6: 339, 368–70; Stirling to Washington, December 12, 1776, Washington Papers, LC; Stirling to David Rittenhouse, December 12, 1776, Schoff Collection, William L. Clements Library.

32. George Washington to Stirling, December 14, 1776, Fitzpatrick, ed., *Washington Papers*, 6: 372; Washington to John Sullivan, December 15, 1776, Otis G. Hammond, ed., *Letters and Papers of Major General John Sullivan, Continental Army*, New Hampshire Historical Society Collections, 12–15 (Concord, 1930–39), 1: 305, hereafter Hammond, ed., *Sullivan Papers*.

33. Stirling to William Heath, December 16, 1776, *Heath Papers*, Massachusetts Historical Society Collections, 5th ser., 4, 7th ser., 4 (Boston, 1878–1905), 2: 313, hereafter *Heath Papers*; Washington to John Sullivan, December 16, 1776, Hammond, ed., *Sullivan Papers*, 1: 305; "Bethlehem During the American Revolution: Extracts from the Diaries in the Moravian Archives at Bethlehem, Pennsylvania," *PMHB*, 12 (1888): 395; Return of Washington's Army, December 22, 1776, Force, ed., *American Archives*, 5th ser., 3: 1401–1402; Lesser, *Sinews*, 43.

34. James Grant to Johann Rall, December 24, 1776, quoted in Stryker, *Trenton and Princeton*, 116; George Washington to Congress, December 27, 1776, Fitzpatrick, *Washington Papers*, 6: 441–44; Theodore Thayer, *Nathanael Greene: Strategist of the American Revolution* (New York, 1960), 138. John R. Alden (*American Revolution*, 109) says Washington intended to attack Von Donlop immediately after Rall's surrender. Freeman, however (*Washington*, 4: 307), says the general's intention was to march on Princeton.

35. Plan of Trenton Campaign, December 25, 1776, George Washington to Congress, December 27, 1776, Fitzpatrick, ed., *Washington Papers*, 6: 441–44; Henry Knox to Lucy Knox, December 28, 1776, Stirling to New Jersey Council of Safety, December 27, 1776, cited in Stryker, *Trenton and Princeton*, 367–68, 371–72; Stirling to William Livingston, December 28, 1776, Livingston Papers, MHS.

36. George Washington to Congress, December 27, 1776, Fitzpatrick, ed., *Washington Papers*, 6: 441–44; Stirling to Governor Livingston, December 28,

1776, Livingston Papers, MHS; Trevelyan, *American Revolution,* 3: 119–20, 120n.

37. Stirling to William Livingston, December 28, 1776, William Livingston Papers, MHS.

38. Stirling to ———, January 4, 1777, Dreer Collection, HSP; Stirling to Congress, January 8, 1777, to Robert Morris, January 8, 1777, PCC, 162, 2: 505–6, 509; Trevelyan, *American Revolution,* 3: 129; Freeman, *Washington,* 4: 368, 393. Henry B. Carrington, in *Battles of the American Revolution* (New York, 1876), 289, incorrectly located Stirling with Washington's army at Princeton.

Chapter 7

1. George Clinton to Stirling, January 22, 1777, New Jersey Letters, Rutgers University Library; Stirling to Robert Morris, January 22, 1777, PCC, 162, 2: 519; Stirling's General Orders, January 23, 1777, Simon Gratz Collection, HSP; Stirling to Theodorick Bland, January 26, 1777, Stirling Papers, NYPL; Thomas Johnson, Jr., to Maryland Council of Safety, January 20, 1777, W. H. Browne, et al., eds., *Archives of Maryland* (65 vols., Baltimore, 1883–1952), 16: 64; George Washington to Stirling, January 19, 1777, Washington Papers, LC.

2. George Washington to Stirling, February 4, 1777, Washington Papers, LC; Ford, ed., *Journals of Congress,* 7: 133, 185; Stirling to Congress, March 3, 1777, PCC, 162, 2: 523–34; John Adams to John Sullivan, June 6, 1777, Hammond, ed., *Sullivan Papers,* 1: 367.

3. George Washington to Stirling, February 25, May 6, 1777, Stirling to Washington, February 26, 1777, Washington Papers, LC; Stirling to William Livingston, March 8, 1777, Livingston Papers, MHS; Stirling to Washington, March 24, 1777, New Jersey Letters, Rutgers University Library; Stirling to Alexander Hamilton, April 12, 1777, Alexander Hamilton Papers, Library of Congress; Stirling to Benjamin Lincoln, April 14, 1777, Chew Family Papers, New Jersey Historical Society, hereafter Chew Family Papers, NJHS; Stirling to Washington, May 6, 1776, Fitzpatrick, ed., *Washington Papers,* 8: 22n; Thayer, *Greene,* 165; Mellick, *Old Farm,* 402.

4. Don Higginbotham, "The American Militia: A Traditional Institution with Revolutionary Responsibilities," in *Reconsiderations on the Revolutionary War,* ed. Don Higginbotham (Westport, Conn., 1978), 90–91; Paul David Nelson, "Citizen Soldiers or Regulars; The Views of American General Officers on the Military Establishment, 1775–1781," *Military Affairs* 43 (1979): 127.

5. William Howe to Lord Germain, July 5, 1777, *New Jersey Archives,* 2d ser., 1: 476–78; George Washington to Congress, June 22, 1777, Fitzpatrick, ed., *Washington Papers,* 8: 283; Washington to Stirling, June 23, 1777, Reeve Schley Autograph Collection, New Jersey Historical Society.

6. George Washington to Joseph Reed, June 24, 1777, to Congress, June 25,

1777, Fitzpatrick, ed., *Washington Papers,* 8: 295–98; Stirling to John Sullivan, June 24, 1777, John Sullivan Papers, New Hampshire Historical Society, hereafter Sullivan Papers, NHHS; William Howe to Lord Germain, July 5, 1777, *New Jersey Archives,* 2d ser., 1: 476–78.

7. George Washington to William Heath, June 27, 1777, to Congress, June 28, 1777, Fitzpatrick, ed., *Washington Papers,* 8: 305–7; William Howe to Lord Germain, July 5, 1777, *New Jersey Archives,* 2d ser., 1: 476–78. Bancroft (*History,* 5: 154) and Trevelyan (*Revolution,* 4: 63) were critical of Stirling for trying to make a stand when he should not have.

8. William Howe to Lord Germain, July 5, 1777, *New Jersey Archives,* 2d ser., 1: 476–78; George Washington to John Langdon, June 29, 1777, Fitzpatrick, ed., *Washington Papers,* 8: 312; Alexander Hamilton to Robert R. Livingston, June 28, 1777, Harold C. Syrett and Jacob E. Cooke, eds., *Papers of Alexander Hamilton* (24 vols. to date, New York, 1961–), 1: 274–75; Stirling to John Sullivan, June 27, 1777, Sullivan Papers, NHHS; *Pennsylvania Journal,* July 2, 1777, cited in Moore, *Diary,* 1: 448–49; Octavius Pickering, ed., *The Life of Timothy Pickering* (4 vols., Boston, 1867–1873), 1: 145; John André, *Major André's Journal: Operations of the British Army Under Lieutenant Generals Sir William Howe and Sir Henry Clinton, June, 1776 to November, 1778* (Tarrytown, 1930), 31–32; Harry Miller Lydenberg, ed., *Archibald Robertson, Lieutenant-General Royal Engineers, His Diaries and Sketches in America, 1762–1780* (New York, 1930), 139; Carrington, *Battles,* 301.

9. General Orders, July 17, 1777, George Washington to Congress, July 22, 1777, Fitzpatrick, ed., *Washington Papers,* 8: 429, 459; Stirling to Washington, July 24, 1777, Washington Papers, LC. Stirling's division went to Peekskill to replace General John Nixon's brigade, which was ordered to join Philip Schuyler's command in the north (Washington to Congress, July 22, 1777, Fitzpatrick, ed., *Washington Papers,* 8: 459).

10. George Washington to Stirling, July 22, 1777, Smith Collection, Morristown; Washington to Stirling, July 28, 1777, Fitzpatrick, ed., *Washington Papers,* 8: 460–62, 487, 492, 505; Stirling to Washington, July 24, 1777, Washington to Stirling, July 26, 27, 30 (2), 1777, Washington Papers, LC.

11. George Washington to Horatio Gates, July 30, 1777, Horatio Gates Papers, Box 5, New-York Historical Society, hereafter Gates Papers, NYHS; Washington to John Langdon, August 4, 1777, Council of War, August 21, 1777, Fitzpatrick, ed., *Washington Papers,* 9: 13, 109–10, 110n; Ford, ed., *Journals of Congress,* 8: 663.

12. General Orders, August 21, 23, 1777, Fitzpatrick, ed., *Washington Papers,* 9: 114, 125.

13. Charles Francis Adams, ed., *Familiar Letters of John Adams and His Wife Abigail Adams, During the Revolution* (New York, 1876), 298.

14. General Orders, August 30, 1777, Fitzpatrick, ed., *Washington Papers,* 9: 149.

15. George Weedon to John Page, September 11, 1777, George Weedon Papers, Chicago Historical Society; Freeman, *Washington,* 4: 471–72.

16. G. C. Scull, ed., *The Montresor Journals,* New-York Historical Society Collections, 14 (New York, 1882), 449; George Washington to Congress, September 11, 1777, Fitzpatrick, ed., *Washington Papers,* 9: 206; George Weedon to John Page, September 11, 1777, George Weedon Papers, Chicago Historical Society.

17. John Sullivan to George Washington, September 11, 1777, Sparks, ed., *Correspondence,* 5: 460; George Weedon to John Page, September 11, 1777, George Weedon Papers, Chicago Historical Society.

18. George Washington to Congress, September 11, 1777, Fitzpatrick, ed., *Washington Papers,* 9: 206; George Weedon to John Page, September 11, 1777, George Weedon Papers, Chicago Historical Society; John Sullivan to Congress, September 27, 1777, Hammond, ed., *Sullivan Papers,* 1: 463–64; Freeman, *Washington,* 4: 481–82.

19. George Washington to Congress, September 11, 1777, Fitzpatrick, ed., *Washington Papers,* 9: 207–8; *Kemble Papers,* 1: 135; Hammond, ed., *Sullivan Papers,* 1: 474.

20. George Washington to Stirling, September 24, 25, 1777, Fitzpatrick, ed., *Washington Papers,* 9: 263–66; Anthony Wayne to Washington, September 21, 23, 1777, Anthony Wayne Papers, 4: 8, 10, Historical Society of Pennsylvania, hereafter Wayne Papers, HSP; Washington to Stirling, September 24, 1777, James S. Schoff Papers, William L. Clements Library; Councils of War, September 23, 28, 1777, Washington Papers, LC.

21. General Orders, [October 3, 1777], George Washington to Congress, October 5, 1777, Fitzpatrick, ed., *Washington Papers,* 9: 307, 308–11; J. W. Fortescue, *A History of the British Army* (13 vols., London, 1899–1930), 3: 221.

22. George Washington to Congress, October 5, 1777, Fitzpatrick, ed., *Washington Papers,* 9: 308–11; Stirling to _____, October 5, 1777, Stirling Papers, NYPL; John Sullivan to Meschech Weare, October 25, 1777, Hammond, ed., *Sullivan Papers,* 1: 544–45; Freeman, *Washington,* 4: 508–9. From Stirling's letter of October 5 I have conjectured that he was with Maxwell. Nowhere does he actually say so, nor does any observer report Stirling's whereabouts during the battle. It would be consistent with the earl's character to find him with Maxwell in the thickest part of the fight.

23. George Washington to Congress, October 5, 1777, Fitzpatrick, ed., *Washington Papers,* 9: 308–11; Stirling to _____, October 5, 1777, Stirling Papers, NYPL; Anthony Wayne to Mary Wayne, October 6, 1777, Wayne Papers, 4: 31, HSP; Henry Knox to Lucy Knox, October 6, 1777, Knox Papers, MHS. On Stirling's loss of a horse in battle, see "Extract of a Letter from Camp," October 5, 1777, *Calendar of Maryland State Papers: The Red Books* (4 vols., Annapolis, 1950–55), 4: 456.

24. *Kemble Papers*, 1: 137; Freeman, Washington, 4: 517; Stirling to _____, October 5, 1777, Stirling Papers, NYPL; Paul David Nelson, "British Conduct of the American Revolutionary War: A Review of Interpretations," *Journal of American History* 65 (1978): 623–53.

25. General Orders, October 10, 11, 16, 1777, Fitzpatrick, ed., *Washington Papers*, 9: 347, 352, 379–80; Hammond, ed., *Sullivan Papers*, 1, 4: 19, 25, HSP; Whittemore, *Sullivan*, 75.

26. Stirling to George Washington, October 29, November 3, 1777, Washington Papers, LC. On Stirling's fall from a horse, see James Wilkinson, *Memoirs of My Own Times* (3 vols., Philadelphia, 1816), 1: 330–32.

27. Stirling to George Washington, November 3, 25, December 3, 1777, Washington Papers, LC; William Livingston to Stirling, November 12, 1777, Princeton University Library; Councils of War, October 27, November 8, 12, 24, 1777, Fitzpatrick, ed., *Washington Papers*, 9: 461, 10: 23–24, 48n, 103n, 106.

28. Council of War, November 30, 1777, Fitzpatrick, ed., *Washington Papers*, 9: 133n; Stirling to George Washington, December 1, 23, 24 (2), 26, 29, 1777, Washington to Stirling, December 17, 1777, Washington Papers, LC; Abraham Clark to Stirling, December 20, 1777, Burnett, ed., *Letters*, 2: 594; Don Higginbotham, *Daniel Morgan: Revolutionary Rifleman* (Chapel Hill, 1961), 81–82.

29. Wilkinson, *Memoirs*, 1: 330–32.

30. Stirling to George Washington, November 3, 1777, Washington Papers, LC; "Historical Notes of Dr. Benjamin Rush, 1777," *PMHB* 27 (1903): 147; Abraham Clark to Stirling, January 15, 1778, Stirling Papers, 4, NYHS; Eliphalet Dyer to William Williams, March 10, 1778, Joseph Reed Manuscripts, Box 4, New-York Historical Society; Higginbotham, *War of Independence*, 216.

31. Stirling to James Wilkinson, January 6, 1778, cited in Wilkinson, *Memoirs*, 1: 382–83; Wilkinson to Stirling, February 4, 1778, Gates Papers, 9, NYHS; James Ripley Jacobs, *Tarnished Warrior: Major-General James Wilkinson* (New York, 1938), 49–50. Jacobs says (54) that Stirling "deceived" Wilkinson. There is no evidence to support such an assertion.

32. James Wilkinson to Horatio Gates, February 22, 1778, to Stirling, March 18, 1778, Gates Papers, 9, NYHS; Stirling to Wilkinson, March 18, 1778, Wilkinson, *Memoirs*, 392; George Washington to Stirling, March 21, 1778, Stirling Papers, 4, NYHS; Jacobs, *Wilkinson*, 51–54.

33. Pierre Étienne DuPonceau, "Autobiography," *PMHB* 63 (1939): 209, 213; General Orders, November 20, 1777, George Washington to Stirling, December 30, 1777, Fitzpatrick, ed., *Washington Papers*, 10: 88, 228–29.

34. Stanislaus Murray Hamilton, ed., *The Writings of James Monroe* (7 vols., New York, 1898–1903), 1: xxvii; Matthew L. Davis, ed., *Memoirs of Aaron Burr, With Miscellaneous Selections from His Correspondence* (2 vols., New York, 1837), 2: 434.

Chapter 8

1. George Washington to General Officers, April 20, 1778, and Responses, Fitzpatrick, ed., *Washington Papers,* 11: 282–83, 283n; Stirling to Washington, April 23, 1778, Washington Papers, LC; Stryker, *Monmouth,* 13; *PMHB* 39 (1915): 221.

2. General Orders, May 5, 7, 1778, Stirling to George Washington, April 30, May 1, 1778, Washington to Stirling, May 1, 1778, Washington to Congress, May 4, 1778, Fitzpatrick, ed., *Washington Papers,* 11: 338, 348, 348n, 354–55, 361; Stirling's Oath of Allegiance, May 12, 1778, Miscellaneous Manuscripts Collection, American Philosophical Society Library.

3. Council of War, May 8, 1778, Fitzpatrick, ed., *Washington Papers,* 11: 363–66; George Washington to Stirling, May 11, 1778, James Lovell to Stirling, June 8, 1778, Stirling Papers, 4, NYHS.

4. Council of War, June 17, 1778, Order of March & Route of Army from Valley Forge, [June 17, 1778], George Washington to Congress, June 22, 1778, Fitzpatrick, ed., *Washington Papers,* 12: 74, 75–78, 109; Stirling to Washington, June 18, 1778, Washington Papers, LC; Reed, ed., *Reed,* 1: 368.

5. Council of War, June 24, 1778, Fitzpatrick, ed., *Washington Papers,* 12: 115–17; Alden, *Lee,* 209; Alexander Hamilton to Elias Boudinot, July 5, 1778, Syrett and Cooke, eds., *Hamilton Papers,* 1: 510–14.

6. Charles Lee to George Washington, June 24, 25, 1778, *Lee Papers,* 2: 417–18; Alexander Hamilton to Elias Boudinot, July 5, 1778, Syrett and Cooke, ed., *Hamilton Papers,* 1: 510–14.

7. George Washington to Congress, July 1, 1778, Fitzpatrick, ed., *Washington Papers,* 12: 139–46; Washington to Stirling, June 27, 1778, Washington Papers, LC.

8. George Washington to Congress, July 1, 1778, Fitzpatrick, ed., *Washington Papers,* 12: 139–46; Philemon Dickinson to Washington, 10:30 A.M., June 28, 1778, Washington Papers, LC.

9. George Washington to Congress, July 1, 1778, Fitzpatrick, ed., *Washington Papers,* 12: 139–46; Stirling to William Henry Drayton, August 15, 1778, Ely Collection, NJHS; Stryker, *Monmouth,* 182.

10. Stirling to William Henry Drayton, August 15, 1778, Ely Collection, NJHS.

11. George Washington to Congress, July 1, 1778, Fitzpatrick, ed., *Washington Papers,* 12: 139–46; Alexander Hamilton to Elias Boudinot, July 5, 1778, Syrett and Cooke, eds., *Hamilton Papers,* 1: 510–14; Stryker, *Monmouth,* 207–9; W. P. Cresson, *James Monroe* (Chapel Hill, 1946), 43–44.

12. George Washington to Congress, July 1, 1778, Fitzpatrick, ed., *Washington Papers,* 12: 139–46; Stirling to William Henry Drayton, August 15, 1778, Ely Collection, NJHS.

13. George Washington to Congress, July 1, 1778, Fitzpatrick, ed., *Washington Papers,* 12: 139–46; Stirling to William Henry Drayton, August 15, 1778, Ely Collection, NJHS. On Henry Clinton's personality, see William B. Willcox, *Portrait of a General: Sir Henry Clinton in the War of Independence* (New York, 1964), and William B. Willcox and Frederick Wyatt, "Sir Henry Clinton: A Psychological Exploration in History," *William and Mary Quarterly,* 3d ser., 16 (1959): 3–26.

14. General Orders, July 1, 3, 1778, Fitzpatrick, ed., *Washington Papers,* 12: 147, 154; Charles Lee to Stirling, July 2, 1778, Stirling to Lee, July 2, 1778, Washington Papers, LC; Alden, *Lee,* 234–35.

15. General Orders, [July 7], July 13, 25, August 14, 1778, Fitzpatrick, ed., *Washington Papers,* 12: 162, 175–76, 228, 324; Charles Lee to Congress, October 13, 1778, and Lee's self-defense, *Lee Papers,* 3: 207–8, 239; Alden, *Lee,* 238; Henry Lee, *Memoirs of the War in the Southern Department of the United States* (New York, 1869), 115.

16. Timothy Pickering to Stirling, August 10, 1778, Israel Shreve Papers, Rutgers University Library; Councils of War, July 25, August 20, September 1, 1778, Fitzpatrick, ed., *Washington Papers,* 12: 229–31, 343–44, 344n, 387–88n; Stirling to George Washington, September 2, 1778, Washington Papers, LC; Stirling to William Livingston, September 7, 1778, Stirling Papers, NYPL.

17. Lady Stirling to Stirling, August 24, 1778, Catherine Alexander to Stirling, September 6, 1778, Stirling Papers, 4, NYHS; Stirling to William Henry Drayton, August 15, 1778, Ely Collection, NJHS.

18. Stirling to Robert Livingston, September 7, 1778, Stirling Papers, NYPL; Cresson, *Monroe,* 45–47.

19. George Washington to Stirling, September 15, 24, 28, 1778, Stirling to Washington, September 24, 28, 1778, Stirling to George Clinton, September 24, 1778, Washington Papers, LC.

20. Stirling to George Washington, October 1, 3, 4, 5, 6, 7, 9, 11, 22, 1778, Washington to Stirling, October 2, 4, 6, 8, 12, 1778, William Livingston to Stirling, October 5, 6, 11, 1778, Washington Papers, LC; Stirling to Congress, October 13, 1778, PCC, 162, 2: 527; Stirling to Stephen Moylan, October 8, 1778, *PMHB* 37 (1913): 349; Stirling to James Abeel, October 8, 1778, James Abeel Papers, Rutgers University Library; Stirling to Elias Dayton, October 12, 1778, Smith Collection, Morristown; Stirling to Dayton, October 13, 1778, Elias Dayton Papers, New Jersey Historical Society; Stirling Papers, NYPL; William Woodford to Stirling, October 5, 1778, Ely Collection, NJHS; Elias Boudinot to Stirling, [1778], Boudinot Family Miscellany, Rutgers University Library.

21. Stirling to George Washington, October 3, 4, 7, 8, 9, 11, 14, 15, 16, 17, 19, 20, 21, 29, 30 (2), November 1, 3, 6, 7, 11, 13, 15, 17, 19, 20, 27 (2), 28, 29, 30, 1778, Washington to Stirling, October 17, 22, 24, 25, 29, November 1, 7, 16, 19, 20,

November 1, 5, December 1, 4, 1778, PCC, 162, 2: 531, 535–36, 537, 543, 547, 551, 559; Stirling to John Sullivan, October 19, 1778, Sullivan Papers, NHHS; Stirling to Congress, November 15, 1778, Emmet Collection, NYPL; Richard Howell to Stirling, November 6, 1778, Ely Collection, NJHS; Henry Laurens to Stirling, November 26, 1778, Misc. MSS, LC; Christian Febiger to Stirling, November 29, 1778, Smith Collection, Morristown; Robert Smith to Richard Caswell, December 11, 1778, Walter Clark, ed., *State Records of North Carolina, 1777–1790* (16 vols., Winston, 1895–1905), 13: 326–27.

22. George Washington to John Augustine Washington, Fitzpatrick, ed., *Washington Papers,* 13: 335; Henry Knox to William Knox, October 28, 1778, Knox Papers, MHS; Washington to Stirling, October 24, 25, 1778, Stirling to Washington, October 29, November 11, 1778, Washington Papers, LC; Stirling to Daniel Morgan, October _____, 1778, Myers Collection, New York Public Library.

23. William Henry Drayton to Stirling, October 29, 1778, Simon Gratz Autograph Collection, Historical Society of Pennsylvania; Cortlandt Skinner to Stirling, November 1, 1778, Smith Collection, Morristown; Stirling to Skinner, November 7, 1778, C. E. French Papers, Massachusetts Historical Society; Henry Clinton to Stirling, October 28, 1778, Stirling Papers, 4, NYHS; Ford, ed., *Journals of Congress,* 12: 1021; Stirling to Congress, October 21, December 1, 1778, PCC, 162, 2: 539–40, 551; George Washington to Stirling, October 21, November 27, 1778, Stirling to Washington, November 24, 1778, Washington Papers, LC; Henry Laurens to Stirling, November 26, 1778, PCC, 162, 2: 559.

24. George Washington to Stirling, October 14, 15, November 1, 27, 1778, Stirling to Washington, October 17, 26, 1778, Washington Papers, LC; Stirling to Congress, December 4, 1778, PCC, 162, 2: 559.

25. Stirling to George Washington, October 16, November 6, 1778, Washington Papers, LC; Stirling to Robert Morris, November 8, 1778, Ely Collection, NJHS; Boyd, *Boudinot,* 76.

26. General Orders, December 16, 1778, February 6, 1779, Fitzpatrick, ed., *Washington Papers,* 13: 407, 14: 70; George Washington to Stirling, December 21, 1778, Stirling to Baron Von Riedesel, December 24, 1778, Stirling to Washington, December 25, 1778, Washington Papers, LC; Stirling to James McHenry, December 25, 1778, James McHenry Papers, Maryland Historical Society.

27. Stirling to George Washington, December 24, 28, 1778, Washington Papers, LC; Nathanael Greene to Stirling, December 27, 1778, Nathanael Greene Papers, Henry E. Huntington Library, hereafter Greene Papers, Huntington Library; Stirling to Greene, December 28, 1778, Chew Family Papers, NJHS.

28. Stirling to George Washington, December 29, 30, 1778, January 3, 4, 1779, Washington to Stirling, January 1, 1779, Washington Papers, LC.

29. Contract for Cannon Balls, January 2, 1779, Smith Collection, Morristown; Stirling to George Washington, December 29, 30, 1778, January 13, 1779, Washington to Stirling, January 2, 8, 26, 1779, Stirling to Caleb North, January 13, 1779, Washington Papers, LC; Stirling to Nathanael Greene, December 28, 1778, Chew Family Papers, NJHS; Stirling to George Clinton, January 7, 1779, New Jersey Letters, Rutgers University Library.

30. General Orders, January 12, 1779, Fitzpatrick, ed., *Washington Papers,* 14: 2; Stirling to George Washington, January 3, 18, 27, 1779, Stirling to William Phillips, January 17, 1779, Washington to Stirling, January 14, 1779, Washington Papers, LC; Stirling to James McHenry, January 26, 1779, Ely Collection, NJHS; Stirling to William Smallwood, January 26, 1779, General Manuscripts, Princeton University Library.

31. General Orders, February 6, 1779, Council of Officers, April 10, 1779, Fitzpatrick, ed., *Washington Papers,* 14: 70, 365–66, 366n; Stirling to George Washington, February 26, March 20, 22, 1779, Washington to Stirling, March 23, 1779, Washington Papers, LC; Bernhard A. Uhlendorf, tr., *Revolution in America: Confidential Letters and Journals, 1776–1784 of Adjutant General Major Baurmeister of the Hessian Forces* (New Brunswick, 1957), 251–52.

32. Stephen Skinner to Stirling, December 14, 1778, Smith Collection, Morristown; Address of New Jersey Officers to New Jersey Council and Assembly, April 17, 1779, Stirling to George Washington, May 10, 1779, Washington Papers, LC; *Selections from the Correspondence of the Executive of New Jersey, from 1776 to 1786* (2 vols., Newark, 1848), 1: 156–57, 161–64; Lundin, *Cockpit,* 436–38.

33. Stirling's Memorial, May 7, 1779, Ely Collection, NJHS; *New Jersey Archives,* 2d ser., 1: 13; Allinson, ed., *Acts of Assembly,* May 31, 1779; Stirling to George Washington, May 24, 1779, Washington Papers, LC.

34. Notices of Sales of Stirling's Property: September 9, October 11, 1779, *New Jersey Archives,* 2d ser., 3: 534, 643–45, and November 1, 1779, Princeton University Library; Stirling to William Paterson, September 15, 1780, February 6, June 5, 1781, William Paterson Papers, Rutgers University Library, hereafter Paterson Papers, Rutgers University Library; Mellick, *Old Farm,* 494.

35. Will of William Alexander, Lord Stirling, January 29, 1780, Will of Sarah Alexander, November 27, 1804, Stirling Papers, NYPL; Jones, *History,* 2: 324.

Chapter 9

1. Stirling to George Washington, May 24, 1779, enclosing Plan of Attack on New York City, Washington Papers, LC.

2. George Washington to Stirling, June 1, 2, 1779, Washington Papers, 4, NYHS.

3. George Washington to Stirling, June 1, 2, 1779, Washington Papers, LC;

Washington to Stirling, June 3, 1779, Stirling Papers, 4, NYHS; Washington to Congress, June 3, 1779, General Orders, June 6, 1779, Fitzpatrick, ed., *Washington Papers*, 15: 238, 269–70; Horatio Gates to Elizabeth Gates, June 14, 1779, Gates Papers, 19, NYHS; Henry Knox to Lucy Knox, June 29, 1779, Knox Papers, MHS.

4. Henry Lee to Stirling, July 3, 1779, John Wanamaker Collection, Historical Society of Pennsylvania; George Washington to Stirling, July 4, 28, August 3, 16, Washington Papers, LC; Washington to Stirling, July 24, 25, 1779, Stirling Papers, 4, NYHS; Nathanael Greene to Stirling, July 4, 25, 1779, Nathanael Greene Papers, William L. Clements Library; Jonathan Stiles to Stirling, July 18, 1779, Stirling Papers, NYPL; Robert Erskine to Stirling, August 21, 1779, Simeon DeWitt Papers, Rutgers University Library.

5. George Washington to Stirling, July 8, 1779, Stirling to Washington, July 11, 1779, Washington Papers, LC; Mellick, *Old Farm*, 493.

6. George Washington to Stirling, August 12, 1779, Washington Papers, LC; Henry Lee to Congress, August 22, 1779, Moore, ed., *Diary*, 2: 207–12; Lee, *Memoirs*, 22.

7. Stirling to Congress, August 20, 1779, PCC, 162, 2: 563; Stirling to Robert Erskine, August 21, 1779, Simeon DeWitt Papers, Rutgers University Library; George Washington to Stirling, August 21, 1779, Washington Papers, LC; Ford, ed., *Journals of Congress*, 15: 1099; President of Congress to Stirling, September 28, 1779, Emmet Collection, NYPL; Thomas E. Templin, "Henry 'Light Horse Harry' Lee: A Biography" (Ph.D. diss., University of Kentucky, 1975), 61–69.

8. George Washington to Stirling, August 28, September 14, 19, 29, 30, 1779, Washington Papers, LC; William Livingston to Stirling, September 25, 1779, New Jersey Letters, Rutgers University Library; Stirling to Anthony Wayne, September 19, 27, 1779, Wayne to Stirling, September 28, October 5, 6, 1779, Wayne Papers, 8: 19, 29, 30, 48, 49, HSP; Copy of Memorial to Congress, Alexander McDougall Papers, Oversize Folder, New-York Historical Society, hereafter McDougall Papers, NYHS; Champagne, *McDougall*, 157–58.

9. George Washington to Stirling, September 25, October 4, 1779, Stirling to Washington, October 5, 1779, Washington Papers, LC; Stirling to Anthony Wayne, October 5, 1779, Chester County Historical Society; Wayne to Stirling, October 5, 1779, Wayne Papers, 8: 47, HSP.

10. George Washington to Stirling, October 7, 1779, Washington Papers, LC; Eugene Parker Chase, ed. and tr., *Our Revolutionary Forefathers: The Letters of François, Marquis de Barbé-Marbois* (New York, 1929), 119; Stirling to Congress, October 17, 1779, PCC, 162, 2: 569.

11. Stirling to William Woodford, October 26, 27, 1779, Woodford to Stirling, October 27, 1779, Park Collection, Morristown; Thomas Jefferson to Washington, November 28, 1779, Julian Boyd, ed., *The Papers of Thomas Jefferson* (21 vols. to date, Princeton, 1950–), 3: 204; Frank Moore, ed., *Songs and Ballads of the American Revolution* (New York, 1856), 209–16.

Notes to Chapter 9

12. George Washington to Stirling, October 29, 1779, Washington Papers, LC; Stirling to Nathanael Greene, November 8, 9, 1779, Park Collection, Morristown.

13. John S. Eustice to Charles Lee, November 28, 1779, *Lee Papers,* 3: 393–94.

14. London, *Evening Post,* August 13, 1779, cited in Moore, ed., *Diary,* 2: 729–30.

15. Stirling to Edward Lewis, December 5, 1779, Washburne Collection, Massachusetts Historical Society; Stirling to George Washington, December 9, 1779, Washington to Stirling, December 9, 1779, Washington Papers, LC; General Orders, December 14, 1779, Fitzpatrick, ed., *Washington Papers,* 17: 265.

16. George Washington to Stirling, January 10, 14, 1780, Stirling Papers, 5, NYHS; Washington to Stirling, January 12, 13, 1780, Washington Papers, LC. On the weather in the winter of 1779–80, consult Jackson, ed., *Washington Diary,* 3: 340–52; Wilson, ed., *Heath's Memoirs,* 239; Thacher, *Journal,* 80–81; and David M. Ludlum, *Early American Winters* (2 vols., Boston, 1966), 1: 111–18.

17. Stirling to George Washington, January 13, 14, 1780, Washington Papers, LC; Stirling to Walter Stewart, January 14, 1780, Park Collection, Morristown.

18. Stirling to George Washington, January 16, 1780, Washington Papers, LC; *New Jersey Journal,* January 18, 1780, cited in Moore, ed., *Diary,* 2: 777–78; George F. Scheer, ed., *Private Yankee Doodle: Being a Narrative of Some of the Adventures, Dangers and Sufferings of a Revolutionary Soldier, by Joseph Plumb Martin* (Boston, 1962), 171–72; Washington to President of Congress, January 18, 1780, Fitzpatrick, ed., *Washington Papers,* 17: 406; Thomas Sterling to Sir Henry Clinton, January 15, 1780, Clinton Papers, Clements Library.

19. Stirling to George Washington, January 16, 1780, Washington Papers, LC; *New Jersey Journal,* January 18, 1780, cited in Moore, ed., *Diary,* 2: 777–78; Scheer, ed., *Private Yankee Doodle,* 171–72; Benson J. Lossing, *The Pictorial Field Book of the Revolution* (2 vols., New York, 1860), 1: 311.

20. John Gibson to Horatio Gates, January 22, 1780, Gates Papers, 14, NYHS; Stirling to George Washington, January 14, 1780, Washington Papers, LC; Washington to Congress, January 18, 1780, Fitzpatrick, ed., *Washington Papers,* 17: 406. For John Adams's comments about New Jersey plunderers, see his letter to W. Carmichael, August 8, 1780, Charles Francis Adams, ed., *The Life and Works of John Adams* (10 vols., Boston, 1854), 7: 145.

21. George Washington to Stirling, March 5, 1780, Washington Papers, LC.

22. Stirling to George Washington, March 19, 1780, Washington Papers, LC.

23. Nathanael Greene to Alexander McDougall, n.d., McDougall Papers, 4, NYHS; George Washington to Stirling, March 22, 1780, Stirling to Washington, March 24, 1780, Stirling Papers, 5, NYHS; Stirling to Washington, March 24, 30, 1780, Washington Papers, LC; Councils of War, March 27, April 1, 1780, Fitzpatrick, ed., *Washington Papers,* 18: 164–66, 166n, 195n.

24. Council of War, June 6, 1780, George Washington to Stirling, June 7, 1780, Fitzpatrick, ed., *Washington Papers,* 18: 482–85, 482n, 488; Miers, *Crossroads,* 220.

25. George Washington to Stirling, June 8, 1780, Fitzpatrick, ed., *Washington Papers,* 18: 490; Washington to Stirling, June 8, 1780 (second letter), Stirling Papers, 5; NYHS.

26. Stirling to Commanding Officers of New Jersey Militia, June 8, 1780, Ely Collection, NJHS; Stirling to George Washington, June 8, 1780, Washington Papers, LC; Joseph H. Jones, ed., *Life of Ashbel Green* (New York, 1949), 11.

27. Robert H. Harrison to Stirling, June 11, 1780, Stirling to Nathanael Greene, June 23, 1780, Stirling to Militia Officers of New Jersey, June 24, 1780, Stirling Papers, 5, NYHS; Stirling to George Washington, June 23, 1780, Washington Papers, LC; Greene to Stirling, June 23, 1780, Greene Papers, Huntington Library.

28. Stirling to George Washington, July 4, 1780, Washington Papers, LC.

29. Memorial of General Officers, July 11, 1780, and General Officers to Alexander McDougall, July 11, 1780, McDougall Papers, 4, NYHS; Champagne, *McDougall,* 160.

30. *Royal Gazette,* August 16, 30, September 30, 1780; Paul David Nelson, *Anthony Wayne: Soldier of the Early Republic* (Bloomington, 1985), 111.

31. Nathanael Greene's Order of the Day, September 26, 1780, cited in Moore, ed., *Diary,* 2, 323; Anthony Wayne to Hugh Sheels, October 2, 1780, Wayne Papers, 1: 86, HSP; Carl Van Doren, *Secret History of the American Revolution* (New York, 1941), 325–54.

32. George Washington to General Officers, September 29, Fitzpatrick, ed., *Washington Papers,* 20: 101; John Laurance, Minutes of André Court Martial, September 29, 1780, Washington Papers, LC; Van Doren, *Secret History,* 355–58.

33. Charles Gray to Sir Henry Clinton, December 29, 1780, Clinton Papers, Clements Library; Thacher, *Journal,* 226–31.

34. Council of War, October 31, 1780, Fitzpatrick, ed., *Washington Papers,* 20: 273–74; Stirling to George Washington, November 2, 1780, January 7, 1781, Washington Papers, LC; Stirling to Anthony Wayne, December 28, 1780, Wayne Papers, 11: 88, HSP; Chastellux, *Travels,* 1: 106–7; Carl Van Doren, *Mutiny in January: The Story of a Crisis in the Continental Army* (New York, 1943), 152, 154–56.

Chapter 10

1. Anthony Wayne to Joseph Reed, December 16, 1780, Reed, ed., *Reed,* 2: 315–17.

2. Stirling to George Washington, January 7 (2), Washington Papers, LC; David Humphreys to George Clinton, January 11, 1781, Hugh Hastings and James A. Holden, ed., *Public Papers of George Clinton, First Governor of New York* (10 vols., New York, 1899–1914), 6: 564; Washington to Arthur St. Clair, January 12, 1781, Fitzpatrick, ed., *Washington Papers,* 21: 92; Van Doren, *Mutiny,* passim.

3. Stirling to George Washington, January 7, 1781, Stirling to Simeon DeWitt, February 17, 1781, Washington Papers, LC; Stirling to William Paterson, July 29, 1781, Paterson Papers, Rutgers University Library; John Pryor to Stirling, January 9, 1781, Stirling Papers, 5, NYHS; Chastellux, *Memoirs*, 1: 142.

4. Board of General Officers, June 12, 1781, Fitzpatrick, ed., *Washington Papers*, 22: 201–4, 204n; Stirling to George Washington, June 16, 1781, Washington Papers, LC; Freeman, *Washington*, 5: 309–10.

5. Stirling to Timothy Pickering, June 17, 1781, George Washington to Stirling, July 14, 1781, Stirling Papers, 5, NYHS; Stirling to Washington, July 6, 1781, Washington Papers, LC; Washington to Robert Howe, September 24, 1781, Fitzpatrick, ed., *Washington Papers*, 23: 131; Jackson, ed., *Washington Diary*, 3: 390, 394; Balch, ed., *Blanchard Journal*, 118–19; Freeman, *Washington*, 5: 310.

6. Stirling to William Paterson, July 29, 1781, Paterson Papers, Rutgers University Library; Stirling to Robert Morris, September 7, 1781, Paterson to Stirling, September 23, 1781, William Duer to Stirling, September 16, 1781, Stirling Papers, 5, NYHS; Thomas Fred. Jackson to _____, October 4, 1781, *PMHB* 39 (1915): 496; Stirling to Thomas Wooster, October 15, 1781, Ely Collection, NJHS.

7. Wilson, ed., *Heath's Memoirs*, 329; Benjamin Tupper to Stirling, October 8, 1781, John Stark to Stirling, October 21, 1781, Stirling to Stark, October 24, 1781, Stirling Papers, 5, NYHS.

8. Stirling to Robert Van Rensselaer and Peter Gansevoort, October 23, 1781, Stirling to John Stark, October 25, 1781, Stirling to Benjamin Tupper, October 25, 1781, Stirling to George Washington, November 20, 1781, Stirling Papers, 5, NYHS; Stirling to George Clinton, October 23, 24, 1781, Hastings and Holden, eds., *Clinton Papers*, 7: 437, 438–39.

9. Stirling to John Stark, October 25, 1781, Stark to Stirling, October 25, 27, 1781, Stirling to George Washington, November 20, 1781, Stirling Papers, 5, NYHS; Stirling to Henry Olin, October 26, 1781, Marinus Willet to Stirling, October 26, 1781, Stirling to George Clinton, October 27, 1781, Hastings and Holden, eds., *Clinton Papers*, 7: 443–44, 447–50; Stirling to William Heath, October 27, 1781, William Heath Papers, 22: 265, Massachusetts Historical Society, hereafter Heath Papers, MHS.

10. Stirling to John Stark, October 28, 1781, Stirling to Peter Gansevoort, October 31, 1781, Stirling to George Washington, November 20, 1781, Stirling Papers, 5, NYHS; Stirling to William Heath, October 29, 1781, Washington Papers, LC; George Clinton to Stirling, October 29, 1781, and to Robert Van Rensselaer, November 2, 1781, Hastings and Holden, eds., *Clinton Papers*, 456–57, 477; Stirling to William Heath, October 31, 1781, Heath Papers, 22: 96, MHS.

11. Stirling to Barry St. Leger, November 1, 1781, Marinus Willet to Stirling, November 2, 1781, Stirling to William Heath, November 3, 1781, St. Leger to Stirling, November 7, 1781, Washington Papers, LC; Stirling to Isra-

el Putnam, November 1, 1781, Miscellaneous Manuscripts, William L. Clements Library; Stirling to George Washington, November 3, 1781, Stirling to George Clinton, November 6, 1781, Schoff Papers, Clements Library; Stirling to George Clinton, November 3, 1781, Hastings and Holden, ed., *Clinton Papers*, 7: 478–79; Stirling to John Stark, November 6, 1781, John Stark Papers, New Hampshire Historical Society, hereafter Stark Papers, NHHS; Stark to Stirling, November 7, 1781, Stirling to Willet, November 9, 1781, Stirling to Washington, November 20, 1781, Stirling Papers, 5, NYHS.

12. Stirling to William Heath, November 9, 10, 18, 1781, Heath Papers, 22: 91, 94, 98, MHS; Stirling to John Stark, November 10, 12, 1781, Stark Papers, NHHS; Stark to Stirling, November 13, 1781, Stirling Papers, 5, NYHS.

13. Stirling to George Washington, November 20, 1781, Stirling Papers, 5, NYHS; Wilson, ed., *Heath's Memoirs*, 339; Duer, *Stirling*, 242n.

14. George Washington to Stirling, November 30, 1781, Stirling Papers, 5, NYHS; Stirling to Washington, December 13, 1781, Washington Papers, LC.

15. William Livingston to Stirling, January 11, 1782, Stirling Papers, 5, NYHS; Philip Schuyler to Stirling, December 8, 1781, George Washington to Stirling, December 25, 1781, Stirling to Washington, January 14, 1782, Washington Papers, LC.

16. General Orders, January 9, 1782, Fitzpatrick, ed., *Washington Papers*, 23: 471; Alexander McDougall to William Heath, January 19, 1782, McDougall Papers, 5, NYHS; McDougall to George Washington, February 8, 1782, Washington Papers, LC.

17. Stirling to William Heath, February 19, 1782, George Washington to Stirling, April 4, 1782, Stirling to Washington, April 5, 1782, Washington Papers, LC; Stirling to Heath, March 31, 1782, Heath Papers, 24, 262, MHS; General Orders, April 7, 1782, Fitzpatrick, ed., *Washington Papers*, 34, 104; Champagne, *McDougall*, 177.

18. Stirling to Alexander McDougall, August 20, December 4, 1782, McDougall to Stirling, November 12, December 14, 1782, McDougall Papers, 5, NYHS; Champagne, *McDougall*, 177.

19. Stirling to William Heath, February 22, 1782, Stirling to George Washington, April 20, 1782, Washington Papers, LC; Stirling to Heath, February 23, 24, 26 (2), 28, March 1, 2, 20, April 27, 28, 30, 1782, Heath Papers, 24: 13, 21, 39, 40, 58, 66, 78, 171, 430, 434, 448, MHS; Memorandum, May 15, 1782, Stirling to Marquis de Bouille, June 25, 1782, Stirling Papers, 5, NYHS; Stirling to Washington, April 19, 1782, Huntington Manuscripts, Henry E. Huntington Library, hereafter Huntington Manuscripts, Huntington Library; Council of General Officers, April 15, 1782, Fitzpatrick, ed., *Washington Papers*, 24: 121–25.

20. Stirling to William Heath, March 16, 1782, Heath Papers, 24: 141, MHS; David Cobb to Stirling, July 28, 1782, Stirling Papers, NYPL; Cession of Cer-

tificates, March 27, 1782, Statesmen Autograph Collection, New Jersey Historical Society; Mr. Jackson to Webb & Talliers, August 19, 1782, Worthington C. Ford, ed., *Correspondence and Journals of Samuel Blachley Webb* (3 vols., New York, 1893–1894), 2: 408n; Stirling to George Washington, August 23, 1782, Washington Papers, LC; Washington to Stirling, August 24, 1782, Smith Collection, Morristown.

21. George Washington to Stirling, August 29, 1782, Stirling to Washington, November 2, 1782, Washington Papers, LC.

22. Stirling to George Washington, September 7, 1782, Washington to Stirling, September 18, 1782, Washington Papers, LC; Stirling to Washington, September 14, 1782, General Manuscripts, Princeton University Library; Stirling to Washington, September 21, 1782, Huntington Manuscripts, Huntington Library.

23. Henry Dearborn to Stirling, September 30, October 14, 23, 1782, John Sullivan to Stirling, October 4, 1782, Stirling Papers, 5, NYHS; Stirling to George Washington, October 6, 12, 1782, Washington to Stirling, October 9, 1782, Henry Dearborn to Stirling, October 14, 1782, Washington Papers, LC; George Clinton to Washington, October 20, 1782, Hastings and Holden, eds., *Clinton Papers,* 8: 78.

24. Stirling to George Washington, October 23, 26, November 2, 8, 12, 1782, Washington Papers, LC.

25. George Washington to Stirling, October 30, November 13, 1782, Washington Papers, LC.

26. Stirling to George Washington, November 2, 23, 1782, Washington Papers, LC; Stirling to Charles Stewart, December 19, 1782, Samuel Hazard, et al., eds., *Pennsylvania Archives* (138 vols. to date, Philadelphia and Harrisburg, 1664–), 2d ser., 9: 675.

27. George Washington to Lady Stirling, January 20, 1783, Stirling Papers, 5, NYHS; Washington to Congress, January 20, 1783, General Orders, January 22, 1783, Fitzpatrick, ed., *Washington Papers,* 26: 53–54, 61; Freeman, *Washington,* 5: 429. Five months later, Washington still missed his friend; "Lord Stirling is no more," he wrote Lafayette on April 5, 1783; "he died at Albany in Jany. last, very much regretted" (Fitzpatrick, ed., *Washington Papers,* 26: 30).

28. Ford, ed., *Journals of Congress,* 24: 96; Elias Boudinot to George Washington, January 29, 1783, Boudinot, ed., *Boudinot Papers,* 1: 288–89.

29. Chastellux, *Travels,* 1: 106–7.

Selected Bibliography

Manuscript Collections

American Philosophical Society, Library, Philadelphia
  Benjamin Franklin Papers
  Royal Society of Arts, London: Selected Material Relating to America, 1754–1806
  Papers on Science
Chester County Historical Society, West Chester (Pennsylvania)
Chicago Historical Society, Chicago
  George Weedon Papers
William L. Clements Library, Ann Arbor (Michigan)
  Sir Henry Clinton Papers
  Nathanael Greene Papers
  James S. Schoff Papers
Detroit Public Library, Detroit
  Burton Historical Collection
Historical Society of Pennsylvania, Philadelphia
  Dreer Collection: Revolutionary Generals
  Etting Collection: Generals of the Revolution
  Franklin Manuscripts
  Simon Gratz Autograph Collection
  Irvine Papers
  Benson J. Lossing Papers
  Penn Papers
  Richard Peters Papers
  John Wanamaker Collection
  Anthony Wayne Papers
Henry E. Huntington Library, San Marino (California)
  Brock Collection
  Nathanael Greene Papers
  Huntington Manuscripts
  Loudoun Collection
Library of Congress, Washington, D.C.
  William Alexander, Lord Stirling Papers
  Peter Force Papers

Selected Bibliography

Alexander Hamilton Papers
Miscellaneous Manuscripts Collection
George Washington Papers
Maryland Historical Society, Baltimore
  James McHenry Papers
Massachusetts Historical Society, Boston
  French Papers
  William Heath Papers
  Henry Knox Papers
  William Livingston Papers
  Washburn Collection
  Washington Manuscripts
Morristown National Historical Park, Morristown (New Jersey)
  Park Collection
  Lloyd W. Smith Collection
National Archives, Washington, D.C.
  Letters of Major General William Alexander, Lord Stirling. Papers of the Continental Congress, No. 162
New Hampshire Historical Society, Concord
  John Stark Papers
  John Sullivan Papers
New Haven Colony Historical Society, New Haven (Connecticut)
  Jared Ingersoll Papers
New Jersey Historical Society, Newark
  Papers of James and William Alexander
  Chew Family Papers
  Elias Dayton Papers
  Edwin Augustus Ely Autograph Collection
  Robert Hunter Morris Papers
  New Jersey Letters
  Reeve Schley Autograph Collection
  Joseph Sherwood Letters
  Statesmen Autograph Collection
New Jersey State Library, Trenton
  New Jersey Colonial Documents
New-York Historical Society, New York
  James Alexander Papers
  William Alexander, Lord Stirling, Papers
  Horatio Gates Papers
  Alexander McDougall Papers
  New York-New Jersey Boundary Papers
  Revolutionary War Papers

Rutherfurd Collection
New York Public Library, New York
    Samuel Adams Papers
    William Alexander (Lord Stirling) Papers
    Emmet Collection
    Myers Collection
    Tomlinson Papers
    D. A. Welch Collection
University of Pennsylvania: Rare Books Collection, Charles Patterson Van Pelt Library, Philadelphia
    Benjamin Franklin Papers
Princeton University Library, Princeton (New Jersey)
    E. Stanley Atkinson Autograph Collection
    General Manuscripts
    Alfred Goddard May Collection
Rutgers University Library, Special Collections, New Brunswick (New Jersey)
    James Abeel Papers
    Samuel Allinson Papers
    Boudinot Family Miscellany
    Simeon DeWitt Papers
    New Jersey Letters
    William Paterson Papers
    Israel Shreve Papers
South Carolina Historical Society, Charleston
    Papers of Henry Laurens

Printed Primary Sources

Adams, Charles Francis, ed. *Familiar Letters of John Adams and His Wife Abigail Adams, During the Revolution*. New York: Hurd and Houghton, 1876.

―――, ed. *The Life and Works of John Adams*. 10 vols. Boston: Little, Brown, 1854.

Albion, Robert G., and Leonidas Dodson, eds., *Philip Vickers Fithian: Journal, 1775–1776, Written on the Virginia-Pennsylvania Frontier and in the Army Around New York*. Princeton: Princeton University Press, 1934.

Alexander, James. *A Brief Narrative of the Case and Trial of John Peter Zenger, Printer of the New York Weekly Journal*. Edited by Stanley N. Katz. Cambridge, Mass.: Belknap Press of Harvard University Press, 1963.

Allinson, Samuel, ed. *Acts of the General Assembly of the Province of New Jersey, 1702–1776*. Burlington: State of New Jersey, 1776.

Selected Bibliography

Almon, J., ed. *The Parliamentary Register: A History of the Proceedings and Debates of the House of Commons.* 25 vols. London, 1775–1804.

André, John. *Major André's Journal: Operations of the British Army Under Lieutenant Generals Sir William Howe and Sir Henry Clinton, June, 1776 to November, 1778.* Tarrytown, N.Y.: William Abbot, 1930.

Archives of the State of New Jersey, 1631–1800. 30 vols. Newark: State of New Jersey, 1800–1949.

Balch, Thomas, ed. *The Journal of Claude Blanchard, Commissary of the French Auxiliary Army Sent to the United States during the American Revolution, 1780–83.* Translated by William Duane. Albany: J. Munsell, 1876.

Baldwin, Thomas Williams, ed. *The Revolutionary Journal of Col. Jeduthan Baldwin, 1775–1778.* Bangor, Maine: C. H. Glass, 1906.

Benson, Adolph B., ed. *The America of 1750: Peter Kalm's Travels in North America: The English Version of 1770.* 2 vols. New York: Wilson-Erickson, 1937.

Boudinot, J. J., ed. *The Life, Public Services, Addresses, and Letters of Elias Boudinot.* 2 vols. Boston: Houghton, Mifflin, 1896.

Boyd, Julian, ed. *The Papers of Thomas Jefferson.* 21 vols. to date. Princeton: Princeton University Press, 1950–.

⸺, and Robert J. Taylor, eds. *The Susquehannah Company Papers.* 11 vols. Wilkes-Barre: Wyoming Historical and Genealogical Society, and Ithaca, N.Y.: Cornell University Press, 1930–71.

Brock, Robert A., ed. *Official Records of Robert Dinwiddie, Lieutenant-Governor of the Colony of Virginia, 1751–1758.* 2 vols. Richmond: Virginia Historical Society, 1883–84.

Browne, W. H., et al., eds. *Archives of Maryland.* 65 vols. Baltimore: The State, 1883–1952.

Burnett, Edmund C., ed. *Letters of Members of the Continental Congress.* 8 vols. Washington, D.C.: Government Printing Office, 1921–38.

Butterfield, Lyman H., ed., *Letters of Benjamin Rush.* 2 vols. Princeton: Princeton University Press, 1951.

Cadwallader Colden Papers. New-York Historical Society Collections, 49–56. New York: The Society, 1917–23.

Calendar of Maryland State Papers: The Red Books. 4 vols. Annapolis: State of Maryland, 1950–55.

Chase, Eugene Parker, ed. and tr. *Our Revolutionary Forefathers: The Letters of François, Marquis de Barbé-Marbois.* New York: Duffield, 1929.

Chastellux, Marquis de. *Travels in North America in the Years 1780, 1781 and 1782.* Translated by Howard C. Rice, Jr. 2 vols. Chapel Hill: University of North Carolina Press, 1963.

Clark, Walter, ed. *State Records of North Carolina, 1777–1790.* 16 vols. Winston: State of North Carolina, 1895–1905.

Clinton, Sir Henry. *The American Rebellion: Sir Henry Clinton's Narrative of*

His Campaigns, 1775–1782. Edited by William B. Willcox. New Haven: Yale University Press, 1954.
Cobbett, William, and John Wright, eds. *The Parliamentary History of England*. 36 vols. London: Hansard, 1806–20.
The Colden Papers. New-York Historical Society Collections, 9–10. New York: The Society, 1876–77.
Columbia University. *Catalogue of Officer and Graduates of Columbia University, from the Foundation of King's College in 1754*. New York: For the University, 1916.
———. *Minutes of the Governors of the College of the Province of New York in the City of New York in America, 1755–1768*. New York: For the University, 1932.
Commanger, Henry Steele, and Richard B. Morris, eds. *The Spirit of Seventy-Six*. 2 vols. Indianapolis: Bobbs-Merrill, 1958.
Conduct of Major General Shirley, Late General and Commander in Chief of His Majesty's Forces in North America, Briefly Stated. London: Private Printing, 1758.
Corner, George W., ed. *The Autobiography of Benjamin Rush*. Princeton: Princeton University Press, 1948.
Davis, Matthew L., ed. *Memoirs of Aaron Burr, With Miscellaneous Selections from His Correspondence*. 2 vols. New York: Harper & Brothers, 1837.
Donnon, Elizabeth, ed. *Documents Illustrative of the History of the Slave Trade to America*. 4 vols. Washington: Carnegie Institute, 1930–35.
DuPonceau, Pierre Étienne, "Autobiography," *Pensylvania Magazine of History and Biography*. 63 (1939): 195–227.
Fitzpatrick, John C., ed. *The Writings of George Washington from the Original Manuscripts, 1745–1799*. 39 vols. Washington, D.C.: Government Printing Office, 1931–44.
Force, Peter, ed. *American Archives: A Documentary History of the Origin and Progress of the North American Colonies*. 9 vols. Washington, D.C.: Government Printing Office, 1837–53.
Ford, Worthington C., ed. *Correspondence and Journals of Samuel Blachley Webb*. 3 vols. New York: Wickersham Press, 1893–94.
———. *Journals of the Continental Congress, 1774–1789*. 34 vols. Washington, D.C.: Government Printing Office, 1904–37.
Grant, W. L., and James Munro, eds. *Acts of the Privy Council of England: Colonial Series*. 6 vols. London: Anthony Bros., 1908–12.
Hamilton, Stanislaus Murray, ed. *Letters to Washington and Accompanying Papers*. 5 vols. Boston: Houghton, Mifflin, 1892–1902.
———, ed. *The Writings of James Monroe*. 7 vols. New York: G. P. Putnam's Sons, 1898–1903.
Hammond, Otis G., ed. *Letters and Papers of Major General John Sullivan, Continental Army*. New Hampshire Historical Society Collections, 12–15. Concord: New Hampshire Historical Society, 1930–39.

Hastings, Hugh, and James A. Holden, eds. *Public Papers of George Clinton, First Governor of New York*. 10 vols. New York: State of New York, 1899–1914.

Hazard, Samuel, et al., eds. *Pennsylvania Archives*. 138 vols. to date. Philadelphia and Harrisburg: The State, 1664–.

Heath Papers. Massachusetts Historical Society Collections, 5th ser., vol. 4, 7th ser., vol. 4. Boston: Massachusetts Historical Society, 1878–1905.

Historical Manuscripts Commission. *The Manuscripts of the Earl of Dartmouth*. 3 vols. London: Eyre and Spottiswoodie, 1887–99.

———. *The Manuscripts of the Marquess Townshend*. London: Eyre and Spottiswoodie, 1887.

Jackson, Donald, and Dorothy Twohig, eds. *The Diaries of George Washington*. 6 vols. Charlottesville: University Press of Virginia, 1976–80.

James, A. P., ed. *The Writings of General John Forbes*. Menasha, Wis.: Collegiate Press, 1938.

Jones, Joseph H., ed. *Life of Ashbel Green*. New York: Private Printing, 1949.

Jones, Thomas. *History of New York During the Revolutionary War*. Edited by Edward Floyd Delancey. 2 vols. New York: New-York Historical Society, 1879.

Journals of the House of Lords. 46 vols. London: The House of Lords, n.d.

Journal of the Commissioners for Trade and Plantations. 14 vols. London: H. M. Stationer's Office, 1920–38.

Kemble Papers. New-York Historical Society Collections, 16–17. New York: The Society, 1884–85.

Labaree, Leonard W., and William B. Willcox, eds. *The Papers of Benjamin Franklin*. 20 vols. to date. New Haven: Yale University Press, 1959–.

Lafayette, Marquis de. *Mémoires, Correspondance et Manuscrits*. 6 vols. Paris: H. Fournier Aîné, Éditeur, 1837–38.

Lee, Henry. *Memoirs of the War in the Southern Department of the United States*. New York: University Publishing, 1869.

Lee Papers. New-York Historical Society Collections, 4–7. New York: The Society, 1872–76.

Lesser, Charles H., ed. *The Sinews of Independence: Monthly Strength Reports of the Continental Army*. Chicago: University of Chicago Press, 1976.

Letters of William Alexander, Lord Stirling. New Jersey Historical Society Proceedings, 1–10, 60. Newark: The Society, 1845–66, 1942.

Lincoln, Charles Henry, ed. *Correspondence of William Shirley*. 2 vols. New York: Macmillan, 1912.

Long Island Historical Society. *Memoirs*, 2–3. Brooklyn: The Society, 1865–69.

Lushington, Stephen R. *Life and Services of General Lord Harris*. 2d ed. rev. London: J. W. Parker, 1845.

Lydenberg, Harry Miller, ed. *Archibald Robertson, Lieutenant-General, Royal*

Engineers, His Diaries and Sketches in America, 1762–1780. New York: The New York Public Library, 1930.

Mackenzie, Frederick. *Diary of Frederick Mackenzie, Giving a Daily Narrative of His Military Service . . . During the Years 1775–1781*. 2 vols. Cambridge, Mass.: Harvard University Press, 1930.

Mauduit, Jasper, Agent in London for the Province of Massachusetts-Bay, 1762–1765. Massachusetts Historical Society Collections, 74. Boston: The Society, 1918.

Miller, George J., ed. *Minutes of the Board of Proprietors of the Eastern Division of New Jersey*. 3 vols. Perth Amboy: Board of Proprietors of the Eastern Division of New Jersey, 1949–60.

Moore, Frank, ed. *The Diary of the Revolution*. 2 vols. Hartford: J. B. Burr, 1876.

―――, ed. *Songs and Ballads of the American Revolution*. New York: D. Appleton, 1885.

Morris, Richard B., ed. *Alexander Hamilton and the Founding of the Nation*. New York: Dial Press, 1957.

―――. *John Jay: The Making of a Revolutionary, Unpublished Papers, 1745–1780*. New York: Harper & Row, 1975.

O'Callaghan, E. B., and Berthold Fernow, eds. *Documents Relative to the Colonial History of the State of New York*. 15 vols. Albany: Weed, Parsons, 1856–87.

Pargellis, Stanley, ed. *Military Affairs in North America, 1748–1765: Selected Documents from the Cumberland Papers in Windsor Castle*. New York: D. Appleton-Century, 1936.

Peckham, Howard, ed. *The Toll of Independence: Engagements & Battle Casualties of the American Revolution*. Chicago: University of Chicago Press, 1974.

Pickering, Octavius, ed. *The Life of Timothy Pickering*. 4 vols. Boston: Little, Brown, 1867–73.

Prince, Carl E., ed. *The Papers of William Livingston*. 2 vols. to date. Trenton: New Jersey Historical Commission, 1979–.

Quincy, Eliza Susan Morton. *Memoir of the Life of Eliza S. M. Quincy*. Boston: J. Wilson and Son, 1861.

Reed, William Bradford, ed. *Life and Correspondence of Joseph Reed*. 2 vols. Philadelphia: Lindsay and Blakiston, 1847.

Ricord, Frederick, and William Nelson, eds. *Archives of the State of New Jersey*. 42 vols. Newark: State of New Jersey, 1880–1949.

Rogers, Robert. *Journals*. London: J. Milla, 1765.

Ryden, George H., ed. *Letters to and from Caesar Rodney, 1765–1785*. Philadelphia: University of Pennsylvania Press, 1933.

Sabine, William H. W., ed. *The New-York Diary of Lieutenant Jabez Fitch of the 17th (Connecticut) Regiment from August 22, 1776 to December 15, 1777*. New York: Colburn & Tegg, 1954.

Selected Bibliography

Scheer, George F., ed. *Private Yankee Doodle: Being a Narrative of Some of the Adventures, Dangers and Sufferings of a Revolutionary Soldier, by Joseph Plumb Martin.* Boston: Little, Brown, 1962.

Schneider, Herbert and Carol, eds. *Samuel Johnson, President of King's College: His Career and Writings.* 4 vols. New York: Columbia University Press, 1929.

Scull, G. C., ed. *The Montresor Journals.* New-York Historical Society Collections, 14. New York: The Society, 1882.

Selections from the Correspondence of the Executive of New Jersey, from 1776 to 1786. 2 vols. Newark: Newark Daily Advertiser Office, 1848.

Showman, Richard K., ed. *The Papers of General Nathanael Greene.* 3 vols. to date. Chapel Hill: University of North Carolina Press, 1976–.

Smith, William. *The History of the Late Province of New York.* Edited by Michael Kammen. 2 vols. Cambridge, Mass.: Belknap Press of Harvard University Press, 1972.

Sparks, Jared, ed. *Correspondence of the American Revolution.* 4 vols. Boston: Little, Brown, 1853.

———. *The Life of Gouverneur Morris, with Selections from His Correspondence and Miscellaneous Papers.* 2 vols. Boston: Gray Bowen, 1832.

———. *The Works of Benjamin Franklin.* 10 vols. Boston: Tappan and Whittemore, 1840.

———. *The Writings of George Washington.* 12 vols. Boston: Little, Brown, 1834–37.

Stark, Caleb, ed. *Memoir and Official Correspondence of General John Stark.* Concord, N.H.: G. P. Lyon, 1860.

Stevens, Benjamin F., ed. *Facsimiles of Manuscripts in European Archives Relating to America, 1773–1783.* 25 vols. London: Malby and Sons, 1889–95.

Stevens, S. K., ed. *Papers of Henry Bouquet.* 2 vols. Harrisburg: Pennsylvania Historical and Museum Commission, 1940–51.

Sullivan, James, et al., eds. *Papers of Sir William Johnson.* 13 vols. Albany: University of the State of New York, 1921–25.

Syrett, Harold C., and Jacob E. Cooke, eds. *Papers of Alexander Hamilton.* 24 vols. to date. New York: Columbia University Press, 1961–.

Tatum, Edward H., ed. *The American Journal of Ambrose Serle, Secretary to Lord Howe, 1776–1778.* San Marino, Cal.: The Huntington Library, 1940.

Taylor, William Stanhope, and John Henry Pringle, eds. *Correspondence of William Pitt.* 4 vols. London: John Murray, 1838–40.

Thacher, James. *A Military Journal During the American Revolutionary War.* Boston: Cottons and Barnard, 1827.

Trumbull Papers. Massachusetts Historical Society Collections, 5th ser., vol. 9–10, 7th ser., vols. 2–3. Boston: Massachusetts Historical Society, 1885–1902.

Uhlendorf, Bernhard, A., tr. *Revolution in America: Confidential Letters and*

Journals, 1776–1784 of Adjutant General Major Baurmeister of the Hessian Forces. New Brunswick, N.J.: Rutgers University Press, 1957.

Waldo, Albigence, "Diary, Valley Forge, 1777–1778," *Pennsylvania Magazine of History and Biography* 21 (1897).

Warren-Adams Letters. Massachusetts Historical Society Collections, 72–73. Boston: Massachusetts Historical Society, 1917–25.

Whitehead, W. A., ed. *Archives of the State of New Jersey, 1631–1800.* 30 vols. Newark, etc.: The State, 1880–1949.

Wilkinson, James. *Memoirs of My Own Times.* 3 vols. Philadelphia: A. Small, 1816.

Willis, William, and James Phinney Baxter, eds. *Documentary History of the State of Maine.* 24 vols. Portland: Maine Historical Society, 1869–1916.

Wilson, Rufus R., ed. *Heath's Memoirs of the American War.* New York: A. Wessels, 1904.

Wroth, Lawrence C. *An American Bookshelf, 1755.* Philadelphia: UPA Press, 1934.

Dissertations

Chase, Philander Dean. "Baron Von Steuben in the War of Independence." Ph.D. diss., Duke University, 1972.

Danforth, George H. "The Rebel Earl." Ph.D. diss., Columbia University, 1955.

Forry, Richard R. "Edward Hand: His Role in the American Revolution." Ph.D. diss., Duke University, 1976.

Templin, Thomas E. "Henry 'Light Horse Harry' Lee: A Biography." Ph.D. diss., University of Kentucky, 1975.

Newspapers

New York Gazette (New York), 1773–75
New York Journal (New York), 1773–74
Pennsylvania Gazeteer (Philadelphia), 1774
Pennsylvania Journal (Philadelphia), 1774
Rivington's New York Gazeteer (New York), 1773–74

Secondary Articles

Adams, Charles Francis. "The Battle of Long Island," *American Historical Review* 1 (1896): 650–70.

Becker, Carl. "Nominations in Colonial New York," *American Historical Review* 6 (1901): 260–75.
Calderhead, William L. "British Naval Failure at Long Island: A Lost Opportunity in the American Revolution," *New York History* 57 (1976): 321–38.
Danforth, George H. "Lord Stirling's Hibernia Furnace," New Jersey Historical Society Proceedings, 71st ser., Newark: New Jersey Historical Society, 1953.
Doerflinger, Thomas M. "Hibernia Furnace During the Revolution," *New Jersey History* 90 (1972): 97–114.
Groce, George E. "Eliphalet Dyer." Edited by Richard B. Morris. *Era of the American Revolution: Studies Inscribed to Evarts B. Greene*. New York: Columbia University Press, 1939.
Higginbotham, Don. "The American Militia: A Traditional Institution with Revolutionary Responsibilities," in *Reconsiderations on the Revolutionary War*, ed. Don Higginbotham. Westport, Conn.: Greenwood Press, 1978, 83–103.
"Historical Notes of Dr. Benjamin Rush," *Pennsylvania Magazine of History and Biography* 27 (1903): 147–48.
Howlett, Ned O. "Lord Stirling in Basking Ridge," New Jersey Historical Society Proceedings, new series 15. Newark: New Jersey Historical Society, 1930.
Lane, William C. "Sir Francis Bernard and His Grant of Mount Desert," Colonial Society of Massachusetts Publications, 24. Boston: The Society, 1895.
Levermore, C. H. "The Whigs of Colonial New York," *American Historical Review* 1 (1896): 238–50.
Longley, R. S. "Lord Stirling, Titled Whig of the American Revolution," Royal Society of Canada Transactions, 3d ser., vol. 56 (1962), 11–22.
McCormick, Richard P. "The Society, the Grape, and New Jersey (i–ii)," *Journal of the Royal Society of Arts* 110 (January–March 1962): 119–21, 265–68.
Nelson, Paul David. "British Conduct of the American Revolutionary War: A Review of Interpretations," *Journal of American History* 65 (1978): 623–53.
———. "Citizen Soldiers or Regulars: The Views of American General Officers on the Military Establishment, 1775–1781," *Military Affairs* 43 (1979): 126–32.
Stockton, Frank R. "An American Lord." In *Stories of New Jersey*, edited by M. V. Gaver. New Brunswick, N.J.: Rutgers University Press, 1961.
Thayer, Theodore. "The Army Contractors for the Niagara Campaign 1755–1756," *William and Mary Quarterly*, 3d ser., vol. 14 (January 1957): 31–46.
Tuttle, J. F. "Hibernia Furnace and the Surrounding Country, in the Revolutionary War," New Jersey Historical Society Proceedings, new series 6. Newark: New Jersey Historical Society, 1879–81.

Willcox, William B., and Frederick Wyatt. "Sir Henry Clinton: A Psychological Exploration in History," *Willam and Mary Quarterly*, 3d ser., 16 (1959): 3–26.

Books

Abbot, Wilbur C. *New York in the American Revolution*. New York: Charles Scribner's Sons, 1929.
Alden, John R. *The American Revolution, 1775–1783*. New York: Harper & Row, 1954.
―――. *General Charles Lee: Traitor or Patriot?* Baton Rouge: Louisiana State University Press, 1951.
―――. *A History of the American Revolution*. New York: Knopf, 1969.
Alexander, Edward Porter. *A Revolutionary Conservative: James Duane of New York*. New York: Columbia University Press, 1938.
Allan, Herbert S. *John Hancock: Portrait in Purple*. New York: Macmillan, 1948.
Andrews, Charles M. *The Colonial Period of American History*. 4 vols. New Haven: Yale University Press, 1934–38.
Aptheker, Herbert. *American Negro Slave Revolts*. New York: Columbia University Press, 1943.
Bancroft, George. *History of the United States from the Discovery of the Continent*. 10 vols. Boston: Little, Brown, 1834–74.
Binger, Carl. *Revolutionary Doctor: Benjamin Rush, 1746–1813*. New York: Norton, 1966.
Billias, George A. *General John Glover and His Marblehead Mariners*. New York: Holt, 1960.
Bonomi, Patricia U. *A Factious People: Politics and Society in Colonial New York*. New York: Columbia University Press, 1971
Bowen, Clarence Winthrop. *The History of the Centennial Celebration of the Inauguration of George Washington as First President of the United States*. New York: Appleton, 1892.
Boyd, George Adams. *Elias Boudinot, Patriot and Statesman*. New York: Greenwood Press, 1952.
Boyer, Charles S. *Early Forges and Furnaces in New Jersey*. Philadelphia: University of Pennsylvania Press, 1931.
Brooke, John. *King George III*. New York: McGraw-Hill, 1972.
Bush, Martin H. *Revolutionary Enigma: A Re-appraisal of General Philip Schuyler of New York*. Port Washington, N.Y.: I. J. Friedman, 1969.
Callahan, North. *Daniel Morgan: Ranger of the Revolution*. New York: A. S. Barnes, 1876.

———. *Henry Knox: General Washington's General*. New York: Rinehart, 1958.
Carrington, Henry B. *Battles of the American Revolution*. New York: A. S. Barnes, 1876.
Champagne, Roger J. *Alexander McDougall and the American Revolution in New York*. Schenectady: New York State American Revolution Bicentennial Commission and Union College Press, 1975.
Clark, Victor S. *History of Manufactures in the United States*. 3 vols. New York: McGraw-Hill, 1929.
Cresson, W. P. *James Monroe*. Chapel Hill: University of North Carolina Press, 1946.
Cuneo, John R. *Robert Rogers of the Rangers*. New York: Oxford University Press, 1959.
Dangerfield, George, *Chancellor Robert R. Livingston of New York, 1746–1813*. New York: Harcourt, Brace, 1960.
Dawson, Henry B. *Battles of the United States by Sea and Land*. 2 vols. New York: Johnson, Fry, 1858.
Dickerson, Oliver M. *The Navigation Acts and the American Revolution*. Philadelphia: University of Pennsylvania Press, 1951.
Dillon, Dorothy R. *The New York Triumvirate: A Study of the Legal and Political Careers of William Livingston, John Morin Scott, and William Smith, Jr.* New York: Columbia University Press, 1949.
Ditmas, Charles Andrew. *The Life and Service of Major-General William Alexander also Called the Earl of Stirling*. Brooklyn: New-York Historical Society, 1920.
Duer, William Alexander. *The Life of William Alexander, Earl of Stirling: Major General in the Army of the United States, during the Revolution*. New York: Wiley & Putnam, 1847.
Dunlap, William. *History of the New Netherlands, Province of New York, and State of New York*. 2 vols. New York: Carter & Thorp, 1839.
Edwards, George Williams. *New York as an Eighteenth Century Municipality, 1731–1776*. New York: Columbia University Press, 1917.
Field, Thomas Warren. *The Battle of Long Island, With Connected Preceding Events and the Subsequent American Retreat*. Brooklyn: Long Island Historical Society, 1869.
Fisher, Edgar Jacob. *New Jersey as a Royal Province, 1738 to 1776*. New York: Columbia University Press, 1911.
Fitzgerald, Percy Hetherington. *Charles Townshend: Wit and Statesman*. London: R. Bentley, 1866.
———. *The Life and Times of John Wilkes*. 2 vols. London: Ward & Downey, 1888.
Fitzmaurice, Edmond George, Lord. *Life of William, Earl of Shelburne*. 3 vols. London: Macmillan, 1875–76.

Fleming, Thomas. *The Forgotten Victory: The Battle for New Jersey—1780*. New York: Reader's Digest Press, 1973.
Flexner, James Thomas. *George Washington: The Forge of Experience, 1732–1775*. New York: Little, Brown, 1965.
———. *George Washington in the American Revolution, 1775–1783*. Boston: Little, Brown, 1968.
———. *Mohawk Baronet: Sir William Johnson of New York*. New York: Harper & Row, 1959.
———. *The Traitor and the Spy: Benedict Arnold and John André*. New York: Harcourt, Brace, 1953.
Fortescue, J. W. *A History of the British Army*. 13 vols. London: Macmillan, 1899–1930.
Fowler, William. *The Baron of Beacon Hill: A Biography of John Hancock*. Boston: Houghton Mifflin, 1979.
Franklin, John Hope. *From Slavery to Freedom: A History of Negro Americans*. 4th ed. New York: Knopf, 1974.
Freeman, Douglas Southall. *George Washington: A Biography*. 7 vols. New York: Charles Scribner's Sons, 1947–57.
French, Allen. *The First Year of the American Revolution*. Boston: Houghton Mifflin, 1934.
Gerlach, Don R. *Philip Schuyler and the American Revolution in New York, 1733–1777*. Lincoln: University of Nebraska Press, 1964.
Gerlach, Larry R. *Prologue to Independence: New Jersey in the Coming of the American Revolution*. New Brunswick, N.J.: Rutgers University Press, 1976.
Gipson, Lawrence H. *The British Empire Before the American Revolution*. 15 vols. New York: Knopf, 1936–70.
———. *Jared Ingersoll: A Study of American Loyalism in Relation to British Colonial Government*. New Haven: Yale University Press, 1920.
Gottschalk, Louis. *Lafayette Comes to America*. Chicago: University of Chicago Press, 1935.
Greene, Francis Vinton. *The Revolutionary War and the Military Policy of the United States*. New York: Charles Scribner's Sons, 1911.
Gruber, Ira D. *The Howe Brothers and the American Revolution*. New York: Atheneum, 1972.
Harrington, Virginia D. *The New York Merchants on the Eve of the Revolution*. New York: Columbia University Press, 1935.
Hayes, John, Lord. *Vindication of the Rights and Titles, Political and Territorial, of Alexander, Earl of Stirling and Dovan and Lord Proprietor of Canada and Nova Scotia*. Washington: Gideon, 1853.
Heusser, Albert H. *George Washington's Map Maker: A Biography of Robert Erskine*. Edited by Hubert G. Schmidt. New Brunswick, N.J.: Rutgers University Press, 1966.

Higginbotham, Don. *Daniel Morgan: Revolutionary Rifleman*. Chapel Hill: University of North Carolina Press, 1961.

———. *The War of American Independence: Military Attitudes, Policies, and Practice, 1763–1789*. New York: Macmillan, 1971.

Horsmanden, Daniel. *The New York Conspiracy*. Edited by Thomas J. Davis. Boston: Beacon Press, 1971.

Hudson, Derek, and Kenneth W. Lockhurst. *The Royal Society of Arts, 1754–1954*. London: John Murray, 1954.

Humphreys, Mary G. *Catherine Schuyler*. New York: Charles Scribner's Sons, 1897.

Jacobs, James Ripley. *Tarnished Warrior: Major-General James Wilkinson*. New York: Macmillan, 1938.

Jensen, Merrill. *The Founding of a Nation: A History of the American Revolution, 1763–1776*. New York: Oxford University Press, 1968.

Kammen, Michael. *Colonial New York: A History*. New York: Charles Scribner's Sons, 1975.

Katz, Stanley Nider. *Newcastle's New York: Anglo-American Politics, 1732–1753*. Cambridge, Mass.: Belknap Press of the Harvard University Press, 1968.

Keep, Austin B. *History of the New York Society Library*. New York: DeVinne Press, 1908.

Klein, Milton M., ed. *The Independent Reflector, or Weekly Essays on Sundry Important Subjects More Particularly Adapted to the Province of New-York*. Cambridge, Mass.: Harvard University Press, 1963.

———. *Politics of Diversity: Essays in the History of Colonial New York*. Port Washington, N.Y.: Kennikat Press, 1974.

Klemmerer, Donald L. *Path to Freedom: The Struggle for Self-Government in Colonial New Jersey, 1703–1776*. Princeton: Princeton University Press, 1940.

Knollenberg, Bernhard. *Growth of the American Revolution, 1766–1775*. New York: Free Press, 1975.

———. *Origin of the American Revolution, 1759–1776*. New York: Macmillan, 1960.

———. *Washington and the Revolution, a Reappraisal: Gates, Conway, and the Continental Congress*. New York: Macmillan, 1940.

Labaree, Benjamin W. *America's Nation-Time, 1607–1789*. New York: Norton, 1972.

Lamb, Martha J. *History of the City of New York*. 2 vols. New York: A. S. Barnes, 1877–80.

Leach, Douglas Edward. *Arms for Empire: A Military History of the British Colonies in North America, 1607–1763*. New York: Macmillan, 1973.

Lossing, Benson J. *The Life and Times of Philip Schuyler*. 2 vols. New York: Sheldon, 1860–72.

———. *The Pictorial Field Book of the Revolution*. 2 vols. New York: Harper & Brothers, 1860.

Lowell, Edward J. *The Hessians and the Other German Auxiliaries of Great Britain in the Revolutionary War*. New York: Harper & Brothers, 1884.

Lundin, Leonard. *Cockpit of the Revolution: The War for Independence in New Jersey*. Princeton: Princeton University Press, 1940.

Lydekker, John Wolfe. *The Life and Letters of Charles Inglis*. London: Society for Promoting Christian Knowledge, 1936.

Mackesy, Piers. *The War for America, 1775–1783*. Cambridge, Mass.: Harvard University Press, 1965.

McCormick, Richard. *New Jersey from Colony to State, 1609–1789*. Newark: New Jersey Historical Society, 1981.

MacCracken, Henry Noble. *Prologue to Independence: The Trials of James Alexander, American, 1715–1756*. New York: James H. Heineman, 1964.

Mason, Bernard. *The Road to Independence: The Revolutionary Movement in New York, 1773–1777*. Lexington: University Press of Kentucky, 1966.

Mellick, Andrew D., Jr. *Lesser Crossroads*. Edited by Herbert G. Schmidt. New Brunswick, N.J.: Rutgers University Press, 1948.

———. *The Story of an Old Farm, or Life in New Jersey in the Eighteenth Century*. Somerville, N.J.: The Unionist-Gazette, 1889.

Miers, Earl Schenck. *Crossroads of Freedom: The American Revolution and the Rise of a New Nation*. New Brunswick, N.J.: Rutgers University Press, 1971.

Miller, John C. *Alexander Hamilton: Portrait in Paradox*. New York: Harper & Brothers, 1959.

———. *Origins of the American Revolution*. Boston: Little, Brown, 1943.

———. *Triumph of Freedom, 1775–1783*. Boston: Little, Brown, 1948.

Montross, Lynn. *Rag, Tag and Bobtail: The Story of the Continental Army, 1775–1783*. New York: Harper & Brothers, 1952.

Namier, Lewis, and John Brooke. *Charles Townshend*. New York: St. Martin's Press, 1964.

Nelson, Paul David. *Anthony Wayne: Soldier of the Early Republic*. Bloomington: Indiana University Press, 1985.

———. *General Horatio Gates: A Biography*. Baton Rouge: Louisiana State University Press, 1976.

Oberholtzer, Ellis Paxson. *Robert Morris: Patriot and Financier*. New York: Macmillan, 1903.

O'Connor, John E. *William Paterson: Lawyer and Statesman, 1745–1806*. New Brunswick: Rutgers University Press, 1974.

Osgood, Herbert L. *The American Colonies in the Eighteenth Century*. 4 vols. New York: Columbia University Press, 1924.

Palmer, John McAuley. *General Von Steuben*. New Haven: Yale University Press, 1937.

Pargellis, Stanley M. *Lord Loudoun in North America.* New Haven: Yale University Press, 1933.
Parkman, Francis. *Montcalm and Wolfe.* 2 vols. Boston: Little, Brown, 1884.
Pearse, John B. *A Concise History of the Iron Manufacture of the American Colonies Up to the Revolution.* Philadelphia: Eggleston, 1876.
Peckham, Howard H. *The Colonial Wars, 1689–1762.* Chicago: University of Chicago Press, 1964.
Pellew, George. *John Jay.* Boston: Houghton Mifflin, 1890.
Pound, Arthur, and Richard E. Day. *Johnson of the Mohawks: A Biography of Sir William Johnson.* New York: Macmillan, 1930.
Rankin, Hugh. *The North Carolina Continentals.* Chapel Hill: University of North Carolina, 1971.
Roberts, Robert B. *New York's Forts in the Revolution.* Rutherford, N.J.: Fairleigh Dickinson University Press, 1980.
Rogers, Charles. *Memorials of the Earl of Stirling and the House of Alexander.* 2 vols. Edinburgh: W. Paterson, 1877.
Rorabaugh, W. J. *The Alcoholic Republic: An American Tradition.* New York: Oxford University Press, 1979.
Rossman, Kenneth R. *Thomas Mifflin and the Politics of the American Revolution.* Chapel Hill: University of North Carolina Press, 1952.
Rutherford, Livingston. *Family Records and Events: Compiled Principally from the Original Manuscripts in the Rutherfurd Collection.* New York: DeVinne Press, 1894.
Schachner, Nathan. *Alexander Hamilton.* New York: D. Appleton-Century, 1946.
Scheer, George F., and Hugh F. Rankin. *Rebels and Redcoats.* Cleveland: World Publishing, 1957.
Schumacher, Ludwig. *Major-General the Earl of Stirling: An Essay in Biography.* New York: New Amsterdam, 1897.
_____. *The Somerset Hills.* New York: New Amsterdam, 1900.
Schutz, John A. *Thomas Pownall, British Defender of American Liberty: A Study of Anglo-American Relations in the Eighteenth Century.* Glendale, Calif.: A. H. Clark, 1951.
_____. *William Shirley: King's Governor of Massachusetts.* Chapel Hill: University of North Carolina Press, 1961.
Sedgwick, Jr., Theodore. *A Memoir of the Life of William Livingston.* New York: J. & J. Harper, 1833.
Sellers, Charles C. *Benedict Arnold: Proud Warrior.* New York: Minton Balch, 1930.
Shy, John. *Toward Lexington: The Role of the British Army in the Coming of the American Revolution.* Princeton: Princeton University Press, 1965.
Smelser, Marshall. *The Winning of Independence.* Chicago: Quadrangle, 1972.

Smith, Page. *A New Age Now Begins: A People's History of the American Revolution*. 2 vols. New York: McGraw-Hill, 1976.
Snell, James P. *History of Hunterdon and Somerset Counties*. Philadelphia: Everts & Peck, 1881.
Sosin, Jack M. *Agents and Merchants: British Colonial Policy and the Origins of the American Revolution, 1763-1775*. Lincoln: University of Nebraska Press, 1965.
Spaulding, E. Wilder. *His Excellency George Clinton, Critic of the Constitution*. New York: Macmillan, 1938.
Stanhope, P. H. *Life of the Right Honourable William Pitt*. 4 vols. London: J. Murray, 1861-62.
Stokes, I. N. Phelps. *The Iconography of Manhattan Island, 1898-1909*. 6 vols. New York: R. H. Dodd, 1915-28.
Stryker, William S. *The Battle of Monmouth*. Princeton: Princeton University Press, 1927.
──────. *The Battles of Trenton and Princeton*. Boston and New York: Houghton Mifflin, 1898.
Thayer, Theodore. *Nathanael Greene: Strategist of the American Revolution*. New York: Twayne, 1960.
Tower, Charlemagne. *The Marquis de Lafayette in the American Revolution*. 2 vols. Philadelphia: J. B. Lippincott, 1901.
Trevelyan, George O. *The American Revolution*. 4 vols. New York: Longmans, Green, 1915.
Tuckerman, Bayard. *Life of General Philip Schuyler, 1733-1804*. New York: Dodd, Mead, 1904.
Tunstall, Brian. *William Pitt, Earl of Chatham*. London: Hudder & Stoughton, 1938.
Valentine, Alan. *Lord Stirling*. New York: Oxford University Press, 1969.
Van Tyne, Claude H. *The War of Independence*. 2 vols. Boston: Houghton Mifflin, 1929.
Van Doren, Carl. *Benjamin Franklin*. New York: Viking, 1938.
──────. *Mutiny in January: The Story of a Crisis in the Continental Army*. New York: Viking, 1943.
──────. *Secret History of the American Revolution*. New York: Viking, 1941.
Van Schaack, Henry C. *Life of Peter Van Schaack*. New York: Appleton, 1842.
Wallace, Willard M. *Appeal to Arms: A Military History of the American Revolution*. New York: Quadrangle, 1964.
──────. *Traitorous Hero: The Life and Fortunes of Benedict Arnold*. New York: Harper & Row, 1954.
Ward, Christopher. *The Delaware Continentals, 1776-1783*. Wilmington: Historical Society of Delaware, 1941.
──────. *The War of the Revolution*. Edited by John R. Alden. 2 vols. New York: Macmillan, 1952.

Wertenbaker, Thomas Jefferson. *Father Knickerbocker Rebels: New York During the Revolution*. New York: Charles Scribner's Sons, 1948.

Whittemore, Charles P. *A General of the Revolution: John Sullivan of New Hampshire*. New York: Columbia University Press, 1961.

Wildes, Harry Emerson. *Anthony Wayne: Trouble Shooter of the American Revolution*. New York: Harcourt, Brace, 1941.

Williams, Basil. *The Life of William Pitt, Earl of Chatham*. 2 vols. London: Longmans, Green, 1913.

Willcox, William B. *Portrait of a General: Sir Henry Clinton in the War of Independence*. New York: Knopf, 1964.

Woodward, Carl Raymond. *Ploughs and Politics: Charles Read of New Jersey and His Notes on Agriculture, 1715-1774*. New Brunswick, N.J.: Rutgers University Press, 1941.

Index

Aberdeen, Lord, 34, 36
Adams, John: praises Stirling, 72; assesses army, 110; criticizes officers, 153
Aix-la-Chapelle, treaty of, 14
Albany Congress, 14–15
Alcide: Stirling sails in, 42
Alexander, Alexander, 38
Alexander, Catherine (sister). *See* Rutherfurd, Catherine Alexander Parker
Alexander, Catherine (cousin's wife), 10
Alexander, Catherine (daughter). *See* Duer, Catherine Alexander
Alexander, Elizabeth (sister). *See* Stevens, Elizabeth Alexander
Alexander, James (father), 16; career of, 1, 5–7, 12; and marriage, 7; and rearing of son, 9; racism of, 11; and Albany Congress, 14–15; death of, 29
Alexander, James, Jr. (brother): death of, 7
Alexander, John, 38
Alexander, Mary (sister). *See* Livingston, Mary Alexander
Alexander, Mary (daughter). *See* Watts, Mary Alexander
Alexander, Mary Sprat Provoost (mother): career of, 1, 7–8; and marriages, 7; and rearing of son, 9; gives son leave, 30; death of, 42
Alexander, Sarah Livingston (wife). *See* Stirling, Sarah Livingston Alexander, Lady
Alexander, Susanna (sister). *See* Reid, Susanna Alexander
Alexander, William. *See* Stirling, William Alexander, Sixth Lord
Alexander, William (cousin), 10

Alexandria conference, 16–17
Allinson, Samuel, 58
American Philosophical Society, 6; Stirling member of, 52
Amherst, Jeffery: ordered to pay claims, 33; and Alexander's militia company, 47
Amherst, William: guest of Stirling's, 51
Anderson, James: and partnership, 55
André, John: satirizes officers, 158; and spy mission, 159–60
Argyle, Duke of, 41; defends Loudoun, 31; friend of Stirling's, 34, 36
Armstrong, John: and Brandywine, 112; and Germantown, 116
Army, Continental: Washington appointed commander of, 65; Stirling given colonelcy in, 65; endangered by Howe, 81; at Morristown, 102–04, 154; marches through Philadelphia, 110; and condition after Germantown, 118; at Whitemarsh, 119; at Valley Forge, 120; commanded by Stirling, 138–41
Arnold, Benedict, 4, 175; treason of, 159; in Virginia, 162
Asia: in New York harbor, 74
Assembly, New Jersey: frees Hibernia of taxes, 55
Atholl, Duke of, 38
Atlee, Samuel: and Long Island, 84–85
Austrian Succession, war of, 10

Ball, Burgess, 146
Barbé-Marbois, Marquis de, 148
Barber, Francis: wounded, 130
Barclay, Thomas: entertains Stirling, 160

Index

Barland, Walter: and Stirling's patronage, 50
Barrington, William Weldman, Viscount: examines Alexander's accounts, 33
Bartram, John, 52
Basking Ridge, N.J.: home of Stirling, 44
Belcher, Jonathan, 29
Bernard, Francis: and Stirling's claims, 54–55
Betts, J., 6
Biddle, Nicholas, 140
Birmingham Meeting House: in battle of Brandywine, 113–14
Blanchard, Claude, 163
Blanchard, Cornelius, 71
Blue Mountain Valley: Stirling seizes, 70–71
Board of Trade: Stirling advises, 46–47
Bollan, William, 54; opposes Alexander's claims, 41
Boudinot, Elias, 176; Stirling's neighbor, 44; buys Stirling's furniture, 60; advises insubordination, 77; mourns Stirling's death, 175
Boudinot, Elisha, 195–96 (n. 22); buys Stirling's furniture, 60; marries, 137
Bouille, Marquis de, 170
Braddock, Edward: and Alexandria conference, 17; death of, 23
Bradley, Richard, 11
Bradstreet, John, 20, 28
Brandywine, battle of, 112–14
Brown, Montfort: exchanged for Stirling, 91
Buildings, The: Stirling's estate, described, 44–45
Burgoyne, John: captures Ticonderoga, 108; abandoned by Howe, 109; surrenders, 121
Burr, Aaron, 134; and Stirling's drinking, 123
Buskirk, Lieutenant Colonel: leads loyalists, 146–47
Bute, Earl of: friend of Alexander's, 35, 36; and Alexander's title claim, 40; and Stirling's petition, 46; supports King's College, 52

Cadwalader, John: the Jockey Club, 51; and Trenton, 99–100
Carlisle Commission: Stirling rejects overtures of, 136
Charles, Robert, 48
Charles I: and Stirling land grant, 36, 40, 45
Chastellux, Marquis de: and Alexander's character, 2–3; and Stirling's drinking, 3; meets Stirling, 160; assesses Stirling's abilities, 176
Chatham, William Pitt, Lord. *See* Pitt, William
Chatterton's Hill: in battle of White Plains, 93
Chew, Joseph, 51
Chew House: in battle of Germantown, 116
Clark, Abraham: and Conway Cabal, 121
Clark, Thomas: and courts-martial, 118
Clarke, George, 6
Clarkson, Matthew, 170
Clinton, George, 165; and news of Riedesel, 172
Clinton, Henry, 133–37 passim, 148–59 passim; friend of Alexander's, 35, 51; and Stirling's captivity, 88; assumes command, 125; and Monmouth, 126–28, 130–31; seizes Stony Point, 145; seduces mutineers, 161–62
Clinton, James: and André trial, 159
Coercive Acts, 61
Colden, Alexander: confronts Alexander, 32; and Stirling's earldom, 37
Colden, Cadwallader, 37; and Stamp Act crisis, 49
Collinson, Peter: and Stirling's personality, 48
Columbia University. *See* King's College
Committee of Safety, New Jersey, 66; and loyalists, 70
Committee of Safety, New York: and loyalists, 70
Commons, House of: Alexander testifies before, 31
Congress, First Continental, 64
Congress, New Jersey Provincial, 65; appoints Stirling colonel, 64; and manpower problems, 74
Congress, New York Provincial, 80; assists Stirling, 71; plans defenses, 74
Congress, Second Continental, 16, 73; appoints Stirling colonel, 65; appoints Washington commander, 65; impressed by Stirling, 67; and importers, 68; and

(*Congress, continued*)
    Franklin's arrest, 68–70; praises Stirling, 71, 147; orders Lee south, 72; appoints Stirling commander at New York, 72; promotes Stirling, 73, 103–04; approves Stirling's plans, 75; and Stirling-Sullivan exchange, 91; rejects Stirling's loss claims, 104, 138; orders general council, 125; and officers' petitions, 147, 157–58; thanks Stirling, 148; and mutiny, 161; mourns Stirling's death, 175
Connecticut Farms, battle of, 155
Continental Army. *See* Army, Continental
Convention army, 138, 140–41
Conway, Thomas: serves with Stirling, 108, 110; and Conway Cabal, 121
Conway Cabal, 120–22, 125
Cooper, Benjamin: and partnership, 55–57
Cooper, Daniel: and Hibernia interest, 55–56
Cornbury, Lord: persecutes Makemie, 180 (n. 25)
Cornwallis, Charles, Lord, 73; pursues Washington, 95, 97; and winter camp, 97; and Woodbridge, 106–07; and Brandywine, 113; and Germantown, 117; in Virginia, 163; and Yorktown, 166
Cosby, William, 6
Council, New Jersey: Stirling serves on, 5–6, 29, 47–50; and Stamp Act crisis, 48–50; chides Stirling, 57, 62; expels Stirling, 65
Council, New York: Stirling serves on, 5–6, 29, 47–50; and Stamp Act crisis, 48–50; expels Stirling, 65
Council of Safety, New Jersey: Stirling member of, 61
Coxe, Daniel: and lottery, 59
Cromwell, Oliver, 12
Crown Point expedition, 21, 23–24
Cruger, Henry, 58
Cumberland, Duke of, 17, 26
Custis, John Parke, 51

Dartmouth, Earl of, 68
Dayton, Elias: and Connecticut Farms, 155
Declaratory Act, 61
DeGrasse, Comte: and French fleet, 162–63
DeHart's Point: and Stirling's operations, 152; and Knyphausen's operations, 155–56

DeKalb, Johann, Baron, 141
DeLance, James, 6, 19; and Alexandria conference, 17; attacked by Shirley's friends, 32; and New York Society Library, 180 (n. 25)
DeLancey family: and New York politics, 5–6, 18, 23, 27, 50
Dempster, James Hamilton, 70
D'Estaing, Comte: and French fleet, 144, 147–49
DeWitt, Charles: and Alexander's army trade, 27
Dieskau, Baron de, 25
Dimler, George, 25
Dinwiddie, Robert, 14, 19; and Alexandria conference, 17
Drummond, Henry: supports King's College, 52; and Stirling's finances, 53
Duane, James: supports Stirling's career, 73
Duer, Catherine Alexander, 134, 139; birth of, 9; and marriage, 9, 146; nicknamed, 43; friendships of, 44; at Valley Forge, 123; visits relatives, 133–34; becomes mother, 164; visited by father, 167–68; home attacked, 167–68
Duer, William (son-in-law): and marriage, 9, 146; in Congress, 9; becomes father, 164; visited by Stirling, 167–68; home attacked, 167–68
Dunmore, John Murray, Earl of: meets Stirling, 89–90
DuPonceau, Pierre Étienne: at Valley Forge, 123
DuPortail, Louis, 127, 133, 149, 163
Dwight, Josiah, 11
Dyer, Eliphalet: and Stirling's rebellion, 63; and Conway Cabal, 121–22

Eagle: Admiral Howe's flagship, 88
Erving, John, Jr.: and army contract, 17
Eustace, John S.: snubs army officers, 149–50
Evening Post: satirizes officers, 150
Ewing, James: and Trenton, 99–100

Faesh, John Jacob: leases Hibernia, 57
Ferguson, Patrick, 135
Fisher, John, 19
Fithian, Philip Vickers: and Long Island, 87
Foord, Jacob: buys Stirling's furniture, 60

Forman, David: and Germantown, 116
Forman, Thomas Marsh: as aide, 140
Fort Crown Point, 34
Fort Duquesne, 34
Fort Frontenac, 34
Fort Mercer, 118
Fort Mifflin, 118
Fort Niagara, 34
Fort Oswego, 34; fall of, 30
Fort Ticonderoga, 34; occupied by St. Leger, 164–65
Fort Washington: fall of, 91, 94
Fox, Henry: as paymaster general, 31, 33
Foy, Edward, 58
Franklin, Benjamin, 7, 35, 48; and Albany Congress, 15; visits Stirling, 51; sponsors Stirling in RSA, 52
Franklin, William, 2, 51; appointed governor, 48; and Wilmot nomination, 48; and Stamp Act crisis, 49–50; and Society for Propagation of Gospel, 50; approves Stirling's lottery, 57; Stirling angry at, 62; and rupture with Stirling, 63–65; expels Stirling from council, 65; opposes Stirling's loyalist policy, 68; ill-treated by Stirling, 68–70
Fry, Joshua, 14

Gage, Lord: friend of Alexander's, 36
Gage, Thomas, 49
Gansevoort, Peter, 165
Gates, Horatio, 103, 133, 150, 153; joins main army, 97–98; and Conway Cabal, 120–31, 125; and duel with Wilkinson, 122; attends council, 125; and Stony Point, 145
George II, 17
George III: supports King's College, 190 (n. 16)
Germain, George: friend of Alexander's, 34
Germantown, battle of, 115–17
Gibson, John: gibes Stirling, 153
Glover, John: and Pelham Bay, 92, 200 (n. 23); and Trenton, 99; and André trial, 159
Gordon, Cosmo: inquires after Stirling, 134
Gordon, Duke of: friend of Alexander's, 35
Gordon, Duchess of: friend of Alexander's, 35
Gordon, Thomas, 6
Graeme, Patrick: friend of Alexander's, 35

Grant, James: and Long Island, 85, 87; alerts Rall, 98; Stirling's dislike of, 199 (n. 15)
Green, Ashbel, 156
Greene, Catherine: visits Stirlings, 104; at Valley Forge, 123
Greene, Nathanael, 4, 79–82 passim, 105, 109, 113, 141; and Long Island, 83; and Trenton, 98; visits Stirlings, 104; and Brandywine, 112, 114; and Germantown, 116; and Conway Cabal, 120–21; at Valley Forge, 123, 125; and Monmouth, 126–28, 130; snubbed, 149–50; at Morristown, 154; and Springfield, 156–57; and Arnold's treason, 159; and André trial, 159; and Guilford Court House, 162
Grenadiers, Independent Company of: Stirling commands, 47
Grenville, George: friend of Alexander's, 34

Halifax, Lord: friend of Alexander's, 36
Hamilton, Alexander: criticizes councils, 126; and Stirling's seniority rights, 127; praises Stirling, 130; snubbed, 149–50; satirized, 150; offered aide's job, 196 (n. 22)
Hamilton, Andrew: defends Zenger, 6
Hamilton, James, 58
Hampden, John, 12
Hancock, John, 75
Hand, Edward, 151; and Trenton, 100; and Knyphausen's operations, 156; and officers' petitions, 147, 158; and André trial, 159
Hardenbergh Patent, 10
Hardy, Charles: approves Alexander's expenses, 27–28
Harlem Heights, battle of, 90
Harley, Thomas: nominated by Stirling, 48
Haslet, John: and Long Island, 84–85; attacks Rogers, 92
Hazen, Moses, 151
Heard, Nathaniel, 70
Heath, William, 77, 79, 80, 92, 167–69 passim; commands at Peekskill, 94, 163; and Trenton, 97–98; orders Stirling to Albany, 164
Hibernia Iron Works, 140; Stirling's interest in, 55–57
Hickey, Thomas: court-martial of, 80
Higginbotham, Don: and militia, 105

Hoff, Joseph: and Hibernia, 55–56
Hopkins, Esek, Commodore, 91
Hopkinson, Francis: and satire, 149
Howe, Richard, Lord, 62; at New York, 81; as peace emissary, 88–91
Howe, Robert: and André trial, 159
Howe, William, 118; evacuates Boston, 78; at New York, 81; and Long Island, 84–85, 87; as peace emissary, 87–91; captures New York, 90; and Stirling-Sullivan exchange, 90–91; at Throg's Neck, 91; at Pell's Point, 92; and White Plains, 93; captures Fort Washington, 94–95; and winter camp, 97; false intelligence about, 102; and Woodbridge, 106–07; sails to Pennsylvania, 107–10; and Brandywine, 112–14; occupies Philadelphia, 115; opens Delaware River, 119; and Whitemarsh, 120
Huntington, Jedediah: and André trial, 159
Hutchinson, Thomas, 63

Irvine, William, 151
Independent Reflector, 13

James II: debt of, 36
Jay, James: and King's College, 52, 190 (n. 16)
Jefferson, Thomas, 63
Jockey Club: Stirling visits, 51
Johnson, John, 172
Johnson, William, 20; and Albany Congress, 15; and Alexandria conference, 17; and Crown Point expedition, 21, 23–24; and anger at Alexander, 23–24; attacked by Shirley's friends, 32
Jones, Thomas: Stirling's treatment of, 81; and Stirling's debts, 143; gibes Stirling, 187–88 (n. 3)

Kalm, Peter, 6
Kelly, William, 58
Kemble, Peter, 47
Kennedy, Samuel, 45
Keppel, Augustus: and Alexandria conference, 17
King's College (Columbia University), 51; founding of, 7, 12; Alexander appointed trustee of, 29; Stirling supports, 52, 190 (n. 16)

Kip's Bay, battle of, 90
Knox, Henry, 109, 133, 141, 148, 175; describes New York, 71; and Trenton, 99; and courts-martial, 118; and Conway Cabal, 120; at Valley Forge, 124; and Monmouth, 126; and officers' petitions, 147, 158; and André trial, 159

Lafayette, Marquis de: and Stirling's military abilities, 4; arrives in America, 109; and Monmouth, 126–28; and officers' petitions, 147, 158; and André trial, 159; in Virginia, 163
Latin High School, 6
Laurance, John: and Lee court-martial, 132; and André trial, 159
Laurens, Henry, 136
Lawrence, John: and lottery, 59
Lee, Charles, 149, 200 (n. 23); and Stirling's character, 2; and New York defenses, 68; and loyalists, 70; orders Stirling to New York, 71; praises Stirling, 71, 73; and retreat, 91–93; and White Plains, 94; ordered to join main army, 95, 97; captured, 98; and seniority rights, 126–27; and Monmouth, 126–28; court-martial of, 131–33; as Stirling's enemy, 133
Lee, Henry, 151, 154; on Lee's sentence, 132; and Paulus Hook, 146–47
Lee, William Philipps: and Stirling land claims, 40–41, 54–55
Legislature, New Jersey: and Stirling's debts, 62, 142–43
Lewis, Edward: criticizes Stirling, 150
Lincoln, Benjamin, 104, 150, 151, 154; commands division, 105; and Brandywine, 112; and Virginia command, 163
Livingston, Henry: and partnership, 10–11
Livingston, Henry Brockholst: pities loyalists, 81
Livingston, Mary Alexander, 7, 8
Livingston, Peter Van Brugh (brother-in-law), 7; studies law, 8; and army contract, 17; and Oswego campaign, 23–25, 29; sues Stirling, 53–54
Livingston, Philip (father-in-law), 9, 15
Livingston, Philip: and Stirling's patronage, 50
Livingston, Robert: and Ancram Furnace, 19; and Alexander's army trade, 27

Livingston, Robert R., 134; nominated by Stirling, 48; and New York Society Library, 180 (n. 25)
Livingston, Sarah. *See* Stirling, Sarah Livingston Alexander
Livingston, William (brother-in-law), 77, 134–37 passim, 153–54; studies law, 7–8; and governorship, 9; and Whig Club, 12–13; defends Shirley, 13; attacks Pownall, 32; exhorted to collect militia, 95; and Trenton, 102; assists Makemie, 180 (n. 25); and New York Society Library, 180 (n. 25)
Livingston family: and New York politics, 5–6, 18, 23, 50
Logan, William, 52
Long Island, battle of, 84–85, 87–88
Lords, House of (English), 1, 41; refuses Alexander's title claim, 39–40, 186 (n. 17); rejects Stirling's petition, 62
Lords, House of (Scots): confirms Alexander's title, 39
Loudoun, John Campbell, Lord, 32; assumes command, 18, 28–30; faults Alexander, 18; denounces Alexander's claims, 33; defended by Argyle, 31
Lovell, James: flatters Stirling, 125
Lyman, John, 11

McDonald, Donald, 90
McDougall, Alexander, 115, 133; and civil-military tensions, 72; suppresses loyalists, 81; and White Plains, 93; and courts-martial, 118; and officers' petitions, 147, 158; court-martial of, 169; challenged by Stirling, 169–70
McEvers, James: and stamps, 49
McHelm, John: and Stirling's debts, 142
McWilliams, William: and Conway Cabal, 120
Makemie, Francis, 180 (n. 25)
Mansion House: described, 7–8; plundered, 90; seized by creditors, 142–43
Martin, Joseph: and Stirling land claims, 54
Martin, Joseph Plumb: and Staten Island raid, 152–53
Mauduit, Joseph: and Stirling land claims, 54
Maxwell, William, 67, 106, 109, 134, 151; appointed to command, 65; and Brandywine, 112, 114; and Germantown, 116, 204 (n. 22); at Valley Forge, 124; and Lee court-martial, 132; as regimental leader, 194 (n. 13)
Mercer, Hugh: and Trenton, 99–100
Middlebrook: army encamps at, 137, 144
Mifflin, Thomas, 80; appointed quartermaster general, 91
Miles, Samuel, 84
Militia: officers' fear of, 105
Miller, Aaron, 52
Monmouth, battle of, 127–31
Monroe, James: as Stirling's aide, 120; and friendship with Stirling, 123; and Monmouth, 130; resigns Stirling's staff, 140
Morgan, Daniel, 106, 136; and withdrawal to Valley Forge, 120; and Conway Cabal, 120; and Lee court-martial, 132
Morris, Lewis, 42; and army contract, 17; sues Stirling, 53–54
Morris, Robert, 138, 164
Morris, Robert Hunter, 28; and Wyoming Valley controversy, 15–16; and Alexandria conference, 17; and friendship with Alexander, 36
Morris, Staats: confronts Alexander, 35; and friendship with Alexander, 39
Morris family: and New York politics, 5
Morristown: as winter encampment, 102, 103, 106, 108, 149, 154–55
Morton, John: as Stirling's neighbor, 44
Muhlenberg, Peter, 124
Murdock, James: censured, 61
Murray, Robert and John: purchasers of Hibernia, 57
Mutiny: in Connecticut line, 155; in Pennsylvania line, 161–62

Neilson, William: loans Stirling money, 55–56
New York City: described, 8, 71; slave rebellion in, 11; welcomes Stirling home, 43; civil-military tensions in, 72
New York State: politics of, 5–6
New York Gazette: and lottery, 58
New York Journal: and lottery, 58
New York Mercury, 13
New York Society Library: Stirling supports, 52, 180 (n. 25)
New York Weekly Journal, 6

Newburgh: army encamps at, 170
Newcastle, Duke of, 28; as secretary of state, 31; friend of Alexander's, 36
Nixon, John: ordered north, 203 (n. 9)
North Castle, 93
Northampton, Lord: friend of Alexander's, 36

Odell, Jonathan: satirizes Stirling, 3–4
Ogden, Samuel: clashes with Stirling, 56–57, 62
Oliver, Colonel: and courts-martial, 118
Oswego campaign, 19–28

Paine, Thomas, 63
Pargellis, Stanley: and Alexander's profiteering, 18, 26–27
Parker, Catherine Alexander. See Rutherfurd, Catherine Alexander Parker
Parker, Elisha III (brother-in-law), 16; death of, 7; studies law, 8
Parsons, Samuel Holden: and André trial, 159
Paterson, John: and André trial, 159
Paulus Hook: storming of, 146–47
Pelham Bay, battle of, 92
Penn, John, 12, 58; and Albany Congress, 15; friend of Stirling's, 35–36
Penn, Richard: and Jockey Club, 51
Penn, Thomas, 16; friend of Stirling's, 35, 36
Pepperell, William, 17, 21
Peters, Richard: and Albany Congress, 15
Peters, Richard: and pastorate, 45
Pettit, Charles, 64; and lottery, 59
Philadelphia: occupied, 125; evacuated, 125
Phillips, William: and Convention army, 138, 140
Phillips family: and New York politics, 5
Phoenix: in New York harbor, 74
Pitt, William: becomes prime minister, 28; friend of Stirling's, 34
Porteous, James: friend of Alexander's, 32
Pownall, John: confronts Alexander, 32
Pownall, Thomas, 23; and Alexandria conference, 17; attacked by Shirley's friends, 32
Prescott, Richard: exchanged, 90
Prevost, Theodosia, 134
Princeton, battle of, 102

Privy Council: denies Stirling's land claims, 41
Provoost, David (half-brother), 7, 10
Provoost, John (half-brother), 12
Provoost, Mary Sprat. See Alexander, Mary Sprat Provoost
Pulaski, Casimir, Count, 135
Putnam, Israel: and Long Island, 82–84, 198 (n. 11)

Quackenbush, Walter, 19
Quebec: seized by British, 34
Quincy, Eliza Susan Morton: describes Stirling's estate, 44; and friendship with Stirling's daughters, 45

Rall, Johann: and Trenton, 98–100
Rawdon, Francis, Lord: leads cavalry, 135
Read, Charles, 52; nominated by Stirling, 48
Read, James: friend of Stirling's, 46; on piracy committee, 47
Reed, Joseph: and Stirling's military abilities, 89; and mutiny, 161
Reid, John (brother-in-law), 7
Reid, Susanna Alexander, 7
Rensselaer, Robert Van, 165
Rhinelander, Frederick: and rebel troops, 72
Rhode Island: Alexander's slave ship, 11
Ritzema, Rudolphus: court-martial of, 82
Rivington's New York Gazeteer: and lottery, 58
Rochambeau, Comte de, 160; joins Washington, 162–63; advises Virginia operations, 163
Rocky Hill mine, 55
Rogers, Robert: in Seven Years' war, 28; attacked by Haslet, 92
Ross, John, 164–65
Royal Society of Arts: awards Stirling prize, 46; receives papers from Stirling, 52
Rush, Benjamin: and Alexander's character, 2–3; on alcohol in army, 3; criticizes officers, 121
Rutherfurd, Catherine Alexander Parker, 80; and marriages, 7, 8
Rutherfurd, Walter (brother-in-law), 7; studies law, 8

Index

Sackville, George Germain, Lord. *See* Germain, George
St. Clair, 141, 150; and André trial, 159
St. Leger, Barry: New York operations of, 164–66
St. Thomas' Church: Stirling subscribes to, 45
Schuyler, Philip, 73, 76, 166; friend of Stirling's, 35; and loss of Ticonderoga, 108; commands Northern Department, 203 (n. 9)
Schuyler family: and New York politics, 5
Scott, Charles: and Monmouth, 126
Scott, John Morin, 80; and Whig Club, 12–13; loses office, 50; and Long Island, 89; and New York Society Library, 180 (n. 25)
Sergeant, Jonathan D.: acts as Ogden's lawyer, 57
Serle, Ambrose: and Stirling's rebellion, 62; contempt for Stirling, 89; cajoles prisoners, 89
Sewall, Jonathan, 63
Sharpe, Horatio: and Alexandria conference, 17
Shelburne, Earl of: friend of Alexander's, 35; Stirling advises, 46–47; and iron industry, 55
Sherwood, Joseph: snubbed by Stirling, 45
Shirley, John, 18
Shirley, William, 13, 65; defended by Alexander, 1, 32, 33; reputation of, 16; and Alexandria conference, 16; and army contract, 17–18; entrusts Alexander, 18–19; and Oswego campaign, 23–30; and army unrest, 26; takes Alexander to England, 30; testifies in Commons, 31; supports Alexander's claims, 33; and Newcastle, 36; attacked in pamphlet, 183 (n. 28)
Skinner, Cortlandt: opposes Stirling, 68; escapes, 69
Smallwood, William: and Long Island, 84–85; and detached service, 114
Smith, William, 6
Smith, William, Jr.: and Whig Club, 12–13; and Stirling's command, 47
Smith, William Peartree: and Whig Club, 12–13

Smith, William Stephens, 170
Smyth, Frederick: and Franklin's arrest, 69–70
Sobieski, John: biography of, 171
Spencer, Joseph, 80, 82; and courts-martial, 118
Springfield, battle of, 157
Stamp Act crisis, 48–50, 61
Stark, John: and André trial, 159; and St. Leger threat, 164, 166
Staten Island raid, 108–09, 139, 148, 151–53
Stephen, Adam, 109; and drinking, 4; warns Stirling, 102; commands division, 105; and Brandywine, 112–13; and Germantown, 116; court-martial of, 118; dismissed from serivce, 118
Stevens, Edward: berated by Rush, 121
Stevens, Elizabeth Alexander, 7
Stevens, James, 19
Stevens, John (brother-in-law), 7; and partnership, 10; and slave trade, 11
Stevens, Richard: and Stirling's debts, 142
Stewart, Charles, 173
Stewart, Walter, 151
Stirling, Henry Alexander, Fifth Lord, 38
Stirling, Sarah Livingston Alexander, Lady, 139; and marriage, 9; description of, 9–10; character of, 9–10; at Valley Forge, 123; visits relatives, 133–34; and destitution, 143; and daughter's wedding, 146; and love for husband, 176
Stirling, William Alexander, First Lord, 37
Stirling, William Alexander, Sixth Lord; defends Shirley, 1, 32–33, 183 (n. 28); financial difficulties of, 1–2, 52–53, 55–57, 59, 142–43, 147, 158; character of, 1–4, 62–63, 88, 175–76; description of, 2; military qualities of, 2, 4; and drinking, 3, 150, 176; anecdotes about, 3, 162; birth of, 4; and Mansion House, 7–8, 43, 90, 142–43; early life of, 7–8; education of, 8; personality of, 9, 48, 63, 73, 88, 117, 175–76; and respect for parents, 9; and marriage, 9; land deals of, 10, 52, 187 (n. 2); as merchant, 10–12; and slave trade, 11–12; racism of, 11; as militia captain, 12; and Whig Club, 12–13; and Albany Congress, 14–15; appointed Shirley's aide, 16; as militia major, 16, 47; and Alexandria conference,

(Stirling, continued)
16–17; and army contract, 17; and army profiteering, 18, 27; blamed for Oswego fiasco, 18; Shirley's trust in, 18–19; and Oswego campaign, 19–28; advises Shirley, 21; and Crown Point expedition, 21, 23–24; angers Johnson, 23–24; and army unrest, 26; and DeLancey's profiteering, 27; and East Jersey Board election, 29, 47; and New Jersey council election, 29, 47; and New York council election, 29, 47; assists Loudoun, 29–30; wardrobe of, 30, 45–46; goes to England, 30–31; testifies in Commons, 31; as agent for East Jersey Board, 31, 185 (n. 1); confronted by Pownall's friends, 32; defends self, 32–33; seeks pay for Oswego campaign, 33–34; follows war news, 34; befriends gentry, 34–36; seeks Scots peerage, 36–40; and Stirling land claims, 40–41, 54–55; considers living in Scotland, 41; returns home, 42–43; adopts title, 43, 186 (n. 17); becomes country gentleman, 43–44; imports carriages, 43–44; country estate of, 44–45; library of, 45; religion of, 45; and viniculture, 46; as agricultural innovator, 46–47; seeks port collectorship, 46; as imperialist, 46–47, 50; on piracy committee, 47; and smuggling, 47; and council business, 47–48; supports William Franklin, 48; and Stamp Act crisis, 48–50, 189 (n. 11); and Navigation Acts, 49; and Quartering Act, 50; and Society for Propagation of Gospel, 50; patronage of, 50; entertains Washington, 51; and Jockey Club, 51; and friendship with Wayne, 51, 147; entertains Amherst, 51; entertains Franklin, 51; and New York Society Library, 51, 180 (n. 25); and Masons, 51; supports King's College, 52; and James Jay, 52, 190 (n. 16); and American Philosophical Society, 52; and science, 52; writes papers for RSA, 52; sued by partners, 53–54; and iron manufacture, 55–57; fights for Hibernia, 56–57; sells Hibernia, 57; and lottery, 57–59; and sales trip, 58; visits Washington, 58; loses household goods, 59–60; and reasons for rebellion, 61–63; embraced by rebels, 63–64; accepts militia colonelcy, 64; and reasons for joining army, 65; and rupture with Franklin, 64–65; expelled from councils, 65; and army administration, 65–67, 79–80, 105, 124, 133, 136–37, 140, 145, 147, 153–54, 163, 170, 173; ordered to New York, 68; seizes ship, 70–71; joins Lee, 71; and New York's appearance, 71; commands at New York, 72; problems with supply, 72; promoted brigadier general, 73; thanks Congress, 73; and manpower problems, 73, 76–77; and civil-military harmony, 73–74; enforces trade laws, 74, 137; and New York's defenses, 74–77; and Boston evacuation, 75; and civil-military problems, 76–77; plans New Jersey defenses, 77; loses New York command, 77; flatters Washington, 77–78; and Hickey court-martial, 80; and Ritzema court-martial, 82; strategic insight of, 82, 117, 118–19, 131, 144, 154–55, 162–63, 168–69, 170–72; and Long Island, 84–85, 87, 89, 198 (n. 11); in captivity, 87–91; muses about bravery, 88; cajoled by Serle, 89; meets Dunmore, 89–90; Mansion House endangered, 90; exchanged, 90–91; retreats of, 91–93, 94–95, 97; attacks Rogers, 92; hangs prisoners, 92; and White Plains, 93–94; and Delaware River line, 97, 102; rides to meet Lee, 97–98; and Lee's capture, 98; and Trenton, 98–100, 102; and ill health, 102, 104, 110, 118–19, 134, 137, 140, 148, 152–53, 163, 170–71, 173–74; visits Philadelphia, 103, 149–50, 168; promoted major general, 103–04; seeks payment for war losses, 104, 138; reprimanded by Washington, 104–05, 153–54; dislikes militia, 105, 119, 135; at Middlebrook, 106; and Woodbridge, 106–07; posted to Highlands, 107–08; and Staten Island raid, 108–09, 139, 148, 151–53; maneuvers in Pennsylvania, 110, 112, 114–15, 120; and Brandywine, 112–14; and Germantown, 115–17, 204 (n. 22); and courts-martial, 118; at Valley Forge, 120, 124–25; berated by Rush, 121; and Conway Cabal, 120–21; quarrels with Wilkinson, 122–23, 205 (n. 3); and friendship with Monroe, 123; and life at Valley

Forge, 123–24; and oath, 124–25; and seniority rights, 126–27, 150–51, 163; and Lee court-martial, 131–33; and family's New York visit, 133–34; and concern for family's safety, 134; thwarts foragers, 134–35, 138; in Elizabethtown, 136–37; commands main army, 138–41; and Convention army, 138; and forage problems, 139–41; furloughs home, 141; lobbies for officers, 141–42; and tender laws, 143; and daughter's wedding, 146; and Paulus Hook, 146–47; and officers' petitions, 147, 158; and cooperation with d'Estaing, 147, 149; cannonaded by *Vulture,* 147; thanked by Congress, 148; and Queen's Rangers, 148–49; and Morristown encampment, 149; snubbed, 149–50; satirized, 150, 158; criticized by preacher, 150; and weather, 151; recruits Jerseyites, 154; and Knyphausen's operations, 155–56; and Springfield, 157; and Arnold's treason, 158–59; and André trial, 159–60; meets Chastellux, 160; visits legislature, 160, 162; and mutiny, 161–62; becomes grandfather, 164; and Albany command, 164–66; and St. Leger threat, 164–66; praises Willet, 166; proposes Canadian campaign, 167, 168, 171–72; visits Duers, 167–68; attacked by loyalists, 167–68; rejoins Heath, 168; and McDougall court-martial, 169; challenges McDougall, 169–70; returns to Albany, 171; and Riedesel threat, 172; inspects Mohawk Valley, 172–73; death of, 174; and burial, 174; and grief for, 174–75; assists Makemie, 180 (n. 25); criticized by Jones, 187–88 (n. 3); imports household goods, 188 (n. 3); offers Hamilton job, 195–96 (n. 22); dislikes Grant, 199 (n. 15); misses Princeton battle, 202 (n. 38); commands at Peekskill, 203 (n. 9)

Stirling land grant, 36, 39–41, 54–55
Stony Point, storming of, 145
Stuart, Andrew: lawyer of Alexander's, 35, 37–40
Sullivan, John, 79, 141; and Long Island, 83–85, 87, 198 (n. 10); in captivity, 88–91; cajoled by Serle, 89; acts as emissary, 89; exchanged, 90–91; joins main army, 98; and Trenton, 98–100; commands division, 105; and Brandywine, 112–14; praises Stirling, 114; and Germantown, 116–17; court-martial of, 118; and Conway Cabal, 120; berated by Rush, 121; warns Stirling, 172
Susquehannah Company: claims Wyoming Valley, 15–16
Sutherland, Samuel: neighbor of Stirling's, 44

Thacher, James: and Stirling's character, 2–3
Thompson, William: commands at New York, 73, 77
Thompson-Neely House: as army headquarters, 98
Tilghman, Tench, 200 (n. 24)
Townshend, Charles: attacks Newcastle, 31; friend of Stirling's, 34–35, 36
Townshend Duties, 61
Trenchard, John, 6
Trenton, battle of, 99–100
Trinity Parish, N.Y.: Stirling member of, 45
Trumbull, Mary: and Stirling land claims, 40–41, 54–55
Trumbull, William, 76
Tryon, William: expels Stirling from council, 65; burns Dobbs Ferry, 145
Tupper, Benjamin: and St. Leger threat, 165–66

United States of America: independence declared, 81–82

Valley Forge: army encamps at, 120, 124–25
Van Cortlandt family: and New York politics, 5
Van Eppes, Joseph, 19
Vaudreuil, Pierre de Rigaud, 25
Verplanck's Point, 145
Von Donlop, Carl, Count: at Bordentown, 99
Von Heister, Philip: and Long Island, 85; captures Stirling, 87
Von Herringen, Colonel: and contempt for Stirling, 87
Von Knyphausen, Wilhelm: and Brandywine, 112; operations around Springfield, 155–57

Von Riedesel, Friedrich, Baron: and Convention army, 138; and Albany expedition, 172

Von Steuben, Wilhelm, Baron, 133; trains army, 124; and officers' petitions, 147, 158; and André trial, 159

Vulture: cannonades Stirling, 147; Arnold escapes to, 159

Waldo, Albigence: and Stirling's character, 2

Wallace, Hugh, 142

Walpole, Robert, 6

Washington, George, 4, 67, 73, 74, 77, 133, 135, 137, 141–42, 150, 157, 162, 167, 172, 173, 175, 176; appreciates Stirling's acquiescence, 2, 126–27, 151, 176; and Seven Years' war, 14; and Shirley's character, 16; and Alexandria conference, 17; addresses Alexander as "Lord Stirling," 43; visits Stirling, 51; and Stirling's visit, 58; wins lottery, 59; orders Stirling to New York, 68; and Boston evacuation, 75; appoints Stirling brigade commander, 79; and Hickey court-martial, 80; suppresses loyalists, 80–81; endangered by Howe, 81–82; and Ritzema court-martial, 82; and Long Island, 82–85, 87–88, 198 (n. 11); loses New York, 90; and Stirling-Sullivan exchange, 91; retreats of, 91–92, 94–95, 97; and White Plains, 93–94; divides army, 94, 154; loses Fort Washington, 95; orders Lee to main army, 95, 97; and Delaware River line, 97; and Trenton, 97–100, 102 (n. 34); and Princeton, 102; and militia, 103, 105, 144–45; reprimands Stirling, 104–05, 153–54; at Middlebrook, 106–07; and Woodbridge, 106–07; and enemy movements, 107–10, 136; in Highlands, 108; maneuvers in Pennsylvania, 110, 112, 114–15; and Brandywine, 112–14; and Germantown, 115–17; and Stirling's advice, 119, 144–45; and Conway Cabal, 120–21; at Valley Forge, 120, 124–25; and French treaty, 124; and Monmouth, 125–28; and Lee court-martial, 131–33; posts Stirling to New Jersey, 134–35; appoints Stirling acting commander, 138; thanks Stirling, 141; and Stony Point, 145; criticizes Tryon, 145; and Paulus Hook, 147; cooperates with d'Estaing, 147–49; and Morristown encampment, 149; and Staten Island raid, 151–53; and army suffering, 154; and Knyphausen's operations, 155–57; and Arnold's treason, 159; and André trial, 159; and winter encampment, 160; and Yorktown campaign, 163; and McDougall court-martial, 169; and Newburgh, 170; sends Stirling regiment, 173; praises Stirling, 174; and Stirling's death, 174–75; comforts Lady Stirling, 174; allows public mourning, 174; and lost correspondence, 185 (n. 7)

Washington, Martha; at Valley Forge, 123

Watts, Mary Alexander, 80, 147; birth of, 9; and marriage, 9; friendships of, 44; visited by relatives, 133–34

Watts, Robert (son-in-law), 80; and loyalism, 9; and marriage, 9; visited by relatives, 133–34

Wayne, Anthony, 106, 151, 160, 175; and friendship with Stirling, 51, 147; and Brandywine, 112, 114; and Paoli ambush, 114; and Germantown, 116; court-martial of, 118; at Valley Forge, 124; and Monmouth, 126; and Lee court-martial, 132; and Stony Point, 145; borrows cannon, 147; and officers' petitions, 147, 158; cooperates with d'Estaing, 148; satirized, 150, 158; and Arnold's treason, 159; and mutiny, 161–62

Wedderburne, Alexander: friend of Alexander's, 34, 36, 37

Weedon, George: and Brandywine, 114

Whig Club, 32; membership of, 12; activities of, 12–13

White Plains, battle of, 93

Whitemarsh: army encamps at, 119

Wilkinson, James: and Conway Cabal, 120–22; quarrels with Stirling, 122–23, 205 (n. 3); and duel with Gates, 122

Willet, Marinus: defeats Ross, 165–66

Williams, William, 20; charges Alexander with abuse of office, 26

Willoughby, Lord, 40

Wilmot, Henry: nominated by Stirling, 48

Winds, William: as Stirling's second in command, 66, 68–69

Winthrop, John, 11

Wolf: Alexander's slave ship, 11

Woodbridge, battle of, 107
Woodford, William, 134–36; and Brandywine, 114; marches south, 151

York, Duke of. *See* James II

Zenger, Peter: trial of, 6

About the Author

Paul David Nelson is professor of history, Berea College, Berea, Kentucky. He received his Bachelor of Arts degree from Berea College and his Master of Arts degree and doctorate from Duke University, Durham, North Carolina. His other publications include *General Horatio Gates: A Biography* and *Anthony Wayne: Soldier of the Early Republic*.